A Concise Dictionary of Indian Philosophy

A Concise Dictionary of Indian Philosphy

Sanskrit Terms Defined in English

John Grimes

State University of New York Press

Published by
State University of New York Press, Albany

Printed in the United States of America

For information, address State University of New York
Press, State University Plaza, Albany, N.Y., 12246

Library of Congress Cataloging in Publication Data

Grimes, John A., 1948—
A concise dictionary of Indian philosophy: Sanskrit terms defined
in English / John Grimes.
p. cm.
Includes index.
ISBN 0-7914-0100-6. — ISBN 0-7914-0101-4 (pbk.)
1. Philosophy, Indic—Dictionaries—Sanskrit. 2. Sanskrit
language—Dictionaries—English. I. Title.
B131.G67 1989
181'.4'03—dc19 88-36717
CIP

10 9 8 7 6 5 4 3 2 1

PREFACE

A Concise Dictionary of Indian Philosophy (*Sanskrit-English*) is the outcome of a personal, experienced need in the field of Indian philosophy. It has been compiled as an introduction to the basic terms found in the major schools of Indian philosophy. The terms fundamental to epistemology, metaphysics, and practical teachings will be found herein. The schools dealt with include: Buddhism, Jainism, Cārvāka, Nyāya, Vaiśeṣika, Sāṅkhya, Yoga, Mīmāṁsā, Vedānta (mainly Advaita, Viśiṣṭādvaita, and Dvaita), Śaiva Siddhānta, Vīra Śaivism, Kashmir Śaivism, and Śivādvaita.

This dictionary, I hope, will serve as an introductory source-book with cross-references wherever relevant. I have attempted to give the common or non-technical definition of a word first, and then, if this word has a special meaning or meanings within a particular philosophical system, I have listed such. For example, a word like *jīva* (individual soul) has fourteen different technical definitions listed since each school conceives of this concept differently

A knowledgeable reader will observe that some systems have been given a deeper and more extensive coverage than others. However, I have endeavored to cover at least the basic concepts fundamental to each individual system. Further, if there is a technical definition given by one school which coincides with that given by another school (*e.g.* Nyāya and Sāṅkhya or Bhāṭṭa Mīmāṁsā and Advaita Vedānta — especially with regard to epistemological matters), I have only listed the most common reference. I have also endeavored to give cross-references wherever appropriate. For instance, consider the close interaction of the term '*avidyā*' with the related terms: *māyā*, *anirvacanīya*, *sadasadvilakṣaṇa*, *anādi*, *bhāvarūpa*, *jñānanivartya*, *āvaraṇa*, and *vikṣepa*.

This book aims at being both basic and comprehensive. It is basic in that (i) it includes virtually all the words basic to the various Indian philosophical systems, and (ii) it defines these terms in their dictionary or common and literal meanings. The book is comprehensive in that it defines many of its terms with the specific meanings that a word has for a specific school.

The purpose of this book is to provide not only the academic community but also the interested lay individual with a comprehensive dictionary of most Indian philosophical terms. The terms are listed both in *devanāgarī* script and roman transliteration along with definitions in English. At the end of the book are given (i) an Index of some important words, and (ii) fourteen charts which provide, at a glance, information regarding relationships, categories, and source-books relevant to the individual schools. These charts are referred to in the main body of the text and the reader can consult them wherever appropriate. There is also a list of words which appear in the body of the text, but which do not merit individual definitions themselves.

Since this book is intended primarily for individuals who are not specialists in Sanskrit, I have compiled the Sanskrit terms in the order of the English alphabets. Wherever relevant, I have illustrated the definitions with the traditional examples used in Indian philosophical texts, *e.g.*, for *savyabhicāra* — fire and smoke, or, for *āśraya-asiddha* — a sky-lotus. One will also find a 'scheme of transliteration' and a 'scheme of pronunciation' to assist the reader.

Acknowledgements

I would like to acknowledge my eternal indebtedness to my teachers — without whom this work would never have been written. First I owe more than words can say to Dr. R. Balasubramanian, Director of the Radhakrishnan Institute for Advanced Study in Philosophy, University of Madras. Not only did he patiently teach me Indian philosophy in the traditional way, but he personally went through every entry in this book, making comments and suggestions. I owe also very much to Dr. P. K. Sundaram, who, along with Dr. Balasubramanian, taught me Advaita Vedānta and spent literally years discussing philosophy and giving me insights into the Indic world.

I would like to thank my other teachers at the RIASP without whose assistance and guidance this volume would not have been possible: Dr. T. P. Ramachandran, Dr. S. Gopalan, Dr. V. Rathinasabapathy, Dr. T. S. Devadoss, (the late) Dr. P. Balasubramanian and Dr. V. K. S. N. Raghavan. I must also acknowledge thanks to Dr. N. Gangadharan for his assistance in writing the terms in *Devanāgarī* script, and to Dr. T. N. Ganapathy for his guidance and encouragement.

To the authorities of the University of Madras, I am very thankful for publishing this under the auspices of the Radhakrishnan Institute for Advanced Study in Philosophy.

Finally, my thanks are due in no small measure to M/s. Avvai Achukkoodam for the neat execution of this work.

JOHN GRIMES

SCHEME OF TRANSLITERATION

अ	a	आ	ā	इ	i	ई	ī
उ	u	ऊ	ū	ऋ	ṛ	ॠ	ṝ
ऌ	ḷ	ए	e	ऐ	ai	ओ	o
औ	au	अं	aṁ	अः	aḥ		

क्	k	ख्	kh	ग्	g	घ्	gh	ङ्	ṅ
च्	c	छ्	ch	ज्	j	झ्	jh	ञ्	ñ
ट्	ṭ	ठ्	ṭh	ड्	ḍ	ढ्	ḍh	ण्	ṇ
त्	t	थ्	th	द्	d	ध्	dh	न्	n
प्	p	फ्	ph	ब्	b	भ्	bh	म्	m
य्	y	र्	r	ल्	l	व्	v		
श्	ś	ष्	ṣ	स्	s	ह्	h		
ळ्	ḷ	क्ष्	kṣ	त्र्	tr	ज्ञ्	jñ		

SCHEME OF PRONUNCIATION

a	like a in organ or the u in but
ā	like a in psalm
i	like i in knit
ī	like ee in meet
u	like u in pull
ū	like u in rule
ṛ	like ri in Rita
e	like e in they
ai	like ai in aisle
o	like o in go
au	like ow in how
ṁ	*anusvāra* is a nasal sound
ḥ	*visarga* is pronounced in the articulating position of the preceding vowel
k	as in kite
kh	as in inkhorn
g	as in give
gh	as in dighard
ṅ	as in sing
c	as in chair
ch	as in church-history
j	as in joy
jh	as in hedgehog
ñ	as in new
ṭ	as in tongue

ṭh	as in anthill
ḍ	as in dark
ḍh	as in God-head
ṇ	as in Monday
t	as in tub
th	as in thought
d	as in dub
dh	as in redhead
n	as in nut
p	as in pan
ph	as in up-hill
b	as in bed
bh	as in clubhouse
m	as in mother
y	as in yes
r	as in race
l	as in light
v	as in vine
ś	as in sure
ṣ	as in bush
s	as in sun
h	as in hall
ḷ	as in curl

A

अबाधित - *Abādhita* - non-contradicted; unsublated

In the epistemology of Advaita, valid knowledge (*pramā*) is new knowledge which has not been contradicted.

आभास - *Ābhāsa* - appearance; semblance

आभासवाद् - *Ābhāsa-vāda* - theory of appearance

1. A theory in Advaita which posits that the individual soul (*jīva*) is an illusory appearance of *Brahman*-intelligence. It is a variation of the *pratibimba-vāda.*

2. The creation theory of the Śaiva and Śākta schools, which posits that the universe consists of appearances which are all real in the sense that they are aspects of the ultimate reality.

अभौतिक - *Abhautika* - non-material

अभाव - *Abhāva* - non-existence

1. The Nyāya, Vais'eṣika, Bhāṭṭa Mīmāṁsā, and Dvaita schools hold that non-existence is a distinct category. The Buddhist schools deny the existence of negation altogether as do the Prābhākara Mīmāṁsā and Vis'iṣṭādvaita schools.

2. Non-existence has two main divisions: (i) the absence of one entity in another (*saṁsarga-abhāva*), which is of three kinds: (a) prior non-existence

(*prāg-abhāva*), (b) annihilative non-existence (*pradhvaṁsa-abhāva*), and(c) absolute non-existence (*atyanta-abhāva*); (ii) one object not being another (*anyonya-abhāva*) or reciprocal non-existence.

अभावरूपधर्म - *Abhāvarūpa-dharma* - a negative attribute

अभावात्मक - *Abhāvātmaka* - a type of *dharma* in Jainism which indicates the distinction of one thing from another

अभय - *Abhaya* - fearlessness

In Advaita, it is equivalent to *mokṣa.*

अभेद् - *Abheda* - non-difference

अभेददर्शन - *Abheda darśana* - cognition or realization of non-duality

अभेदसंसर्ग - *Abheda-saṁsarga* - relation of non-duality; relationship of identity

Vide *vākyārtha.*

अभेदश्रुति - *Abheda-śruti* - a scriptural text whose purport is non-duality

The Upaniṣadic texts which express non-difference between the individual soul (*jīvātman*) and the supreme Being (*paramātman*).

अभिधा - *Abhidhā* - primary meaning; literal sense

अभिधेय - *Abhidheya* - nameable or denotable thing

अभिगमन - *Abhigamana* - morning worship

अभिघात - *Abhighāta* - a type of contact producing sound; striking; impact

अभिहितान्वयवाद - *Abhihitānvaya-vāda* - the theory of the construction of the uttered

The Bhāṭṭa Mīmāṁsā theory holds that words independently signify their own separate meanings and subsequently these isolated meanings combine again to produce the single meaning of a sentence. Thus a sentence-sense is a later cognition coming from the construction of the meanings of the words (which express one connected idea). One first remembers the isolated meanings of the words and then a simultaneous collective memory gives the same a collective meaning.

अभिलाप - *Abhilāpa* - the association of name and permanence to objects perceived

अभिमान - *Abhimāna* - conceit; attachment

1. The function of the ego (*ahaṅkāra*).

2. A state of mind which interprets experience as 'mine'.

अभिमानद्रव्य - *Abhimāna-dravya* - the ego

अभिमुक्ति - *Abhimukti* - turned toward liberation

1. The stage of the *arhat.*

2. Vide *bodhisattva.*

अभिनव अन्यथाख्याति - *Abhinava-anyathā-khyāti* - the neo-theory of 'apprehension-otherwise'

Dvaita theory of error. It is a combination of *asat-khyāti,* in that the object of the erroneous cognition is held to be unreal, and of *anyathā-*

khyāti, in that the object of error appears as otherwise than what it is. Thus what is seen in erroneous cognition is unreal, but it is seen in a substrate which is real.

अभिनिवेश - *Abhiniveśa* - will-to-live; strong desire

1. One of the five types of afflictions (*kleśa*) according to the Yoga school. It is an instinctive clinging to life and a dread of death.

2. Vide *kleśa.*

अभिन्न - *Abhinna* - undifferentiated

अभिन्ननिमित्तोपादान - *Abhinna-nimittopādāna* - non-different efficient and material (cause)

1. The Advaita theory that the efficient and material causes are one and non-different: both causes are *Brahman* since there is ultimately nothing but *Brahman.*

2. Viśiṣṭādvaita also accepts this theory.

अभिप्राय - *Abhiprāya* - intention; opinion

अभिसन्धान - *Abhisandhāna* - co-ordination; binding together

अभिसङ्क्रान्ति - *Abhisaṅkrānti* - synthesis

अभिव्यक्त - *Abhivyakta* - manifested

अभिव्यक्तियोग्यता - *Abhivyakti-yogyatā* - fitness for manifestation

That part of the internal organ which pervades the object, assumes the form of the object, and invests the object with the character of objectness (is known as fitness for manifestation).

आभोग - *Ābhoga* - immediate experience

अभ्रान्त - *Abhrānta* - non-illusory

अभूत - *abhūta* - non-existent

अभ्यनुज्ञा - *Abhyanujñā* - a logical concession

अभ्यास - *Abhyāsa* - continuous endeavour; constant practice; repetition

Vide *ṣaḍ-liṅga.*

अभ्यासप्रत्यय - *Abhyāsapratyaya* - repetitional cognition

अभ्युदय - *Abhyudaya* - prosperity

The purpose of life as related to material prosperity and individual and social welfare. It is enjoined by the ritual section of the *Vedas* (*karma-kāṇḍa*) and is the empirical objective of everyone.

अभ्युपगमसिद्धान्त - *Abhyupagama-siddhānta* - for the sake of argument the opponent's views are granted uncritically thereby establishing a conclusion the consequences of which will then be refuted

Vide *siddhānta.*

अचक्षुदर्शन - *Acakṣu-darśana* - indeterminate understanding

Vide *upayoga.*

अचल - *Acala* - the immovable

Vide *bodhisattva.*

आचार - *Ācāra* - conduct; good behavior

आचारलिङ्ग - *Ācāra-liṅga*

Vide *liṅgasthala*.

आचारमूल - *Ācāra-mūla* - source of (religious) conduct

आचार्य - *Ācārya* – preceptor; teacher; spiritual guide

1. A title affixed to the names of learned spiritual individuals.

2. According to Jainism, one stage of the ascetic order. Their duties are: to initiate people in the spiritual path; to guide, instruct, and correct those aspirants; and to govern and regulate the monks of the Order.

आचार्याभिमान - *Ācārya-abhimāna* - devotion to the teacher

अचेतन - *Acetana* - non-conscious; inanimate; inert

अचिन्त्य - *Acintya* - unthinkable; incomprehensible; inexplicable

1. A name denoting the Divine because it is said that the mind cannot cognize the Ineffable.

2. A type of power (vide *śakti*).

अचिन्त्य भेदाभेद वेदान्त - *Acintya-bhedābheda-vedānta* - a school of philosophy founded by Śrī Caitanya (unthinkable dualistic non-dualism)

It propounds that there is both difference and non-difference between all individual souls (*jīva*) and *Brahman*, but that this dualistic relation of both difference and non-difference is logically unthinkable.

अचित् - *Acit* - insentient; inert; non-conscious; matter

1. According to Vīra Śaivism, it comprises the twenty-four *tattvas* beginning from *prakṛti.*

2. Vide chart no. 12.

3. Vide *tattvatraya.*

आदरप्रत्यय - *Ādarapratyaya* - regardful cognition

आदेश - *Ādeśa* - command; instruction

अधम - *Adhama* - the low

अधमाधम - *Adhamādhama* - the lowest (of the low)

आधार - *Ādhāra* - support; substratum

अधर्म - *Adharma* - demerit; unrighteousness; medium of motion

1. Jainism understands this concept totally different from what it means in all the other systems of Indian philosophy. According to Jainism, it means the principle of rest which pervades the entire universe. It is one of the five categories included in the term '*ajīva*'. Along with the medium of motion (*dharma*), it is considered to be responsible for the systematic character of the universe. Without it, no substance could remain at rest.

2. Vide *astikāya* and *ajīva.*

अधर्मास्तिकाय - *Adharmāstikāya*

Vide *adharma.*

आधेय - *Ādheya* -- occasioned; dependent upon; supported

A type of power (*śakti*) that is occasioned in a thing by some new operation (as in an idol when it is consecrated).

आधिभौतिक – *Ādhibhautika* – of inanimate objects; of elements

According to Sāṅkhya, one of the three types of sorrows. These are miseries caused by extrinsic, natural influences inflicted by other individuals beasts, birds, and inanimate objects.

आधिदैविक - *Ādhidaivika* - cosmic; super-natural

According to Sāṅkhya, one of the three types of sorrows. These are miseries caused by extrinsic supernatural influences such as spirits, demons, ghosts, etc. Gauḍapāda also included herein miseries due to heat and cold, wind and rain, etc. This he did due to the theory that these phenomena, in their origination, are presided over by deities. (See also *ādhyātmika*)

अधिकार - *Adhikāra* - chapter; authority

अधिकारमुक्त - *Adhikāra-mukta* - pure soul

1. A term used in Śaiva Siddhānta to denote a state of the soul.

2. Vide *jīva.*

अधिकरण - *Adhikaraṇa* – topic; set of arguments

1. A *sūtra*-work is divided into chapters (*adhyāya*); each chapter is divided into sections

(*pāda*); and each section is divided into topics (*adhikaraṇa*). The procedure of exposition for an *adhikaraṇa* is fivefold. First, a Vedic sentence is taken up as the subject for investigation (*viṣaya-vākya*). Then a doubt (*saṁśaya*) is raised regarding the correct meaning of the sentence. Then the *prima facie* view (*pūrva-pakṣa*) is stated. This is then refuted (*uttara-pakṣa*). And finally the conclusion (*nirṇaya*) is established. These are the five limbs of a topic.

2. These five limbs of a topic are also listed as *viṣaya, viśaya, saṁśaya, pūrva-pakṣa*, and *siddhānta.*

अधिकरणसिद्धान्त - *Adhikaraṇa-siddhānta* - an established conclusion which once being accepted, other conclusions will naturally follow

Vide *siddhānta.*

अधिकारिन् - *Adhikārin* - eligible person; a qualified aspirant after liberation; a fit student who has shown his deservedness to be taught

अधिकारिभेद - *Adhikāri-bheda* - the difference of the qualified aspirants

1. Aspirants are distinguished by different qualifications. All are not capable of apprehending the same truth. Thus some are taught action (*karma*), others are taught devotion (*bhakti*), and still others are taught wisdom (*jñāna*).

2. Vide *arundhatī-darśana-nyāya.*

अधिकारिव्यवस्था - *Adhikāri-vyavasthā* - determining the qualified

The individual soul identified with the gross body.

अधिष्ठान - *Adhiṣṭhāna* - basis; substratum, ground

अधोलोक - *Adholoka* - the region where the denizens of hell reside

अधोनियामकशक्ति - *Adhoniyāmaka-śakti* - the power of impurity of ignorance (*āṇava*) which misdirects the soul and leads it to degrade itself; the power which deludes the soul

अध्वन् - *Adhvan* - evolution; way; time

The six ways that God is declared to be connected to the soul in Śaiva Siddhānta. They are: mystic formula (*mantra*), letters (*varṇa*), words (*pāda*), world (*bhuvana*), categories (*tattva*), and constrictors (*kalā*). These six ways help the soul experience and attain the Lord. The Lord takes form on the basis of these six, and gives results to the soul according to its aspiration.

अध्वर - *Adhvara* - sacrifice

अध्वर्यु - *Adhvaryu* - chief priest of the sacrifice who lays out the measure of the ritual

अध्यारोप - *Adhyāropa* - superimposition; incorrect attribution

अध्यारोपापवाद - *Adhyāropāpavāda* - the method of prior superimposition and subsequent denial

1. By this method, one first superimposes illusory attributes on an attributeless entity and then subsequently denies or removes them. This technique is used by Advaita to lead an aspirant to the knowledge of the non-dual Self.

2. Vide *apavāda*.

अध्यास - *Adhyāsa* - superimposition; false attribution; illusion

1. The imposition of a thing on what is not that thing (*atasmiṁs-tad-buddhiḥ*). It is of two kinds: *svarūpa-adhyāsa* and *saṁsarga-adhyāsa*. The former consists in superimposing an illusory (*mithyā*) object on something real, i.e., superimposing an illusory snake on a real rope, which is an example of an ordinary error; or of superimposing ignorance (*avidyā*) and the empirical world upon *Brahman*, which is an example of a foundational error. *Saṁsarga-adhyāsa* is the superimposition of an attribute on an object. This relation is false (*mithyā*), i.e., to superimpose redness upon a crystal which is in the immediate physical proximity of a red object.

2. It may also be divided into: (i) *artha-adhyāsa* - the superimposition of an object upon a substratum, and (ii) *jñāna-adhyāsa* - superimposition of the knowledge of the former upon the knowledge of the latter.

3. A third division of *adhyāsa* is: (i) *dharma-adhyāsa* (superimposition of objects) and (ii) *dharmi-adhyāsa* (superimposition of attributes).

अध्यासभाष्य - *Adhyāsa-bhāṣya* - commentary on superimposition

Śaṅkarācārya's famous introductory part of his commentary on the *Brahma-sūtra* which precedes the commentary on the text itself.

अध्यात्म - *Adhyātma* - personal; individual; of the supreme Self

अध्यात्मविद्या - *Adhyātmavidyā* - metaphysics; study of the self

आध्यात्मिक - *Ādhyātmika* - internal

1. According to Sāṅkhya, one of the three types of sorrows. These are miseries caused by intrinsic influences, bodily and mental, such as the presence of bile or phlegm or desire, anger, etc. They are generated internally by illness of the body or by unsatisfied passions of the mind.

2. Vide *ādhibhautika* and *ādhidaivika*.

अध्यवसाय - *Adhyavasāya* - affirmative process; conviction; determinative cognition; apprehension

अध्याय - *Adhyāya* - chapter; section

अध्ययन - *Adhyayana* - learning, study

आदि - *Ādi* - first; origin; beginning

आदित्य - *Āditya* - the sun

अद्रव्य - *Adravya* - non-substence

One of the two main categories of Viśiṣṭādvaita.

It has ten members: *sattva*, *rajas*, *tamas*, *śabda*, *sparśa*, *rūpa*, *rasa*, *gandha*, *saṁyoga*, and *śakti*. They are all considered as attributes and always dependent upon substances (*dravya*).

अदृष्ट - *Adṛṣṭa* - unseen potency; destiny; influence

1. It is generated by actions for helping to bring about their respective fruits in a hereafter.

2. The unknown quality of things which arranges for later experiences in accordance with merits and demerits.

3. The unseen power of one's past good and bad deeds.

4. It is also called *apūrva.*

5. According to Vaiśeṣika, it is the cause of the world process.

अदृष्टकारण - *Adṛṣṭa-kāraṇa* - an unknown cause

अदृष्टफल - *Adṛṣṭa-phala* - unseen fruit

The results of (Vedic) actions are imperceptible and manifest at a future time.

अदृष्टार्थ - *Adṛṣṭārtha* - imperceptible results; super-sensuous; trans-empirical

अद्वैत - *Advaita* - non-dualism

1. One of the six orthodox schools of Indian philosophy. It has no founder, for its roots are to be found in the *Vedas,* and particularly the *Upaniṣads.* Its central teaching is the oneness of the individual soul (*jīva*) with *Brahman.* It affirms the non-duality of *Brahman,* the non-reality of the empirical world, and the non-difference between the individual soul and *Brahman* (*brahma satyam, jagan-mithyā, jīvo brahmaiva nāparaḥ*).

2. Its basic source-books are the *Upaniṣads,* the *Bhagavad-gītā,* and the *Brahma-sūtra.* Vide *prasthāna-traya.*

3. The key concept in the system is ignorance (*avidyā/māyā*). This explains the otherwise per-

plexing distinction between the *nirguṇa-* and the *saguṇa Bṛahman*, between the non-dual Reality appearing as individuals and as God (*Īśvara*). It accounts for Advaita's metaphysics, epistemology, and ethics.

4. Vide chart no. 4.

अद्वय - *Advaya* - one; oneness; unique

अद्वयमजातम् - *Advayam-ajātam* - one non-coming-into-being

अद्वयता - *Advayatā* - oneness

अद्वितीय - *Advitīya* - without a second

आद्यावस्था - *Ādyāvasthā* - first state

A technical term in Yādava's cosmology.

आगम - *Āgama* - scripture; what has come down from tradition

1. They are divided into three main branches according to the deity that is worshipped therein. *Pāñcarātra* and *Vaikhānasa Āgamas* are the Vaiṣṇava scriptures which extol *Viṣṇu*. The *Śaiva Āgamas* extol *Śiva*. And the *Śakta Āgamas* extol *Devī*.

2. An *Āgama* deals with four topics: temple construction, making idols, etc.; philosophichl doctrines; meditative practices; and methods of worship (*kriyā*, *jñāna*, *yoga*, and *caryā*). These are divided into three divisions: *tantra* which teaches rituals; *mantra* which teaches the *yoga* stage of worship; and *upadeśa* which expounds the existence and nature of the three eternal entities — *paśu*, *pāśa*, and *pati*.

आगमापायि - *Āgamāpāyi* - that which appears and that which disappears

आगामि - *Āgāmi* - *karma* yet-to-come

Vide *karma*.

अघातिकर्म - *Aghāti-karma* - non-obstructive *karmas*

According to Jainism, non-obstructive *karmas* are of four types which determine: the length of life in any given birth (*āyus*); the particular body with its general and special qualities and faculties (*nāma*); the nationality, caste, family, etc. (*gotra*); and the inborn energy of the soul by the obstruction (*antarāya*) of which it prevents the doing of a good action when there is a desire to do it.

अघटितघटना - *Aghaṭitaghaṭanā* - accomplishment of the unaccomplished

अग्नि - *Agni* - fire

1. Fire is of five kinds: the fire of time (*kāla-agni*) the fire of hunger (*kshudhā-agni*); the cold fire (*śīta-agni*); the fire of anger (*kopa-agni*); and the fire of knowledge (*jñāna-agni*). These five fires reside respectively in the feet, navel, stomach, eye, and heart.

2. Vide *tejas*.

अग्निहोत्र - *Agni-hotra* - the name of an obligatory rite enjoined on all twice-born persons, so long as they live

अग्र - *Agra* - foremost; chief

आग्रह - *Āgraha* - anger

अग्रहण - *Agrahaṇa* - non-apprehension; not knowing the truth

1. According to Advaita, it is an aspect of ignorance which remains even in the deep sleep state, though in a latent form. This explains how deep sleep differs from liberation.

2. Non-apprehension is negative (*abhāva*) and what is negative cannot be the cause of anything according to Advaita.

अग्राह्यम् - *Agrāhyam* - ungraspable

अहं - *Aham* - ' I '; the notion of the ego; the individual soul

अहं ब्रह्मास्मि - *Aham-brahmāsmi* - I am *Brahman*

1. A *mahāvākya* which occurs in the *Bṛhadāraṇyaka Upaniṣad* of the *Yajur-veda.*

2. Vide *mahāvākya.*

अहङ्कार - *Ahaṅkāra* - 'I'-ness; egoism; the concept of individuality

In the evolutionary process *ahaṅkāra* is said to evolve from the intellect (*buddhi*) and give evolution to the senses (*indriya*) and the subtle essence of the elements (*tanmātra*) in turn. Its function is self-assertion. It is an aspect of the inner organ (*antaḥkaraṇa*) and it has the three aspects of: *vaikārika* or *sattva*, *taijasa* or *rajas*, and *bhūtādi* or *tamas.*

आहार - *Āhāra* - food

आहार्य - *Āhārya* - adventitious

आहार्यारोप - *Āhāryāropa* - adventitious assumption

आहार्यशङ्का - *Āhārya-śaṅkā* - adventitious doubt

अहिंसा - *Ahiṁsā* - non-injury; non-violence

1. One of the great vows (*mahāvrata*) of the Jainas. It is the law of compassion in body, mind, and spirit. Negatively it means refraining from causing any injury and positively it stands for the practice of love towards all living beings.

2. Vide *mahāvrata.*

3. One of the abstentions (*yama*) of the Yoga school.

4. Vide *yama.*

अह्रीक - *Ahrīka* - shamelessness

ऐक्य - *Aikya* - oneness

Vide *sthala*

ऐक्यसामानाधिकरण्य - *Aikya-sāmānādhikaraṇya* - grammatical co-ordination in the sense of oneness

1. In the sentence, "This is a cow," the word 'this' refers to an individual object and the word 'cow' refers to the generic attribute of cowness. In this example, the two words are equated due to their being in grammatical co-ordination to each other.

2. Vide *sāmānādhikaraṇya.*

ऐश्वर्य - *Aiśvarya* - dominion; power; lordship

1. An attribute of *Īśvara* or any theistic deity.

2. Vide *Īśvara.*

ऐतिह्य - *Aitihya* - tradition

1. A traditional belief or beliefs which have been handed down from generation to generation.

2. One of the means of valid knowledge (*pramāṇa*) according to the Paurāṇikas.

अज - *Aja* – unborn; unproduced

अजड - *Ajaḍa* - immaterial; non-material

According to Viśiṣṭādvaita, immaterial substance is of two kinds: external (*parāk*) and internal (*pratyak*). The external is of two kinds: eternal manifestation (*nitya-vibhūti*) and attributive consciousness (*dharma-bhūta-jñāna*). The internal is also of two kinds: individual self (*jīva*) and God (*Īśvara*).

अजहल्लक्षणा - *Ajahal-lakṣaṇā* - non-exclusive implication

1. When the primary meaning of a sentence is not adequate to convey a coherent idea, then the secondary meaning is resorted to. In this case, the primary meaning is not totally rejected, but is retained and added to by the implied meaning, e.g., 'The red runs' means that the red horse runs. The primary meaning of 'red' is retained, and clarified by adding to it the implied meaning, namely 'horse'.

2. Vide *lakṣaṇā*.

अजातिवाद - *Ajāti-vāda* - the theory of non-origination

The Advaita theory, especially associated with Gauḍapāda, which denies any causal change. That which is non-existent in the beginning and non-existent at the end, is also non-existent in the middle and therefore completely non-existent.

अजाति - *Ajāti* - non-origination

A term employed by both Gauḍapāda and the Mādhyamika school of Buddhism to mean that nothing is born and nothing dies (though for different reasons).

अजीव - *Ajīva* - non-soul; what is inert or non-conscious

One of the two principles which constitute reality according to Jainism. It is comprised of the five categories: matter (*pudgala*), medium of motion (*dharma*), medium of rest (*adharma*), space (*ākāśa*), and time (*kāla*).

अज्ञ - *Ajña* - ignorant

अज्ञान - *Ajñāna* - ignorance; nescience

1. One of the five types of delusion (*mithyātva*) according to Jainism.

2. According to Advaita, it is defined as: beginningless (*ānādi*), positive (*bhāva-rūpa*), removable by right knowledge (*jñāna-nivartya*), having its locus either in *Brahman* or in the individual soul (*jīva*), having the two powers of concealment (*āvaraṇa*) and projection (*vikṣepa*), and indeterminable (*anirvacanīya*).

3. Vide *avidyā*.

अज्ञातज्ञापन - *Ajñāta-jñāpana* - knowing what is not otherwise known; the unknown becoming known

अकल्पित - *Akalpita* - unimagined

अकाम - *Akāma* - desireless

आकाङ्क्षा - *Ākāṅkṣā* - expectancy; mutual affinity between words; syntax

1. One of the material conditions or causes which brings about a valid cognition from a proposition. Words must be compatible in order to fulfil this condition, e.g., a mere string of words such as man, horse, dog, cow, etc. does not produce a valid sentence.

2. Vide *āsatti*, *yogyatā*, and *tātparya*.

आकार - *Ākāra* - form

आकरज - *Ākaraja* - mineral; one of the four kinds of fire

Vide *tejas*.

आकारजबन्ध - *Ākāraja-bandha* - limitation by form

अकर्मकृत - *Akarma-kṛta* - non-karmically made

1. According to Viśiṣṭādvaita, those bodies which are non-eternal and non-*karma* made. These include the forms of *Īśvara* such as *mahat*, etc., and the forms of *avatāras* assumed at their will (*saṅkalpa*).

2. Vide *anitya-śarīra*.

अकर्तृ - *Akartṛ* - not an agent

आकाश - *Ākāśa* - ether; space

1. One of the five elements. Vide *mahābhūta*.

2. In Buddhism, one of the 3 *asamskṛta-dharmas*. It is held to be a permanent, omnipresent, immaterial substance. Its essence is free from obstruction. Vide *asamskṛta-dharma*.

3. In Jainism, it is an all-pervasive, subtle, existent substance which provides the ground for all other substances to exist.

4. According to Nyāya-Vaiśeṣika, it is what is inferred as the eternal and all-pervasive substratum in which sound inheres.

5. According to Sāṅkhya and Advaita, it is one of the five elements which are produced and destroyed.

अकेवलत्व - *Akevalatva* - manifoldness

अखण्ड - *Akhaṇḍa* - indivisible; whole; undivided

अखण्डदेश - *Akhaṇḍa-deśa* - indivisible space

अखण्डकाल - *Akhaṇḍa-kāla* - impartite time; indivisible time

It is held to be eternal and all-pervasive.

अखण्डाकारवृत्तिज्ञान - *Akhaṇḍākāra-vṛtti-jñāna* - the modal cognition through which *Brahman* is apprehended; direct knowledge of the Self (*ātman*) in Advaita

This is knowledge which arises through a mental mode, the object of which is the impartite *Brahman.* This modification (*vṛtti*) is called *antya-vṛtti.* It destroys every other *vṛtti*, giving rise to the direct perception of Reality (*sākṣātkāra*), and then perishes itself as well, leaving only the Reality.

अखण्डार्थ - *Akhaṇḍārtha* - impartite.

अखण्डार्थ-वाक्य - *Akhaṇḍārtha-vākya* - identity statement

1. A sentence where the subject and the predicate refer to the same entity. Each word has its own

meaning and yet, both of them refer to one entity, e.g., "That thou art" (*tat tvam asi*) or "This is that Devadatta" (*so'yaṁ devadattaḥ*).

2. According to Advaita, it is a literal expression of the non-dual Reality.

3. Viśiṣṭādvaita holds that the grammar of language is the grammar of Reality and thus, unlike Advaita, it posits that identity statements indicate a qualified Reality.

अखण्डोपाधि - *Akhaṇḍopādhi* - an attribute which is not a generic or class attribute but which is similar to it

आख्यात - *Ākhyāta* - verbal suffix

अख्याति - *Akhyāti* - non-apprehension

The theory of error of the Sāṅkhya and the Prābhākara-Mīmāṁsā schools. Error is conceived as a case of omission or non-observation. When an individual mistakes a snake for a rope and makes a judgment, 'This is a snake,' the error lies in the non-apprehension of the non-relation between the perceived 'this' and the remembered snake. There is no error in respect of the object which is seen, nor in respect of the snake remembered. The error is in one's failure to realise that they are non-related as subject and predicate. Thus error is due to incomplete knowledge and arises from non-discrimination.

अकिञ्चनत्व - *Akiñcanatva* - absolute want

आकिञ्चन्य - *Ākiñcanya* - sense of meekness

अक्लिष्ट - *Akliṣṭa* - non-afflicted

According to the Yoga school, a state of the mind which leads one towards liberation.

आकृति - *Ākṛti* - form

आक्ष – *Ākṣa* - pertaining to the senses

अक्षपाद - *Akṣapāda* - name of Gautama, author of the *Nyāya-sūtras*

अक्षर - *Akṣara* - imperishable; immutable

A name for the Reality in its transcendent immutable aspect.

आक्षेप - *Ākṣepa* - objection

आकुञ्चन - *Ākuñcana* - contraction

1. One of the five types of action.
2. Vide *karma.*

आकूत - *Ākūta* - idea; intention

अलाभ - *Alābha* - loss

अलक्षण – *Alakṣaṇa* - indefinable; without any sign or mark

आलम्बन - *Ālambana* - support

आलस्य - *Ālasya* - idleness; apathy; sloth

अलातचक्र - *Alāta-cakra* - fire-brand circle

अलातशान्ति - *Alāta-Śānti* - quenching of the fire-brand

The title of Chapter IV of the *Māṇḍūkya-kārikā* in which Gauḍapāda explains the illusoriness of the phenomenal world by comparing it to the illusory designs produced by the waving of a fire-brand.

अलौकिक - *Alaukika* - transcendental; super-normal

अलौकिकमुख्यविशेष्यता - *Alaukika-mukhya viśeṣyatā* - super-normal principal substantiveness

अलौकिकसाक्षात्कार - *Alaukika-sākṣātkāra* - super-normal immediate apprehension

अलौकिकसन्निकर्ष - *Alaukika-sannikarṣa* - super-normal contact

अलौकिकविषयता - *Alaukika-viṣayatā* - super-normal objectness

आलयविज्ञान - *Ālaya-vijñāna* - store-consciousness

A term used in Yogācāra Buddhism to indicate the store-house consciousness. The Yogācāras posit a reality of nothing but ideas, consciousness (*vijñāna*), and this store-house is the carrier of all latent potencies and the receptacle for all accumulating tendencies. It can also mean the transcendent and eternal Reality which is the Absolute Consciousness. Thus, depending upon one's perspective, it is either the continually changing stream of consciousness or the Absolute Being itself. As it is always changing, dynamic, and a continuum which is one and homogenous, it is unanalyseable by the faculty of reasoning.

अलिङ्ग - *Aliṅga* - without any characteristic or mark

Sometimes used in reference to one perspective of the Sāṅkhyan *prakṛti* in which no characteristic may be affirmed of it.

अलोभ - *Alobha* - disinterestedness

आलोचन - *Ālocana* - bare awareness; simple perception; non-determinate cognition

आलोचनज्ञान - *Ālocana-jñāna* - sense cognition

अलोक - *Aloka* - the transcendent region of liberated souls according to Jainism

(आळ्वार्) - *Āḻvār* - (Tamil) - one who has taken a deep plunge into the ocean of divinity

1. In the *Bhāgavata-purāṇa* it is said that the devotees of Lord *Viṣṇu* would appear in South India on the banks of rivers. This reference is to the twevle *Āḻvārs* who were wandering saints dedicated to spreading *Viṣṇu's* glory by songs. They propagated the path of devotion. Their compositions are collected in the *Nālāyira-divya-prabandha* (The Book of Four-thousand Divine Stanzas).

2. The twelve *Āḻvārs* are: Periy–aḻvār, Āṇḍāḷ, Kulaśekhara Āḻvār, Tirumaḻiśai Āḻvār, Toṇḍaraḍippoḍi Āḻvār, Tiruppāṇaḻvār, Madhurakavi Āḻvār, Tirumaṅgai Āḻvār, Nammāḻvār, Poygai Āḻvār, Bhūdattāḻvār and Pēy Āḻvār.

अमल - *Amala* - pure

अमात्रा - *Amātrā* – modeless; the fourth (*turīya*) state

Vide *turīya.*

अम्भः - *Ambhaḥ* - a form of laziness

Vide *tuṣṭi.*

आम्नाय - *Āmnāya* - tradition; scripture

अमोषधर्म - *Amoṣa-dharma* - that which is not lost

अमृत - *Amṛta* - immortality; divine nectar; juice of divine delight

अंश - *Aṁśa* -- part; component; limb

अंशत्रय - *Aṁśa traya* - the triple aspects

They are the method, the means, and the end.

अंशिन् - *Aṁśin* - whole

1. One of the ten categories in Dvaita. It is not the parts, nor their relation, nor both.

2. Vide *padārtha* and chart no. 6.

अमूर्त - *Amūrta* - formless; without form; void; subtle

अनभिभव - *Anabhibhava* - not being overcome

अनभिव्यक्त - *Anabhivyakta* - potential; not manifest

अनधिगत - *Anadhigata* - previously unacquired; original

अनधिगतार्थ - *Anadhigata-artha* - what is not known

अनध्यवसाय - *Anadhyavasāya* - want of definite knowledge; indefinite correlation

Vide *saṁśaya*.

अनादि - *Anādi* - beginningless; eternal

According to Advaita, six things are eternal: *Brahman*, *Īśvara*, *jīva*, *avidyā*, the difference between the *jīva* and *Īśvara*, and the relation between pure consciousness and *avidyā*.

अनागामिन् - *Anāgāmin* - never-returner

1. A Buddhist aspirant who has destroyed all the obstacles to perfection (*nirvāṇa*). Such a one will never be born into the cycle of birth and death again.

2. Vide *bodhisattva.*

अनागत - *Anāgata* - future; not yet come into existence

अनैकान्तिकहेतु - *Anaikāntika-hetu* - non-absolute reason

1. A type of fallacy in inferential reasoning wherein the concomitance of the middle term (*hetu*) with the major term (*sādhya*) is not absolute, e.g., sound is eternal since it is an object of knowledge. (Being an object of knowledge is found present in eternal as well as non-eternal things.)

2. Vide *hetvābhāsa.*

अनैकान्तिकत्व *Anaikāntikatva* – inconclusiveness

अनक्षर – *Anakṣara* - without letters; non-alphabetic

आनन्द - *Ānanda* - bliss; delight; a type of *samādhi* in which the mind concentrates on the intellect

आनन्दमयकोश - *Ānandamaya-kośa* - the sheath of bliss

1. The innermost of the five sheaths enveloping the self.

2. Truly speaking it is infinite, transcendent, and perfect and not really a sheath but the very essence of the Self according to some schools.

3. It is also known as the causal body (*kāraṇa-śarīra*), according to Advaita.

आनन्दतारतम्य - *Ānanda-tāratamya* - gradation of bliss

The nature of release is graded in Dvaita according to the soul's level of knowledge. The four levels are: entering the abode of *Viṣṇu* (*sālokya*), proximity to God (*sāmīpya*), having the form of God (*sārūpya*), and united to God (*sāyujya*).

अनन्त - *Ananta* - infinite

अनन्तदर्शन - *Ananta-darśana* - infinite perception

According to Jainism, the soul, in its pure state, possesses infinite perception.

अनन्तज्ञान - *Ananta-jñāna* - infinite knowledge

According to Jainism, the soul, in its pure state, possesses infinite knowledge.

अनन्तर - *Anantara* - immediate

अनन्तसुख - *Ananta-sukha* - infinite bliss

According to Jainism, the soul, in its pure state, possesses infinite bliss.

अनन्तवीर्य - *Ananta-vīrya* - infinite power

According to Jainism, the soul, in its pure state, possesses infinite power.

अनन्य - *Ananya* - similar but not equal; non-different; identical; non-separate

अनन्यार्हशेषत्व - *Ananyārha-śeṣatva* - absolute serviceability to one only

अनन्यथासिद्ध - *Ananyathā-siddha* - indispensable antecedent

A technical term employed by the Vaiśeṣika school. The cause is the indispensable or necessary antecedent of the effect.

अनपदेश - *Anapadeśa* - fallacious middle

An instance of fallacious reasoning wherein there is no connection between the major and middle terms.

अनपेक्ष - *Anapekṣa* - independent

अनर्थ - *Anartha* - suffering; evil

अनर्थदण्डव्रत - *Anartha-daṇḍa-vrata* - a Jaina ethical code of conduct which enjoins one to abstain from harmful activities

अनर्थहेतु - *Anartha-hetu* - undesired middle term

Vide *anumāna.*

अनर्वाचीन - *Anarvācīna* - ancient determinate and indeterminate perception

1. A type of perception which does not need the help of the sense organs. Vide *pratyakṣa.*

2. It is the knowledge possessed by *Īśvara*, eternals (*nityasūris*), and liberated souls (*mukta*) according to Viśiṣṭādvaita.

अनार्य - *Anārya* - ignoble; unholy

अनशन - *Anaśana* - an external penance in Jainism; fasting

अनाश्रव - *Anāśrava* - undefiled

अनाशृततत्त्व - *Anaśṛta-tattva* - independent categories (unaffected by *māyā*)

1. The first five categories in Kashmir Śaivism.

Vide chart no. 9.

2. An act of cognising consciousness in which there is no objective content as yet.

अनाथ - *Anātha* - without a protector

अनात्मन् - *Anātman* - without substance; not-self

The Buddhist theory of the non-existence of the soul.

अनत्त - *Anatta* - (Pāli term) same as *anātman*

अनौपाधिक - *Anaupādhika* - unconditional; necessary

Vide *vyāpti*.

आणव - *Āṇava* - impurity of ignorance

1. In Śaiva Siddhānta, it is the root impurity (*mūla-mala*). It is the cause of delusion by which the infinite soul becomes finite. It is beginningless and a positive entity which is the original cause of the soul's bondage. It is due to *āṇava* that the other two *malas*, *karma* and *māyā*, get tainted and become fetters for the soul. It has two powers called *āvāraka-śakti* (concealing) and *adhoniyāmaka-śakti* (projecting).

2. Vide *mala*.

अनवकाश - *Anavakāśa* – that whose scope remains unfulfilled

अनवसाद - *Anvasāda* - cheerfulness

Vide *sādhana-saptaka*.

अनवस्था - *Anavasthā* - infinite regress; *regressus ad infinitum*

Vide *tarka*.

आणवोपाय - *Āṇavopāya* - one of the four steps to liberation according to Kashmir Śaivism

Vide *upāya.*

आनय - *Ānaya* - bring

अण्ड - *Aṇḍa* - cosmic sphere(s); the whole

They are infinite in number according to some traditions.

अण्डज - *Aṇḍaja* - egg-born body

अन्धतामिस्र - *Andha-tāmisra* - a type of false knowledge; self-love

Vide *viparyaya.*

अनेकान्त - *Anekānta* - manifoldness

1. According to Jainism, nothing can be affirmed absolutely as all affirmations are true only under certain conditions.

2. Vide *anekānta-vāda.*

अनेकान्तवाद - *Anekānta-vāda* - the theory of relative pluralism; manifoldness

1. According to Jainism, all things are relatively manifold. Nothing can be affirmed absolutely as all affirmations are true only under certain conditions. Thus the nature of Reality can only be expressed in several steps — no single definition is adequate to describe all of its manifoldness.

2. Vide *sapta-bhaṅgi.*

अङ्ग - *Aṅga* - individual; part; limb; accessory

1. There are eight limbs to Patañjali's *rāja-yoga.*

Vide *aṣṭāṅga-yoga.*

2. According to Buddhism, the name of each member of the twelve links in the causal chain of existence. Vide *pratītyasamutpāda.*

3. According to Jainism, the *Aṅgas* are its chief scriptures. Vide *Aṅgāḥ.*

अङ्गबाह्य - *Aṅga-bāhya* - not incorporated in the twelve *Aṅgas*

1. One of the two classes of knowledge contained in the Jaina scriptures. This class has twelve varieties within it.

2. Vide *śruta-jñāna.*

अङ्गाः - *Aṅgāḥ* - the name of the Jaina sacred books or canonical literature

1. There are eleven *Aṅgas* which constitute the oldest existing Jaina canon.

2. Vide chart no. 2.

अङ्गप्रविष्ट - *Aṅga-praviṣṭha* - incorporated in the twelve *Aṅgas.*

1. One of the two classes of knowledge contained in the Jaina scriptures.

2. Vide *śruta-jñāna.*

अङ्गस्थल - *Aṅga-sthala* - part of the classification scheme of Vīra Śaivism

Vide *ṣaṭ-sthala, liṅga-sthala,* and chart no. 14.

अङ्गत्वबोधकप्रमाण - *Aṅgatva-bodhaka-pramāṇa* - according to Mīmāṁsā, the list of principles by which one could decide whether there obtains a subsidiary relation or not

They are: direct assertion (*śruti*), indication or capability (*liṅga*), context (*prakaraṇa*), position or proximity (*sthāna*), syntactical relation (*vākya*), and designation (*samākhyā*).

अङ्गि - *Aṅgi* - the whole

According to Viśiṣṭādvaita, the individual is a part (*aṅga*) or mode (*prakarā*) of God who is the whole (*aṅgi*). God, together with individuals and matter, is an organic whole.

अङ्गुलित्व - *Aṅgulitva* - fingerness

अनिच्च - *Anicca* - (Pali term) - vide *anitya*

अणिमा - *Aṇimā* - little; minute

1. The capacity to become small like an atom and to be invisible.

2. Vide *aṣṭa-aiśvarya*.

अनिमित्त - *Animitta* - no cause; uncaused

अनिन्द्रिय - *Anindriya* - not a sense organ

अनिर्मोक्षप्रसङ्ग - *Anirmokṣa-prasaṅga* - impossibility of release from the cycle of birth and death

अनिरुद्ध - *Aniruddha* - one of the four *vyūhas* of the theistic systems

1. He emanates from *Pradyumna* and rules over ego (*ahaṅkāra*). He protects the creation and makes known liberation which results from practice (*sādhana*). He has consummate potency and splen-

dour. He is the origin of the sub-*vyūhas*, viz., *Hṛṣīkeśa*, *Padmanābha*, and *Dāmodara.*

2. Vide *vyūha.*

अनिर्वचनीय - *Anirvacanīya* - indeterminable as either real or unreal; indeterminability

अनिर्वचनीय अनुपपत्ति - *Anirvacanīya-anupapatti* - the untenability of the indefinability of ignorance (*avidyā*)

1. One of Rāmānuja's seven major objections against the Advaita theory of *avidyā.*

2. Vide *saptavidha-anupapatti.*

अनिर्वचनीयख्याति - *Anirvacanīya-khyāti* - the indefinability of apprehension

1. The theory of error of Advaita. Advaita holds that the object of error is neither real nor unreal. As the object of error is sublatable it is not ultimately real. And as the object of error is perceivable, it cannot be said to be totally unreal. It cannot be both real and unreal for that amounts to a violation of the law of contradiction. For perceptual error to take place, two main factors are necessary. There must exist a substratum (*adhiṣṭhāna*) on which the false is superimposed, and there must be a defect (*doṣa*) called ignorance. This ignorance projects the false object upon the substratum.

2. Vide *khyāti.*

अनिर्वाच्यवाद् - *Anirvācyā-vāda* - the doctrine of the indeterminable or the indefinable

अनिसर्गज - *Anisargaja* - not natural

अनिष्ट - *Aniṣṭa* – undesirable

अनित्य - *Anitya* - impermanent

अनित्यदोष - *Anitya-doṣa* - occasional defect

अनित्यफल - *Anitya-phala* - non-eternal results; transitory fruits

अनित्यशरीर - *Anitya-śarīra* - non-eternal bodies

They are twofold: non-*karma*-made bodies (*akarma-kṛta*) and *karma*-made bodies (*karma-kṛta*). Again, they are classified as either non-ambulent or ambulant.

अनित्यता - *Anityatā* - transitoriness

अनित्यवाद - *Anitya-vāda* - the doctrine of momentariness

Vide *kṣaṇika-vāda.*

अङ्कुर - *Aṅkura* – sprout

अन्नमयकोश – *Annamaya-kośa* - the sheath of food

1. It is the outermost sheath enveloping the individual soul. It is made of food and is also called the physical body or the gross body.
2. Vide *sthūla-śarīra.*

अनोत्तप - *Anottapa* - hardness of heart

अनृत - *Anṛta* - falsehood

अन्त - *Anta* - extremity; end

अन्तःकरण - *Antaḥ-karaṇa* - the internal organ

1. It is comprised of the intellect, the mind, the ego, and the consciousness (*buddhi*, *manas*, *ahaṅkāra*, and *cit*) according to Advaita. The Sāṅkhya school recognises only the intellect, mind, and ego as comprising the inner organ.

2. It is the seat of the functions of the senses as distinct from their outer organs. It receives and arranges what is conveyed to it through the senses. It reflects objects by its relation with the self (*puruṣa*) according to Sāṅkhya or by its relation to the Self (*ātman*) according to Advaita.

3. According to Advaita, the variations of different individuals' cognitions are due to the differences in their respective *antaḥ-karaṇas*.

4. The inner organ functions by streaming out to an object, illumining it, assuming its shape, and then cognizing it according to Advaita.

अन्तःकरणवृत्ति - *Antaḥ-karaṇa-vṛtti* - mental mode; modification of the internal organ

In perception, the mind becomes identified with the object perceived and takes its form.

अन्तःप्रज्ञ - *Antaḥ-prajña* - inwardly cognitive

The dream state wherein consciousness still funtions, but is not externally manifested. This dream consciousness is technically called *taijasa*. Here the dreamer experiences subtle objects which are projections of the mind.

अन्तःप्रवेश - *Antaḥ-praveśa* - entering into

अन्तर - *Antara* - internal; interior; inside

अन्तरा-भव - *Antarā-bhava* - an intermediate state between death and rebirth according to Buddhism

अन्तरङ्गसाधन - *Antaraṅga-sādhana* - proximate aid to liberation

1. In *rāja-yoga*, the last three limbs of the *aṣṭāṅgayoga*, i.e. *dhāraṇā*, *dhyāna* and *samādhi*, are known as the internal spiritual disciplines.

2. Vide *sādhana-catuṣṭaya.*

अन्तराय - *Antarāya* - a sub-type of *karma* particle which binds the soul

1. According to Jainism, they are of five types and are responsible for obscuring the inherent power of the soul. They obscure respectively: charity, profit-making, enjoyment, will-power, and circumstances under which enjoyment will be possible. These *karmas* determine the inborn energy of the soul by the obstruction of which it prevents the doing of a good action when there is a desire to do it.

2. Vide *aghāti-karma.*

अन्तर्भूतकारयिता - *Antarbhūta-kārayitā* - immanent cause of creation

अन्तरिक्ष - *Antarikṣa* - sky

अन्तर्मुख - *Antar-mukha* - inward vision

According to Kashmir Śaivism, Śiva limits His powers through inward vision so that the withdrawal of the world is effected.

अन्तर्व्याप्ति - *Antar-vyāpti* – inner concomitance

Concomitance between that which has the characteristic of the mark (*liṅga*) and that which has the characteristic of the subject (*sādhya*), e.g., fire, in the sentence "Where there is smoke there is fire."

अन्तर्यामिन् - *Antaryāmin* - indweller; inner guide; inner ruler

1. The immanent form of God.

2. The cosmic form of the Self as associated with *māyā*.

3. Vide *Īśvara*.

अन्त्यविशेष - *Antya-viśeṣa* - ultimate particularity

For example, the atoms (*aṇu*) of the Vaiśeṣika system.

अणु - *Aṇu* - atomic; elementary particle; that which cannot be further divided

1. The smallest indivisible particle of matter of which all material things are ultimately produced. They are said to be eternal.

2. Viśiṣṭādvaita calls the size of the soul, 'atomic'.

3. According to Jainism, atoms have touch, taste, smell, and colour. Two atoms form a compound (*skandha*). They maintain that atoms are in contact with one another (a fact which Buddhists deny).

4. According to the Vaiśeṣikas, they are insentient. Two of them grouped together form a dyad and three dyads together form a triad, which is the smallest visible substance. The four elements, earth, air, fire, and water are atomic in their

primary form. The variety seen in the universe is due to the number of atoms in a particular object's composition. Atoms are eternal and qualitatively differ as smell, taste, colour, and touch. Atoms have no parts, are non-spatial, and are globular (*pārimāṇḍalya*).

अनुबन्धचतुष्टय - *Anubandha-catuṣṭaya* - four prerequisites

There are four preambulary factors to a philosophical work: the subject matter (*viṣaya*), the aim (*prayojana*), the relation (*sambandha*), and the persons for whom the work is meant (*adhikārīn*).

अनुभाग - *Anubhāga* - intensity

According to Jainism, one of the four *bandhas*.

अनुभव -- *Anubhava* - perception; direct presentation; knowledge; experience

अनुभाव - *Anubhāva* - that which indicates a feeling

According to Indian aesthetics, this is one of the three factors regarded as the efficient cause of *rasa*. It is the effect or manifestation of an emotion. All the physical changes that accompany an emotion come under this term. They are of two main types: *sāttvika-bhāvas*, which are involuntary expressions ofan emotion which cannot be produced at will, and *bhāvas* other than *sāttvika-bhāvas*. Bharata enumerated eight *sāttvika bhāvas*: stupefaction (*stambha*), perspiration (*sveda*), horripilation (*romāñca*), change of voice (*svara-bheda*), trembling (*vepathu*), change of colour (*vaivarṇya*), shedding tears (*aśru*), and fainting (*pralaya*). Vide *rasa*.

अनुभूत - *Anubhūta* - sub-perceptional

अनुभूति - *Anubhūti* - direct apprehensions; experience which reveals new knowledge; experience

अनुद्भूतत्व - *Anudbhūtatva* - non-manifestedness

अनुद्धर्ष - *Anuddharṣa* - not overjoyed

Vide *sādhana-saptaka.*

अनुग्रह - *Anugraha* – grace

आनुकूल्यस्य सङ्कल्पः - *Ānukūlyasa saṅkalpaḥ* - to conceive what is in conformity with the will of Īśvara

Vide *prapatti.*

अनुलोम - *Anuloma* – in a natural order

अनुमान - *Anumāna* - inference; syllogism; instrument of inference

1. Literally it means 'after-knowledge', that is, knowledge which follows other knowledge. Inferential knowledge is knowledge that results through the instrumentation of some other knowledge (*jñāna-karaṇaka-jñānam*)

2. It is the efficient instrument of inferential cognition.

3. It is divided intoknowledge for others (*parārtha*) and knowledge for oneself (*svārtha*), due to distinctions according to purpose or it is divided into: *parvavat, śeṣavat,* and *sāmānyatodṛṣṭa,* due to distinctions according to the kinds of relation (*vyāpti*), or it is divided into: *kevalānvayi, kevala-vyatireki,* and *anvaya-vyatireki* due to distinctions according to the establishment of the *vyāpti.* Vide *vyāpti.*

4. Nyāya claims there are five members of a syllogism: thesis (*pratijñā*), reason (*hetu*), exemplification (*udāharaṇa*), subsumptive correlation (*upanaya*) and the conclusion (*nigamana*).

5. Mīmāṁsā claims there are needed only three members in a syllogism and they may be comprised of either the *pratijñā*, *hetu* and *udāharaṇa* or of the *udāharaṇa*, *upanaya*, and *nigamana*.

6. Buddhism claims that only two members of a syllogism are necessary: the *udāharaṇa* and *upanaya*.

7. There are five conditions to be fulfilled in a valid inference. The reason must be present in the minor term; the reason must be found wherever the major term is found; the reason must not be found wherever the major term is not found; the reason must not be related to something absurd; and the reason must not be contradicted by an equally strong middle term.

8. Vide *liṅga-parāmarśa–vyāpti*, and *hetvābhāsa*.

9. Some old Naiyāyikas claimed there were ten members of an inference: desire to know the truth (*jijñāsā*), doubt about the real nature of a thing (*saṁśaya*), capacity of the *pramāṇas* to lead to true knowledge (*śakyaprāpti*), the purpose of making an inference (*prayojana*), removal of all doubts about the truth of an inference(*saṁśaya-vyudāsa*), thesis (*pratijñā*), reason (*hetu*), example (*udāharaṇa*), application of the example (*upanaya*), and the final conclusion (*nigamana*).

आनुमानिक - *Ānumānika* - inferential

अनुमेय - *Anumeya* - object of inference

अनुमिति - *Anumiti* - inference

अनुमितिकरण - *Anumiti-karaṇa* - prime cause of inference

अनुपलब्धि - *Anupalabdhi* - non-cognition

1. The Bhāṭṭa Mīmāṁsakas and the Advaitins hold that non-existence (*abhāva*) is known through non-cognition. The absence of an object is known due to its non-perception. It is the specific cause of an immediate knowledge of non-existence. It is based upon the presumption that non-existence is a separate category. The above two schools are the only schools to accept non-cognition as a separate valid means of knowledge (*pramāṇa*). Even as positive apprehension of some existent through a valid means of knowledge is a way of cognizing, so is the non-apprehension of something another way of cognizing according to these two schools. The critics say that this is merely a variant of perception and not really a separate source of cognition. However, as it is the specific cause of an immediate knowledge of non-existence, which is not produced by any other means of knowledge, it deserves a place in the list of valid *pramāṇas* — thus claim the Bhāṭṭa Mīmāṁsakas and the Advaitins.

2. Vide *pramāṇa*.

अनुपलम्भ - *Anupalambha* - non-apprehension

अनुपपत्ति - *Anupapatti* - untenability

Vide *saptavidha-anupapatti*.

अणुपरिमाण - *Aṇuparimāṇa* - size of the atom; atomic measurement

अनुपसंहारिन् - *Anupasamhārin* - non-conclusive reason

1. A type of fallacious reasoning in which the reason has no affirmative or negative example, e.g., all things are non-eternal because they are knowable.

2. Vide *savyabhicāra.*

अनुपाय - *Anupāya* - one of the four steps to liberation according to Kashmir Śaivism

Vide *upāya.*

अनुप्रमाण - *Anu-pramāṇa* - secondary means of knowledge

1. The sources of valid knowledge are held to be secondary means according to Dvaita. They are the means (of acquiring valid knowledge) though they reveal an object only indirectly. These means include: perception, inference, and verbal testimony. It is *kevala-pramāṇa* which is defined as giving knowlede of an object as it is.

2. Vide *kevala-pramāṇa.*

अनुप्रेक्षा - *Anuprekṣā* - a process to stop the inrush of *karma* particles

1. According to Jainism, it is one of the *bhāva-samvaras.* It consists of meditation about the transient character of the world, about one's helplessness without the truth, about the cycles of birth and death, about one's duties and responsibilities for one's good and bad actions, about the distinction between the soul and non-soul, about the defects of the physical body, about the influx of *karma* and its stoppage and destruction, and

about the essential principles of the soul, the world, knowledge, faith, and conduct.

2. Vide *bhāva-saṁvara.*

आनुपूर्वी - *Ānupūrvī* - particular order; regular

अनुसन्धान - *Anusandhāna* - subsumptive correlation; the application

The Vaiśeṣika technical term for *upanaya*, one of the five members of a syllogism.

अनुस्मृति - *Anusmṛti* - remembrance

अनुस्मृतिनिर्देश - *Anusmṛti-nirdeśa* - reminiscent discrimination referring only to the past

Vide *nirdeśa.*

अनुष्णाशीत - *Anuṣṇāśīta* - lukewarm

अनुष्ठान - *Anuṣṭhāna* - observance; pursuit

अनुष्ठिति - *Anuṣṭhiti* - action

अनुत्तमाम्भस् - *Anuttamāmbhas* - increase of desires leading to greater disappointments

Vide *tuṣṭi.*

अनुत्तर - *Anuttara* - a name for Reality according to Kashmir Śaivism

According to Kashmir Śaivism, there is nothing beyond this great Reality.

अणुत्व - *Aṇutva* - smallness

According to Nyāya-Vaiśeṣika, smallness (*aṇutva*) and largeness (*mahattva*) are the two main varieties of size.

अनुवाद् - *Anuvāda* - restatement ; translation

अनुवादक - *Anuvādaka* - corroborative; translator

अणुव्रत - *Aṇu-vrata* – the lesser vows

1. The five vows which a householder is prescribed to observe in Jainism. These observances consist of non-violence, truthfulness, non-stealing, celebacy, and non-covetousness. These vows are the same in form as those enjoined upon the monks and nuns, with the exception that they are milder and a less scrupulous observance is expected and enjoined.

2. Vide *mahā-vrata* and compare with *yama.*

अनुवृत्त - *Anu-vṛtta* - continuity; persistence

अनुव्यवसाय - *Anu-vyavasāya* - recognition; re-perception; reflexive cognition

अनुव्यवसायज्ञान - *Anu-vyavasāya-jñāna* - after-cognition; reflexive cognition; aware of awareness

1. According to Nyāya, a cognition wherein both knowledge and the knowing subject get revealed. A cognition wherein the mind comes into contact for a second time with a cognition which has already been perceived.

2. A second-order knowledge.

अनुयोगिन् - *Anuyogin* - correlate

1. The ground or substrate of non-existence. The locus of non-cognition. When two things are related, the correlate exists in the counter-correlate or locus; e.g., between a pot and the floor,

the floor is the locus or ground for the pot. It is also known as *pratiṣedha-viṣaya*.

2. Vide *pratiyogin*.

अन्वागत - *Anvāgata* - connected

अन्वय - *Anvaya* - positive; affirmative

अन्वयदृष्टान्त -*Anvaya-dṛṣṭānta* - affirmative example

अन्वयसहचार - *Anvaya-sahacāra* - sequence of positive factors

अन्वयव्याप्ति - *Anvaya-vyāpti* - positive concomitance

अन्वयव्यतिरेक - *Anvaya-vyatireka* - positive and negative concomitance

1. A type of inference based upon the invariable concomitance of agreement in presence and agreement in absence. In this type of inference, the reason (*hetu*) is both co-present and co-absent with the major term (*sādhya*), e.g., smoke is both positively and negatively concomitant with fire. In a hearth, smoke is co-present with fire, and in a lake, smoke is co-absent with fire.

2. Vide *anumāna*.

अन्वयव्यतिरेकि - *Anvaya-vyatireki* - vide *anvaya-vyatireka*

आन्वयिक - *Ānvayika* - directly connected

आन्वीक्षिकी - *Ānvīkṣikī* - the science of logic

अन्विताभिधानवाद - *Anvitābhidhāna-vāda* - expression of the construed

1. The Prābhākara Mīmāṁsā theory that words convey their own meanings as well as the construed meaning of the sentence.

2. Vide *abhihitānvaya-vāda.*

अन्यतरकर्मज - *Anyatara-karmaja* - one of the two actions

1. A type of conjunction where one substance comes and conjoins another. Vide *saṁyoga.*
2. A type of disjunction where the action of one of the conjoined substances leads to separation, e.g., a leaf falling from a tree. Vide *vibhāga.*

अन्यथा - *Anyathā* - otherwise than what it is

अन्यथाभान - *Anyathā-bhāna* - becoming otherwise

One thing appears as another without really changing, e.g., a straight stick appears bent when seen through water.

अन्यथाभाव - *Anyathā-bhāva* - existing otherwise

When an object changes, it is no more as it was. When gold is made into a bangle, it no longer appears as a lump of gold.

अन्यथाग्रहण - *Anyathā-grahaṇa* - otherwise-than-what-it-is apprehension; misapprehension

अन्यथाज्ञान - *Anyathā-jñāna* - false cognition; otherwise-than-what-it-is cognition

अन्यथाख्याति - *Anyathā-khyāti* - apprehension otherwise

The theory of error propounded by the Nyāya school. The object of error exists, but not in the place where it is perceived. The 'this' of error is proximate, but the object of error is elsewhere.

Error consists in wrongly synthesising the 'this' with the object of error.

अन्यथासिद्ध - *Anyathā-siddha* - dispensable antecedent; accidental circumstance

A dispensable antecedent is not the true cause of an effect.

अन्यथासिद्धशून्य - *Anyathā-siddha-śūnya* - not being established as other than indispensable

अन्यत्वभावन - *Anyatva-bhāvana* - to meditate on the fact that all individuals are different

अन्योन्याभाव - *Anyonya-abhāva* - reciprocal non-existence

1. It is also called difference (*bheda*). In stating 'A is not B', the significance of 'not' is reciprocal non-existence or difference. This type of non-existence is eternal.

2. Vide *abhāva*.

अन्योन्याश्रय - *Anyonya-āśraya* - reciprocal dependence; mutual support

1. The fallacy of mutual dependence, i.e., 'A is dependent on B and B is dependent upon A'. This leads to fallacious reasoning.

2. Vide *tarka*.

अप् (आपः) - *Ap* (*āpaḥ*) - water

1. One of the five elements. It possesses colour, taste, and touch.

2. Vide *mahābhūta*.

अपचार - *Apacāra* - beginningless impurity; disobedience to Śiva's will

अपच्छेदन्याय - *Apacchedanyāya* - the principle of the subsequent sublating the earlier

It is so called because it was expounded by the Pūrva Mīmāṁsā school in connection with the expiatory rites which are to be performed when the various priests let go their hold of the tucked-up waist cloth of the priest in front while going around the sacrificial fire.

आपद्धर्म - *Āpad-dharma* - the law (*dharma*) of calamity

1. During times of distress, there is a certain laxity in the rules and regulations of the law. This is based upon the idea that before a good life may be secured, life itself must be preserved.

2. Vide *dharma*.

अपदेश - *Apadeśa* - middle term; second step in a syllogism; statement of the reason

A Vaiśeṣika term corresponding to the Nyāya term '*hetu*'.

अपध्यान - *Apadhyāna* - cessation from inflicting any bodily injuries, killing, etc.

आपः - *Āpaḥ* - water

Vide *ap*.

अपहतपाप्मन् - *Apahatapāpman* - sinless

अपहतपाप्मत्व - *Apahatapāpmatva* - purity

अपकर्ष - *Apakarṣa* - subtraction

अपान - *Apāna* - carrying-downwards breath

1. The life-breath which removes out of the human system all that is waste material. It is one of the five vital airs.

2. Vide *prāṇa*.

अपर - *Apara* - lower

A term employed in the *Upaniṣads* to describe knowledge relating to the phenomenal world.

अपरजाति - *Apara-jāti* - (vide *jāti*).

अपरत्व - *Aparatva* - spatial or temporal proximity

1. According to the Vaiśeṣika school, one of the categories (*padārtha*) is qualilty (*guṇa*). The twelfth quality is *aparatva* and it gives rise to perceptions of spatial and temporal nearness.

2. Vide chart no. 7.

अपरब्रह्मन् - *Apara-brahman* - the supreme Reality as conditioned by attributes

It is immanent, limited, and with name and form. It is master of the universe and within the cause-effect sphere. It is eternal, omnipresent, omnipotent, omniscient, creator, sustainer, and destroyer — according to Advaita.

अपरमार्थ - *Aparamārtha* - not-real

अपरमार्थरजत - *Aparamārtha-rajata* - not-real silver

अपारमार्थिक - *Apāramārthika* - unreal

अपरमुक्त - *Apara-mukta* - souls failing to understand
Vide *jīva* per Śaiva Siddhānta.

अपरा विद्या - *Aparā vidyā* - lower knowledge

अपरिग्रह - *Aparigraha* - non-possession; non-grasping

1. It is to accept only that which is absolutely necessary, in thought, word and deed.
2. One of the limbs of *cāritra* (right conduct) and also one of the great vows (*mahā-vrata*) in Jainism.
3. One of the abstentions (*yama*) in the Yoga school.
4. Vide *cāritra*, *mahā-vrata*, and *yama*.

अपरोक्ष - *Aparokṣa* - immediate; direct

अपरोक्षज्ञान - *Aparokṣa-jñāna* - direct intuition; Brahman-khowledge; immediate cognition

अपरोक्षप्रतिभास - *Aparokṣa-pratibhāsa* - an object of immediate perception

अपौरुषेय - *Apauruṣeya* - impersonal; not the composition of any person

The *Vedas* are said to be impersonal as they were revealed to *ṛṣis* and not composed by them. They are held to be eternal and authorless. Not even God is considered their author according to Advaita.

अपवाद - *Apavāda* - statement; recession; subsequent denial

Vide *adhyāropa-apavāda*.

अपवर्ग - *Apavarga* - liberation; release; escape from pain

1. The Nyāya-Vaiśeṣika term for liberation.

2. The Sāṅkhya-Yoga term for liberation.

3. Ultimate cessation from pain. Vātsyāyana expounded that liberation was only cessation from pain and not a positive state of bliss.

अपाय - *Apāya* - annihilation; losing

अपेक्षाबुद्धि - *Apekṣābuddhi* - enumerative cognition

1. A cognition which has the notion of relativeness, of two-ness.

2. The Vaiseṣika school uses this term to account for the conception of numbers.

अपोह - *Apoha* - exclusion; negation

The Buddhist theory of word-meaning based on the principle of negation. Words, when applied to unique particulars, mean only exclusion.

अप्रचरितशून्यता - *Apracarita-Śūnyatā* - an unknown type of nothingness

अप्रधान - *Apradhāna* - secondary

अप्राकृत - *Aprākṛta* - non-material

अप्रमा - *Apramā* - invalidity

Nyāya defines invalidity as: not truth, not untruth, but invalidity, i.e. doubt.

अप्रमत्त - *Apramatta* - without losing oneself

अप्रमेय - *Aprameya* - not an object of valid knowledge; immeasurable

अप्राप्यकारि - *Aprāpyakāri* - not remaining in its place

1. All the sense organs except the visual sense remain in their respective places and perceive objects which come within their reach. The visual organ streams out towards its object.

2. Vide *prāpyakāri.*

अप्रसिद्ध - *Aprasiddha* - not well-established; non-existent; unknown

अप्रतिसङ्ख्यानिरोध - *Apratisaṅkhyā-nirodha* - natural annihilation

1. One of the three unconditional (*asaṁskṛta*) *dharmas* of Buddhist metaphysics. It is non-substantial, non-existent, and illusory. It means the destruction of a thing brought about naturally. It is cessation brought about by the absence of conditioning factors.

2. The Sautrāntika school does not make so much of a difference between *pratisaṅkhyā-nirodha* and *apratisaṅkhyā-nirodha* as the Vaibhāṣika school does.

3. Vide *pratisaṅkhyā-nirodha.*

अप्रत्यक्ष - *Apratyakṣa* - imperceptibility

अप्रवृत्ति - *Apravṛtti* - involution

अपृथक्सिद्धविशेषण - *Apṛthak-siddha-viśeṣaṇa* - inseparable attribute

अपृथक्सिद्धि - *Apṛthak-siddhi* - internal relation of inseparability

The key concept of Viśiṣṭādvaita. It is the relation that obtains between *Brahman* on the one hand and souls (*cit*) and matter (*acit*) on the other. This internal, inseparable relation connotes that one of the two entities related is dependent upon the other in such a way that it cannot exist without the other also existing. Thus the relation between substance and attribute, between body and soul, and between *Brahman* and the soul, or the world, is necessarily inseparable according to Viśiṣṭādvaita. The dependent entity cannot be rightly known without the other also being known at the same time.

आप्त - *Āpta* - trustworthy person

One who knows the truth and conveys it correctly.

आप्तकाम - *Āpta-kāma* - the state of having attained one's desires

आप्तवचन - *Āpta-vacana* - words of reliable authority or trustworthy person; testimony

The Nyāya school defines *śabda* or verbal testmony as the testimony of a reliable authority.

आप्तवाक्य - *Āpta-vākya* - the testimony of a trustworthy person

आप्ति - *Āpti* - attainment

1. One of the fourfold effects of *karma*.
2. Vide *karma*.

अपुनरावृत्ति - *Apunarāvṛtti* - non-return

अपूर्व - *Apūrva* - unseen potency; new

Vide *adṛṣṭa*.

अपूर्वविधि - *Apūrva-vidhi* - unknown or unseen injunction

1. A type of injunction which enjoins something not otherwise known.

2. Vide *vidhi.*

आराधना - *Ārādhanā* - worship of the divine; adoration; self-surrender

आरादुपकारक - *Ārād-upakāraka* - indirect means; a subsidiary action which is directly helpful to something else; an accessory

अराग - *Arāga* - dispassion

आराग्रमात्र - *Ārāgramātra* - atomic; point-sized

आरम्भवाद - *Ārambha-vāda* - the theory of origination

The Nyāya-Vaiśeṣika theory of causation which states that the effect is a new production from the cause. The cause is one thing, the effect is another. The effect is held to be non-existent before its production by the cause. This theory is also called *asatkārya-vāda.*

अरणि - *Araṇi* - wooden piece; tinder-stick

आरण्यक - *Āraṇyaka* - scriptural text

That section of the *Vedas* which gives philosophical prose treatises. It interprets the ritual section by allegorizing them and prescribing various modes of meditation. It was mainly meant for ascetics who lived in the forest.

अर्चा - *Arcā* - worship; adoration; image

Vide *arcāvatāra.*

अर्चनम् - *Arcanam* - worshipping an image or idol of the divine

Vide *bhakti.*

अर्चावतार - *Arcāvatāra* - sacred images or idols

1. That special form which the divine, without remoteness of space and time, accepts for its body as a substance chosen by the devotees and descends into it with a non-material body.

2. It is fourfold: self-manifested, consecrated by divine beings, consecrated by sages, and consecrated by human beings.

3. It is God in the spape of sacred idols and one of the fivefold forms of *Īśvara.*

4. Vide *vyūha.*

अर्चिरादिमार्ग - *Arcirādi-mārga* - the path to liberation; the passage through which *jīva* journeys to the Supreme Being/Abode

अर्चिष्मति - *Arciṣmati* - radiant insight

Vide *bodhisattva.*

आर्द्रेन्धन - *Ārdrendhana* - green wood; wet fuel

अर्हन्त - *Arhanta* - enlightened one; holy one

According to Jainism, this is the fourth stage in an ascetic's spiritual evolution. In this stage all traces of anger, pride, greed, deceit, attatchment, hatred, and ignorance are destroyed. The practice of non-violence is now perfect. At this stage, one's very presence is able to convert and uplift the people.

अर्हत् - *Arhat* - enlightened one; holy one

1. One of the stages of the Jaina ascetic order. *Arhat* is an intensely spiritual being who radiates purity to all. Vide *arhanta.*

2. In Hīnayāna Buddhism, an *arhat* is one who is an enlightened saint who has obtained his deliverance through instruction.

3. According to Buddhism, there are three stages: *srotāpatti-mārga* or the stage of entering the stream; *sakṛdāgāmi-mārga* or the stage of the once-returner; and *anāgāmi-mārga* or the stage of the never-returner.

आर्जव - *Ārjava* - straight-forwardness

आरोह - *Āroha* - ascent

आरोप - *Āropa* - hypothetical admission; superimposition

आरोपित - *Āropita* - appearance; assumed

आर्ष - *Ārṣa* - authority; sagelike intuition

अर्थ - *Artha* - wealth

1. One of the goals of life (*puruṣārtha*) sought by individuals. It is the secular value which is both desired and desirable. It satisfies the acquisitive tendency in individuals. It is the economic value.

2. Vide *puruṣārtha.*

अर्थाधिगति - *Arthādhigati* - attaining what one wishes to attain

अर्थाध्याहारवाद - *Arthādhyāhāra-vāda* - the theory of supplying the meaning

अर्थक्रियाज्ञान - *Artha-kriyā-jñāna* - knowledge attained by practical efficiency

अर्थक्रियाकारित्व - *Artha-kriyā-kāritva* - the power of performing actions and purposes of some kind; practical efficiency; the doctrine of causal efficiency

1. A criterion of right knowledge according to the Nyāya school.

2. A criterion of existence according to Buddhism.

अर्थक्रियासिद्धि - *Artha-kriyā-siddhi* - the fulfillment of any need; the accomplishment of producing any action or event

अर्थनय - *Artha-naya* - the viewpoint which is concerned with the meaning of objects

Vide *naya*.

अर्थानुपपत्ति - *Arthānupapatti* - contradiction of the present perception with a previously acquired certain knowledge

अर्थापत्ति - *Arthāpatti* - postulation; presumption

1. Postulation is a valid source of knowledge (*pramāṇa*) for the Mīmāṁsā schools and for Advaita. It is the postulation of what explains through the knowledge of what is to be explained. It is the process of knowledge which makes something intelligible by assuming something else.

2. It is of two kinds: postulation from what is heard (*śruta-arthāpatti*) and postulation from what is seen (*dṛṣṭa-arthāpatti*).

3. The Prābhākara school says that it involves an element of doubt and postulation's job is to

remove that doubt. The Bhāṭṭa school says that it involves a conflict between two wellknown facts. Advaita says that there is neither a doubt nor a conflict, but merely an inexplicable fact which needs explaining. Presumption is the framing of an explanatory hypothesis on the basis of the knowledge of the fact to be explained, posits Advaita.

अर्थप्रकाश - *Artha-prakāśa* - that which reveals others

अर्थप्रापकत्व - *Artha-prāpakatva* - practical experience

अर्थप्राप्ति - *Artha-prāpti* - a synonym of postulation (*arthāpatti*)

A term found in the *Caraka-saṁhitā.*

अर्थवाद् - *Artha-vāda* - eulogistic meaning; corroborative sentence; supplimental texts which are explanatory to injunctive texts

1. Sentences in the *Vedas* which, occurring in context, may either describe existing things, praise, or denounce some deed of injunction. They are held to be subordinate to injunctive sentences, according to the Mīmāṁsakas. They indicate their meaning only as syntactically connected with the injunctive sentences.

2. They are of three kinds: *guṇa-vāda* or figurative statements; *anu-vāda* or statements which reiterate what is already known; and *bhūtārtha-vāda* or a statement of a fact which is not already known and which is not contradictory to known facts.

अरुळ - *Aruḷ* - (Tamil) divine grace

अरुन्धतीदर्शनन्याय - *Arundhatī-darśana-nyāya* - the method of spotting the tiny star, *Arundhatī*, with the help of larger stars near it, by calling each one *Arundhatī* as it is pointed out until one actually arrives at the tiny star itself

1. The process of moving from the known to the unknown.

2. The process of moving from a prelimininary definition to a final definition.

अरूप - *Arūpa* - formless

अरूपलोक - *Arūpa-loka* – realm of incorporeality

अर्वाचीन - *Arvācīna* - recent determinate and indeterminate perception

1. They are twofold: dependent on senses (*indriya-sāpekṣa*) and independent of the senses (*indriya-anapekṣa*).

2. Vide *pratyakṣa*.

आर्य अष्टाङ्गमार्ग – *Ārya aṣṭāṅga-mārga* - the noble eightfold path

It is the fourth of Buddha's four noble truths embodying the path that leads to the ending of sorrow. It is the middle way which leads to *nirvāṇa*. The path consists of eight steps which are to be cultivated together. The eight steps are: right view (*samyag-dṛṣṭi*), right speech (*samyag-vāk*), right resolve (*samyak-saṅkalpa*), right conduct (*samyak-karmānta*), right livelihood (*samyag-ājīva*) right effort (*samyag-vyāyāma*), right recollection (*samyak-smṛti*), and right contemplation (*samyak-samādhi*).

आशा - *Āśā* - hope

असदकारणात् - *Asad-akāraṇāt* - that which has no existence does not possess the capacity to create

One of the proofs for *satkārya-vāda* found in the *Sāṅkhya-kārikā.* Thus the effect must exist previously, potentially in the cause before it is produced.

असद्भाव - *Asad-bhāva* - non-being

असाधारण - *Asādhāraṇa* - special; uncommon; strange; extra-ordinary; too restricted

1. That which is free from the three faults of a definition viz., over-applicability (*ati-vyāpti*); partial inapplicability (*a-vyāpti*); and total inapplicability (*asambhava*).

2. A type of fallacious reasoning in which the reason is fallacious due to its being present only in the subject and not present in any example; e.g., "Sound is eternal because it is sound."

3. Vide *savyabhicāra.*

असाधारणधर्म - *Asādhāraṇa-dharma* - specific feature

असाधारणकारण - *Asādhāraṇa-kāraṇa* - special cause; specific cause

असद्रूप - *Asadrūpa* - existing in a place in a negative relation; imperceptible to the senses

असाध्य - *Asādhya* - that which cannot be accomplished through actions

असहिष्णुभेदवादिन् - *Asahiṣṇu-bheda-vādin* - the followers of Sāṅkhya

They are called *asahiṣṇu-bhedavādin* because they refuse to recognize the distinct existence of cause and effect.

अशक्ति - *Aśakti* - inability

असमानजातीयद्रव्यपर्याय - *Asamāna-jātīya-dravya-paryāya* - (vide *paryāya*)

असमवायिकारण - *Asamavāyi-kāraṇa* - non-inherent cause

1. One of the three types of causes. Vide *kāraṇa*.

2. It is that cause which produces its characteristics in the effect through the medium of the material cause (*upādāna*); e.g., clay is not the cause of the colour of the pot, but the colour of the clay is the cause of the colour of the pot.

3. It is never the inherent cause, but that which inheres in the inherent cause.

असम्भव - *Asambhava* - total inapplicability

1. The third fault of a definition that stultifies the latter. It is the absence of definition anywhere in the thing defined.

2. Vide *asādhāraṇa*.

असम्भावना - *Asaṃbhāvanā* - doubt

Doubt is of two types: doubt per the source of knowledge (*pramāṇa*) which is removed by hearing (*śravaṇa*); and doubt per the object of knowledge (*prameya*) which is removed by reflection (*manana*).

असम्भावना शङ्का - *Asambhāvanā śaṅkā* - doubt which questions whether what the scripture tells one is possible or not

It is removed by repeated contemplation (*nididhyāsana*).

असंज्ञिन् - *Asaṁjñin* - without rationality

According to Jainism, the lower animals have no faculty of reason.

असम्प्रज्ञासमाधि - *Asamprajñā-samādhi* - a stage in *samādhi* wherein one is not conscious of any object

1. In this stage the mind ceases to function.

2. Vide *samādhi*.

असम्प्रज्ञात - *Asamprajñāta* - without knowledge of objects

असंस्कृत - *Asaṁskṛta* - non-originated; non-constructed; eternal

असंस्कृतधर्म - *Asaṁskṛta-dharma* - non-originated *dharma*

1. That which is eternal, permanent, unchanging, and pure, according to Buddhism. It does not originate from a cause nor is it destroyed.

2. It is of three types according to the *Sarvāstivādins*: *pratisaṅkhyā-nirodha*, *apratisaṅkhyā-nirodha*, and *ākāśa*.

आसन - *Āsana* - posture; seat

1. One of the eight limbs of *rāja-yoga*. Vide *aṣṭāṅga-yoga*.

2. External aids which constitute the physical culturing of the individual.

3. A name for the small mat upon which one sits during meditation.

4. A posture that is stable and conducive to bliss.

असन्दिग्ध - *Asandigdha* - an assured definite cognition

आशङ्का - *Āśaṅkā* - doubt

One of the members of the ten-membered syllogism. Vide *saṁśaya.*

आशङ्काप्रतिषेध - *Āśaṅkā-pratiṣedha* - removal of doubt

One of the members of the ten-membered syllogism. Vide *saṁśaya-vyudāsa.*

असङ्ख्येयकल्प - *Asaṅkhyeya-kalpa* - a very vast period of time

असार - *Asāra* - worthless

अशरण - *Aśaraṇa* - without help; helpless

अशरणभावना - *Aśaraṇa-bhāvanā* - a meditation on helplessness

अशरीरत्व - *Aśarīratva* - formless; bodiless

अशाश्वत - *Aśāśvata* - non--eternal

असत् - *Asat* - non-being; non-existence; false

असत्कार्यवाद - *Asat kārya-vāda* - the theory of the non-pre-existent effect

1. The Nyāya-Vaiśeṣika theory of causation which states that the effect is a new production from the cause. The cause is one thing, the effect is another. The effect is held to be non-existent prior to its production by the cause.

2. This theory is also known as *ārambha-vāda.*

असत्ख्याति - *Asat-khyāti* – apprehension of the non-existent

The theory of error held by the Mādhyamika Buddhist school. According to them, the object of error is totally non-existent. Error is the cognition of a totally non-existent object as being existent. There is no substrate whatever for delusive cognitions and the sublation of these delusions is without limit. Vide *khyāti-vāda.*

असत्प्रतिपक्ष - *Asat-pratipakṣa* - absence of opposite probans

An inference in which the reason (*hetu*) is such that it may establish an opposite conclusion as equally strong as the one it attempts to establish is called *satpratipakṣa.* The inference in which the reason is not so is *asat-pratipakṣa.*

आसत्ति – *Āsatti* - proximity

1. The formal condition which words must possess to constitute a sentence. The words that go to make up a sentence must be proximate or contiguous in time when they are spoken, or in space when they are written. Thus it consists in the articulation of words without undue delay. It is also called *sannidhi.*

2. Vide *ākāṅkṣā*, *yogyatā*, *tātparya*, and *sannidhi.*

असत्य - *Asatya* - unreal; untrue

आशौच - *Āśauca* - impurity

आसव - *Āsava* – depravities

The Buddhists classify them as: *kāmāsava*, *bhavā-sava*, *ditthāsava*, and *avijjāsava*. (Compare this with the Jaina term: *āsrava*).

असिद्ध - *Asiddha* - unestablished (reason); untrue

1. A fallacious reason. It is of three kinds: unestablished in respect of abode (*āśraya-asiddha*), unestablished in respect of itself (*svarūpa-asiddha*), and unestablished in respect of its concomitance (*vyāpyatva-asiddha*).

2. Vide *hetvābhāsa*.

अस्मिता - *Asmitā* - egoism; state of concentration

1. One of the five afflictions of the mind. It is the erroneous identification of the self with the mind-body complex.

2. According to the Yoga school, it is a state of unifying concentration (*samādhi*). In this state the intellect (*buddhi*) concentrates on pure substance as divested of all modifications.

3. Vide *kleśa*.

अस्पर्शयोग - *Asparśa-yoga* - the *yoga* of no contact

1. The *yoga* of transcendence whereby one realizes the supra-rational Reality. The path to the realization of non-duality.

2. It is prescribed in the *Māṇḍūkya-kārikā* of Gauḍapāda.

आश्रम - *Āśrama* - a halting place; stage of life

There are four stages of life's journey. They delineate the individual's vertical ascent to liberation.

These four are: the student stage (*brahmacarya*), the householder stage (*gṛhastha*), the forest-dweller (*vānaprastha*), and the renunciant (*sannyāsa*). These emphasize the individual aspect of one's personal development. They are stages of strife when selfishness is slowly but steadily rooted out.

अश्रौत - *Aśrauta* - non-scriptural

Vide *āgama*.

आस्रव - *Āsrava* - influx of karmic matter

1. The entrance of *karma* particles into the body of the individual soul. It is a cause of human bondage. It acts as a channel through which the *karma* may enter the soul and these channels are said to be of forty-two types according to Jainism.

2. It is of two types: it is *bhāva-āsrava* when the soul loses its resistence to the inflow of *karma* particles and *dravya-āsrava* when the actual influx of *karma* binds the soul.

3. There are five main sources from which matter flows into the soul: perversity of outlook (*mithyātva*), absence of self-control (*avirati*), negligence of duties (*pramāda*), passions (*kaṣāya*), and actions of the body, mind and speech (*yoga*).

आश्रय - *Āśraya* - support; ground; locus

आश्रय-अनुपपत्ति - *Āśraya-anupapatti* - untenability of locus

1. One of Rāmānuja's seven major objections against the Advaita theory of *avidyā*.

2. Vide *saptavidha-anupapatti*.

आश्रयासिद्ध - *Āśraya-asiddha* - unestablished in respect of abode; the fallacy of reason (*hetu*) which is not in the locus

1. One type of an unestablished reason. An example of this type of fallacy would be: "A sky-lotus is fragrant because it is a lotus, like the lotus in a pond." In this example, the sky-lotus is the abode or subject and as such it does not exist at all.

2. Vide *asiddha.*

आश्रिततत्त्व - *Āśrita tattva* - dependent categories

1. The latter thirty-one categories of Kashmir Śaivism. Vide chart no. 9.

2. Consciousness which admits the existence of other objects.

अश्रुतकल्पना - *Aśruta-kalpanā* - extra-textual assumption made to suit one's own ideas

अष्ट-ऐश्वर्य - *Aṣṭa-aiśvarya* - the eight powers

1. According to the Yoga school, eight super-normal powers may be attained by practising the Yoga path. These are: *aṇimā*, *laghimā*, *mahimā*, *prāpti*, *prākāmya*, *vaśitva*, *īśitva*, and *yatrakāmā-vasāyitva.*

2. Vide *siddhi.*

अष्ट-आवरण - *Aṣṭa-āvaraṇa* - the eight aids or protections; rules to be observed

According to Vīra Śaivism, there are eight protections by which an individual self protects itself from the three fetters (*mala*). They are necessary prerequisites to *ṣaṭ-sthala*. They are: obedience to a teacher (*guru*); worship of the divine Self (*liṅga*); reverence for a person who moves from place to place (*jaṅgama*); sipping the water in which the feet of a *guru* or *jaṅgama* have been ceremoniously washed (*pādodaka*); offering food to a *guru*, *jaṅgama*, or *liṅga* and then partaking sacramentally of what is left over (*prasāda*); smearing of the sacred ash (*vibhūti*, or *bhasma*); wearing of the sacred rosary beads (*rudrākṣa*), and uttering the five-syllabled formula '*namaḥ śivāya*' (*mantra*).

अष्टमूर्ति - *Aṣṭa-mūrti* - eight forms

The eight forms of God as described in Śaiva Siddhānta. God is said to pervade the earth, water, air, fire, sky, sun, moon, and mankind.

अष्टाङ्गयोग - *Aṣṭāṅga-yoga* - the eight-limbed *yoga*

According to the Yoga school, a discipline to remove afflictions and lead to the discriminative knowledge (of the Self and the not-Self) which gives liberation. The eight limbs are: abstentions (*yama*), observances (*niyama*), postures (*āsana*), control of breath (*prāṇāyāma*), withdrawal of the senses from their objects (*pratyāhāra*), fixing one's attention (*dhāraṇā*), meditation (*dhyāna*), and meditative trance, a state of oneness, or unifying concentration (*samādhi*). The first five limbs are external aids, and the last three are the internal aids.

अस्तेय - *Asteya* - non-stealing

1. One of the abstentions (*yama*) of the Yoga school.

2. It means not only not to take what does not belong to oneself, but also not to covet another's property, even mentally. Greed and envy are thus to be totally shunned. Vide *yama*.

3. In Jainism, it constitutes one of the great vows and one type of right conduct. Vide *mahāvrata* and *cāritra*.

अस्थान - *Asthāna* - without abode; not established

अस्थूल - *Asthūla* - not gross

आस्तिकदर्शन - *Āstikadarśana* - a name of the *Vaidika* systems

1. The schools of Indian philosophy which regard the *Vedas* as infallible and authoritative are called *āstika*. These orthodox schools (*āstika-mata*) are six: Nyāya, Vaiśeṣika, Sāṅkhya, Yoga, Mīmāṁsā and Vedānta. Vide *ṣaḍ-darśana*.

2. They are of two types: those which are directly based upon the *Vedas* (Mīmāṁsā and Vedānta), and those which are not directly based on the *Vedas* but which do accept their testimony and try to show how their systems are harmonious with the *Vedas* (Nyāya, Vaiśeṣika, Sāṅkhya, and Yoga).

अस्तिकाय - *Asti-kāya* - extended real

Anything that occupies space or has pervasiveness. It is a form of substance. The *astikāyas* are: matter (*pudgala*), medium of motion (*dharma*), medium of rest (*adharma*), and space (*ākāśa*), according to Jainism.

अस्ति-नास्ति - *Asti-nāsti* - either is or is not

Vide *syād-vāda.*

अशुभ - *Aśubha* - inauspicious

अशुचिभावना - *Aśuci-bhāvanā* - meditation on the impurity of the body

अशुद्ध - *Aśuddha* - impure; incorrect

अशुद्धाध्वन् - *Aśuddhādhvan* - impure way

1. The impure creation (the latter thirty-one categories of Kashmir Śaivism). Vide chart no. 9.

2. Vide *tattva.*

अशुद्धजीव - *Aśuddha-jīva* - impure individual

According to Jainism, this is an inidvidual in the state of bondage. As it is associated with *karma*, it is considered impure.

अशुद्धमाया - *Aśuddha-māyā* - impure *māyā*

1. According to Śaiva Siddhānta, *māyā* is twofold in nature. Impure *māyā* is that which is mixed with the impurities of ignorance (*āṇava*) and action (*karma*). From impure *māyā* evolve the bodies, organs, worlds, and objects of enjoyment for the impure souls. It may be equated with the Sāṅkhyan *prakṛti*. For pure *māyā*, vide *śuddha-māyā.*

2. Vide chart no. 9.

अशुद्धनिश्चय -- *Aśuddha-niścaya* - impure determination

Vide *naya-niścaya.*

अशुक्लाकृष्ण - *Aśuklākṛṣṇa* - neither white nor black

1. A type of *karma* according to the Yoga school.

2. Vide *karma.*

असुर - *Asura* - demon

असुरभि - *Asurabhi* - non-fragrant

आसुरी - *Āsurī* - demoniac

अश्वमेध - *Aśvamedha* - horse sacrifice

अश्वत्थ - *Aśvattha* - pipal tree

The eternal tree of life whose roots are in heaven.

अतल - *Atala* - nether world

1. One of the seven lower worlds. It is the nether pole of *Satya-loka.* It is a state of spiritual annihilation.

2. Vide *loka* and *tala.*

अतस्मिन्-तद्बुद्धिः - *Atasmin-tad-buddhiḥ* - the cognition of something as something else

Śaṅkarācārya's definition of superimposition (*adhyāsa*) as given in his *Brahma-sūtra-bhāṣya* introduction.

अथर्ववेद - *Atharva-veda* - (vide *Veda*)

अथातो ब्रह्मजिज्ञासा - *Athāto brahma-jijñāsā* - now, therefore, the inquiry into the real nature of *Brahman*

The first *sūtra* of the *Brahma-sūtra.*

अतिचार - *Aticāra* - transgressions of one type of ethical code

Vide *digvirati-vrata.*

अतिदेश - *Atideśa* - a type of injunction; analogy

For example, "Achieve heaven through charity for a whole month."

अतिदेशवाक्य - *Atideśa-vākya* - assimilative proposition

Vide *upamāna*.

अतीन्द्रिय - *Atīndriya* - trans-sensuous; infra-sensible; transcendental

अतिप्रसङ्ग - *Atiprasaṅga* - undue extension; unwarranted discussion

अतिरात्र - *Atirātra* - an optional part of the *jyotiṣṭoma* sacrifice

अतिरेक - *Atireka* - excess

अतिशय - *Atiśaya* - peculiarity; superiority

According to Jainism, a super-human quality of an *arhat*.

अतिथिसंविभाग - *Atithi-saṁvibhāga* – a Jaina ethical code of conduct enjoining honouring of one's guests

अतिथिसंविभागव्रत - *Atithi-saṁvibhāga-vrata* - making gifts to others

Vide *śikṣā-vrata*.

आतिवाहिकपुरुष - *Ātivāhika-puruṣa* - one who conducts the released individual self to the world of *Brahman*

अतिवर्णाश्रमिन् - *Ativarṇāśramin* – one beyond the rules of caste and the stages of life

अतिव्याप्ति - *Ativyāpti* - over-application; being too wide; over-pervasion

1. A fallacy in a definition which tries to say too much. It is the presence of the definition of something other than the thing sought to be defined.

2. Vide *asādhāraṇa*.

आत्मा - *Ātmā* - (vide *ātman*)

आत्मभाव - *Ātmabhāva* - the nature of the Self

आत्मैकप्रकारत्व - *Ātmaika-prakāratva* - deriving its modal existence from the Self

आत्मैकप्रयोजनत्व - *Ātmaika-prayojanatva* - entirely subserving the needs of the Self

आत्मैकाश्रयत्व - *Ātmaikāśrayatva* - dependent entirely on the Self

आत्मैकत्व - *Ātmaikatva* - unity of the Self

आत्मज्ञान - *Ātma-jñāna* - knowledge of the Self

आत्मकाम - *Ātma-kāma* - desirous of the Self

आत्मख्याति - *Ātma-khyāti* - the apprehension of the Self

1. The theory of error of Yogācāra Buddhism. Error is said to consist in mistaking what is internal to be external. All determinate cognitions of objects are erroneous as there are no external objects at all. What exists is only cognition, idea. The object of error is real, but not as existing outside in space. It is real as a mode of the mind.

2. Vide *khyāti-vāda*.

आत्ममनोवादिन् - *Ātma-manovādin* - a type of Cārvāka who considers the mind as the Self

आत्मन् - *Ātman* - Self

1. The Reality which is the substrate of the individual and identical with *Brahman*, according to Advaita. It cannot be doubted, for it is the basis of all experience. It cannot be known by thought as the knower cannot be the known. Yet there is no experience without it. It is the basis of all proofs, but cannot be proved itself, though it can be experienced.

2. Nyāya and Vaiśeṣika call it the substratum in which cognition inheres. It is of two kinds: supreme Soul and individual soul. It is a substance which is revealed in one's inner perceptual experience arising through the inner sense of mind, independently of the external senses.

3. Sāṅkhya and Yoga define it as an unrelated, attributeless, self-luminous, ominipresent entity which is identical with consciousness.

4. The *Upaniṣads* say that it denotes the ultimate essence of the universe as well as the vital breath in human beings.

5. It is the unseen basis which is the reality within the five sheaths. It is the spark of the divine within. It is the reality behind the appearance and universal and immanent in every entity. It is not born nor does it die. It is imperishable according to the *Upaniṣads*.

6. In the Indian philosophical systems, the Self is said to be of one of three sizes: Dvaita and Viśiṣṭādvaita call it atomic (*aṇu-parimāṇa*); Advaita and Sāṅkhya call it all-pervasive (*vibhu-parimāṇa*); Jainism calls it neither atomic nor all-pervasive but of medium size (*madhyama-parimāṇa*).

7. Buddhism denies any reality to the Self altogether. Vide *anātman*.

आत्मनिक्षेप - *Ātmanikṣepa* - to surrender oneself to *Īśvara* in all meekness

Vide *prapatti*.

आत्मनिवेदन - *Ātma-nivedana* – dedicating thought, word, and deed to God

Vide *bhakti*.

आत्मानुभव - *Ātmānubhava* - self-realization

आत्मसाक्षात्कार - *Ātma-sākṣātkāra* - realization of the true nature of the Self; Self-realization

आत्माश्रय - *Ātmāśraya* - self-dependence

A type of fallacy.

आत्मवाद - *Ātma-vāda* - the theory of the Self

A belief in the abiding reality of the Self. Sometimes the Advaitin is called an *ātma-vādin*.

आत्मविचार - *Ātma-vicāra* - enquiry into the nature of the Self

आत्मविद्या - *Ātma-vidyā* - knowledge of the Self

Realization of the reality of the Self.

अत्यन्त-अभाव - *Atyanta-abhāva* - absolute non-existence

1. One of the four types of non-existence. If in a locus, a thing is never present, then it is said that there is in that locus the absolute non-existence of that thing. This type of non-existence is held to be eternal by the Logicians, though this is denied by the Advaitins.

2. Vide *abhāva*.

अत्यन्त-अभेद् - *Atyanta-abheda* - absolute non-difference

अत्यन्तभिन्न - *Atyanta-bhinna* - absolute difference

अत्यन्तासत् - *Atyanta-asat* - complete non-being; non-existence

आत्यन्तिकदुःखध्वंस - *Ātyantika-duḥkha-dhvaṁsa* - final annihilation of sorrows

आत्यन्तिकप्रलय - *Ātyantika-pralaya* - the state wherein the individual obtains release from the bondage of matter

औदर्य - *Audarya* - the fire in the stomach; the fire of appetite

Vide *tejas*.

औदयिक - *Audayika* - the state in which *karma* takes its effect and produces its proper results in the ordinary manner

औपचारिकवृत्ति - *Aupacārika-vṛtti* - the secondary denotation of words; metaphorical

It is of two types: *lakṣaṇā* (e.g. the village is on the river), and *gauṇī* (e.g. the boy is a lion).

औपाधिक - *Aupādhika* - due to limiting adjuncts

औपम्य - *Aupamya* - comparison; analogy; resemblance

औपशमिक - *Aupaśamika* - complete subsidence of vision-deluding *karmas*

According to Jainism, by proper efforts *karma* may be prevented from taking effect though it still continues to exist. This is one of the 'states of being' within the doctrine of *guṇasthāna*. Vide *guṇasthāna*.

अवभास - *Avabhāsa* - appearance

अवच्छेदक - *Avacchedaka* - delimiting; limitation

The delimitant serves the purpose of specifying which attribute is referred to.

अवच्छेदकसम्बन्ध - *Avacchedaka-sambandha* - delimiting relation

Each delimited attribute has a specific relation and this relation must be stated to avoid any ambiguity.

अवच्छेदवाद - *Avaccheda-vāda* - the theory of limitation

1. The individual is but an abridgement of the supreme Brahman, according to Advaita. The body-mind complex seemingly limits the infinite *ātman*, just as a pot seemingly limits the infinite space. When the adjunct is dispensed with, one realizes the non-difference between the two.

2. This view is attributed to Vācaspati in Advaita.

अवच्छिन्न - *Avacchinna* - delimited

The object delimited, e.g., a pot is delimited by potness.

अवधान - *Avadhāna* - concentration; attention

अवधारण - *Avadhāraṇa* - assertion

अवधि - *Avadhi* - supernatural cognition; transcendental knowledge; clairvoyance; limit

1. According to Jainism, it refers to an individual's ability to perceive without the help of the sense organs and the mind, things which have shape and form. All living beings possess this capacity in varying degrees, with limitations appropriate to each, imposed due to *karmic* veils.

2. It is of three types: limited by space and time (*deśa-avadhi*), not limited by space and time (*parama-avadhi*), and apprehension of all modes of physical objects (*sarva-avadhi*).

अवधिदर्शन - *Avadhi-darśana* - a type of determinate understanding

Vide *upayoga.*

अवग्रह - *Avagraha* - sense-object contact devoid of particularity

1. The first stage in *mati-jñāna* according to Jainism. It is of two types: only contact between the subject and object (*vyañjana-avagraha*) and the subject both apprehends and feels the object (*artha-avagraha*).

2. Vide *mati.*

अवक्षेपण - *Avakṣepaṇa* - downward motion

Vide *karma.*

अवक्तव्य - *Avaktavya* - unspeakable; inconceivable; indescribable

अवाक्यार्थ - *Avākyārtha* - a sentence conveying a non-verbal sense

E.g., *tat tvam asi* - that thou art, according to Advaita.

अवलम्बन - *Avalambana* - basis

अवान्तरवाक्य - *Avāntara-vākya* - subsidiary text

A branch of the Upaniṣadic texts which do not give liberating knowledge. They are the intermediary texts which give knowledge about the Reality with form and attributes (*saguṇa-brahman*). This is a view held by Advaita.

अवाप्तसमस्तकाम - *Avāpta-samasta-kāma* - one whose desires are ever fulfilled

अवर - *Avara* - lower

आवारकशक्ति - *Āvāraka-śakti* - the power of *āṇava* which covers the cognitive, conative, and affective energies of the individual and renders them inoperative (*Śaiva siddhānta*)

आवरण - *Āvaraṇa* - concealment

1. The veiling power of ignorance. According to Advaita, one of the twofold powers of *avidyā.*

2. Vide *avidyā.*

आवरणशक्ति - *Āvaraṇa-śakti* - capacity to conceal

अवरोह - *Avaroha* - descent

अवस्था - *Avasthā* - state of experience; state of consciousness; condition

They are three in number: waking (*jāgrat*), dreaming (*svapna*), and deep sleep (*suṣupti*). Also vide *turīya.*

अवस्थाभेद - *Avasthā-bheda* - difference in condition

अवस्थाज्ञान - *Avasthā-jñāna* - any individual state or experience of ignorance

अवस्थापरिणाम - *Avasthā-pariṇāma* - change of experience or appearance with regard to the past, present, and future

अवस्थात्रयविचार - *Avasthā-traya-vicāra* - enquiry into the three states of experience

This is a technique used in Advaita to reveal the real nature of the individual. In its empirical existence, the individual has three kinds of experience — waking, dreaming, and deep sleep. The Self is involved in these three states through the adjunct of the body-mind complex with which it is associated. This enquiry is meant to reveal that the Self is not really affected by the triple stream of experience. It is adventitious and not natural to it. To realize this is to realize the fourth (*turīya*) state, or *Brahman*.

अवस्तु - *Avastu* - non-substantial

अवतार - *Avatāra* - divine incarnation; the descent of God into the world in a tangible form

1. According to Tradition there are ten *avatāras* of Viṣṇu: *Matsya*, *Kūrma*, *Varāha*, *Narasiṁha*, *Vāmana*, *Paraśurāma*, *Rāmacandra*, *Balarāma*, *Kṛṣṇa*, and *Kalki*. A variation of this list replaces *Balarāma* with *Buddha*.

2. They are of two types: principal and subordinate. The former is when Viṣṇu himself incarnates and the latter is the incarnation of inspired saints.

अवाय - *Avāya* - perceptual judgement

A stage in *mati-jñāna* wherein the object is known definitely. Vide *mati*.

अवयव - *Avayava* - premise; member; component part

1. The five premises (members) in a syllogism.
2. One of the sixteen categories in the N/ì system.
3. Vide *padārtha* and chart no. 6.

अवयावयवि - *Avayavāvayavi* - part and whole; mem and non-member

अवयविन् - *Avayavin* - the whole; composite structure

अविभाग - *Avibhāga* - inseparability

अविभागाद् वैश्वरूपस्य - *Avibhāgād-vaiśvarūpasya*-the unmanifest is that in which all effects dissolve

A Sāṅkhyan proof for the existence of *prakṛti.* As there is an identity between cause and effect, if one traces each effect backwards into its cause, eventually one will reach the unmanifest *prakṛti*.

अविचारसिद्ध - *Avicāra-siddha* - non-enquiry into the nature of the Ultimate

अविद्वान् - *Avidvān* - one who has no knowledge of the Ultimate.

अविद्या - *Avidyā* - ignorance; nescience

It is the key concept in the Advaita system. It serves as the corner-stone for Advaita metaphysics, epistemology, and ethical disciplines; thus its role cannot be belittled. It is characterized by six marks: it is beginningless (*anādi*); it is removed by right knowledge (*jñāna-nivartya*); it is a positive entity of the nature of an existent (*bhāva-rūpa*); it is indescribable (*anirvacanīya*); it has the two powers of concealment and projection which respectively represent the truth and suggest the false (*āvaraṇa* and *vikṣepa*); and its locus is either in the individual self (*jīva*) or in Brahman.

2. One of the twelve links in the causal chain of existence (vide *pratītyasamutpāda*). It is the root of all and the primary cause of existence according to Buddhism.

अविद्यादोष - *Avidyā-doṣa* - defect of ignorance

अविद्यानिवृत्ति - *Avidyā-nivṛtti* - removal of ignorance

अविद्यास्वभाव - *Avidyā-svabhāva* - nature of ignorance

अविद्यावृत्ति - *Avidyā-vṛtti* - a mode of ignorance

A modification of ignorance. It gives knowledge of illusory objects; internal states of the mind like pleasure and pain; and knowledge (*jñāna*) and ignorance (*avidyā*), according to Advaita. This knowing is done by the witness consciousness (*sākṣin*).

अविघात – *Avighāta* - non-obstruction

अविज्ञाता - *Avijñātā* - one who does not know; an epithet of Lord Viṣṇu

अविकल्पित - *Avikalpita* - indeterminate

अविकारि - *Avikāri* - not subject to change

अविनाभाव - *Avinābhāva* - invariable relation

अविरति - *Avirati* – lack of control

आविर्भूत - *Āvirbhūta* – manifest

अविरोध - *Avirodha* - non-conflict

अविशेष - *Aviśeṣa* - indeterminate

A technical term in Sāṅkhya for the ego (*ahaṅkāra*) and the five subtle essences of the elements (*tanmātra*).

अवीत - *Avīta* - a type of inference which proceeds by denying the consequent

1. A type of inference according to Sāṅkhya. It is called *śeṣavat.* It is essentially negative in nature as it is based on the co-absence of the major term (probandum) and the middle term (probans). In this type of inference, no positive instance is possible and only negative instances may be given; e.g., the effect (cloth) is non-different from the cause (threads), for the former inheres in the latter, as a property of it. No positive instance can be given because all instances will fall within what is sought to be proved. If the effect and the cause were different, inherence would be impossible.

2. Vide *śeṣavat.*

अविवेक - *Aviveka* - non-discrimination

अव्यभिचारि – *Avyabhicāri* - unalterable

अव्याकृत - *Avyākṛta* – unanswerable questions

They are the questions which Buddha refused to answer. They are ten (sometimes fourteen) questions on causality which Buddha answered by, 'Do not say so.'

अव्याकृताकाश - *Avyākṛtākāśa* - unmanifested ether

अव्यक्त - *Avyakta* - unmanifest

The Sāṅkhya term for *prakṛti.*

अव्यपदेश्य - *Avyapadeśya* - unspeakable; non-verbalizable

अव्याप्ति - *Avyāpti* - inapplicability; non-pervasion

1. A fallacy which attempts to give a definition which says too little. It is the absence of the definition in a thing sought to be defined.

2. Vide *asādhāraṇa.*

अव्याप्यवृत्ति - *Avyāpya-vṛtti* - non-pervasive

अव्याप्यवृत्तित्व - *Avyāpya--vṛttitva* - partial extensity

अव्यवहार्य - *Avyavahārya* - unrelatable

अव्यय - *Avyaya* - eternal; imperishable

आयाम - *Āyāma* - length; expansion; extension

अयमात्मा ब्रह्म - *Ayam-ātmā brahma* - this Self is *Brahman*

A great saying (*mahā-vākya*) which occurs in the *Māṇḍūkya Upaniṣad* of the *Atharva Veda.*

अयन - *Ayana* - solstice; a period of time; way

आयतन – *Āyatana* - field of operation

1. The sense organs *viz.*, mind, eyes, nose, mouth, ears, organ of elimination, and organ of generation.

2. Vide *pratītyasamutpāda.*

अयथार्थ - *Ayathārtha* - erroneous

अयथार्थानुभव - *Ayathārthānubhava* - erroneous experience

अयौगपद्य - *Ayaugapadya* - non-simultaneity

अयोनिज - *Ayonija* - origin unknown; not born of mortal beings

1. Bodies whose birth (origin) is unknown.

2. Those individuals not born of mortal beings e.g., Sītā.

आयुः - *Āyuḥ* (*āyus*) - age-determining

One of the eight main types of obscuring *karmas* in Jainism. It is subdivided into four types as relating to the duration of life (longevity) in the four states of the individual (*jīva*): celestial (*deva-āyus-karma*), human (*manuṣya-āyus-karma*), animal (*tiryag-āyus-karma*), and hell-being (*nāraka-ayus-karma*).

आयुहन - *Āyuhana* – conglomeration

आयुर्वेद - *Āyur-veda* - the scripture dealing with medicine

अयुतसिद्ध - *Ayuta-siddha* - the establishment of absolutely different things appearing as one inseparable whole; inseparable

1. This relation means that of the related entities one is invariably found associated with the other.

2. There are five types of *ayuta-siddha* objects according to Nyāya–Vaiśeṣika: *dravya* and *guṇa*; *dravya* and *karma*; particular (*vyakti*) and universal (*jāti*); ultimate things and *viśeṣa*; and whole (*aṁśin*) and parts (*aṁśa*).

अयुतसिद्धावयव - *Ayutasiddha-avayava* - the combination of parts which exist close together; a conglomeration of interrelated parts

B

बद्ध - *Baddha* - bound

बद्धजीव - *Baddha-jīva* - bound individual soul

Vide *jīva.*

बाध - *Bādha* - cessation; contradiction; fallacy

बाधक - *Bādhaka* - sublator

बाधकप्रतीति - *Bādhaka-pratīti* - sublating cognition

बाधायां सामानाधिकरण्य - *Bādhāyāṁ sāmānādhikaraṇya* - grammatical co-ordination in the sense of sublation

A theory used by the Advaitins to interpret the great sayings (*mahāvākyas*); e.g., originally one perceived the object as a post, but later realized that it was a man. The original perception of the post is thus sublated.

बाधित - *Bādhita* - sublated; stultified reason; contradictory reason

1. A logical fallacy which tries to prove a thesis which is contrary to direct experience; e.g., when someone says, 'fire is not hot because it is a substance' the thesis is wrong because of stultified reason.

2. This fallacy is also known as: *kālātīta* and *kālātyayāpadiṣṭa.*

3. Vide *hetvābhāsa.*

बहिःप्रज्ञा - *Bahiḥ-prajñā* – outer knowledge

In the waking state, an individual's awareness extends outside. One operates (knows) through one's ten senses (*indriyas*), five vital airs (*prāṇas*) and the internal organ (*antaḥ-karaṇa*). Through these, one receives stimuli from the external world and reacts to them in diverse ways.

बहिरङ्गसाधन - *Bahiraṅga-sādhana* - the remote aid to spiritual practices

1. It is comprised of daily and occasional actions (*nitya* and *naimittika-karmas*).

2. According to the Yoga system, the first five limbs of *aṣṭāṅga-yoga* are known as the external spiritual disciplines. These are: *yama, niyama, āsana, prāṇāyāma* and *pratyāhāra.*

बहिर्द्रव्यत्व - *Bahir-dravyatva* - external substanceness

बहिर्मुख - *Bahir-mukha* - outward vision

The cause for the exhibition of the universe according to Kashmir Saivism. Lord Śiva turns his vision outwards.

बाह्य - *Bāhya* - external

A type of perception in Nyāya.

बल - *Bala* - strength; force; vigour

Vide *bhaga.*

बलवदनिष्टाननुबन्धिन् - *Balavad-aniṣṭānanubandhin* - that which does not entail great harm

बन्ध - *Bandha* - bondage

1. According to Jainism, bondage is due to *karma* particles. It is caused by activities of the body-mind complex as influenced by passions. This bondage has two stages. *Bhāva-bandha* is a change in an individual's consciousness due to passions (*kaṣāya*). It prepares the individual for the actual bondage which follows (*dravya-bandha*). This latter stage is when there is an actual contact of the *karma* particles with the individual.

2. Bondage is of four kinds: nature bondage (*prakṛti-bandha*), space-quantity bondage (*pradeśa-bandha*), duration-quality bondage (*sthiti-bandha*), and intensity of fruition bondage (*anubhāga-bandha*).

बर्हिः - *Barhiḥ* - a kind of sacrificial grass

भग - *Bhaga* - six glorious features of God

They are: *jñāna* (wisdom), *śakti* (potency), *bala* (strength), *aiśvarya* (lordship), *vīrya* (valour), *tejas* (splendour).

भागत्यागलक्षणा - *Bhāga-tyāga-lakṣaṇā* - another name of *jahad-ajahal-lakṣaṇā*

Vide *jahad-ajahal-lakṣaṇā.*

भगवान् - *Bhagavān* - Lord; God; revered person

Vide *Īśvara.*

भगवदनुभव – *Bhagavad-anubhava* - God-realization

भागवत - *Bhāgavata* - devotee of God; name of a *Purāṇa*

भागवतकैंकर्य - *Bhāgavata kaiṅkarya* - service to the devotees of God

भगवत्पाद् - *Bhagavatpāda* - a term of respect applied to Śaṅkarācārya

भाग्य - *Bhāgya* - salvation worked out by fate; fortune Vide *tuṣṭi*.

भक्त - *Bhakta* - devotee; lover of God

1. According to Viśiṣṭādvaita, a devotee is one type of votary of liberation. They are those who have read the *Veda* together with its auxiliaries and the *Upaniṣads*, and who, from the knowledge of the earlier and later parts of the Mīmāṁsā, have determined the nature of *Brahman* as different from *cit* and *acit*. They are of the nature of bliss and know *Brahman* as of the nature of bliss, infinitude, and unsurpassability.

2. A stage of consciousness. Vide *sthala*.

भक्ति - *Bhakti* - loving devotion

1. It is of two types: *sādhana-bhakti* which is comprised of *aṣṭāṅga-yoga*, *sādhana-saptaka*, etc.; and *phala-bhakti* which is received by God's grace spontaneously.

2. It is also divided into nine forms: *śravaṇa*, *kīrtana*, *smaraṇa*, *pāda-sevana*, *arcana*, *vandana*, *dāsya*, *sakhya*, and *ātma-nivedana*. Vide *navavidhā bhakti*.

3. Devotion to God can assume many forms and the devotee can be related to God in one of many attitudes. The chief ones are: *dāsya*, the attitude

of a servant to his master; *sakhya*, the attitude of a friend to a friend; *vātsalya*, the attitude of a parent to a child; *śānta*, the attitude of a child to a parent; *kānta*, the attitude of a wife to a husband; *rati*, the attitude of a beloved to her lover; and *dveṣa*, the attitude of an atheist towards God.

भक्तिरूपापन्नज्ञान - *Bhakti-rūpāpanna-jñāna* - love of God; knowledge turned into devotion

भामतीप्रस्थान - *Bhāmatī-prasthāna* - the *Bhāmatī* school

1. One of the two schools within Advaita. Its most important works are: the *Bhāmatī* of Vācaspati, the *Kalpataru* of Amalānanda, and the *Parimala* of Appayya Dīkṣita.

2. The school derives its influence and inspiration from Maṇḍana Miśra.

भाषा - *Bhāṣā* - gentle and holy talk

Vide *samiti*.

भासक - *Bhāsaka* - revealer

भास्वर - *Bhāsvara* - brilliant

भाष्य - *Bhāṣya* – commentary

भाष्यकार - *Bhāṣyakāra* - commentator

1. The most well-known commentators on the *Brahma-sūtra* include: Śaṅkarācārya for Advaita, Rāmānuja for Viśiṣṭādvaita, and Madhvācārya for Dvaita.

2. Rāmānuja is familiarily known as 'the *bhāṣyakāra*' in Vedāntic literature of Viśiṣṭādvaita.

भाति - *Bhāti* - shining

In Advaita, *Brahman* is described as: *asti* (is), *bhāti* (shines), *priyam* (pleasure).

भट्ट - *Bhaṭṭa* - Kumārila Bhaṭṭa

1. The originator of one of the two main schools of Pūrva Mīmāṁsā.

2. Advaitins usually follow the Bhāṭṭa view in all matters empirical.

भौम - *Bhauma* - terrestrial

1. One of the four kinds of fire.

2. Vide *tejas*.

भौतिक - *Bhautika* - formed of matter; constituted of the gross elements

भव - *Bhava* - becoming; an epithet of Śiva

भाव - *Bhāva* - state of being; existence; emotion

1. Existence: that from which everything comes.

2. One of the twelve links in the causal chain of existence. Vide *pratītyasamutpāda*.

3. Becoming or a state of flux.

भावना - *Bhāvanā* - reminiscent impression; meditation; consideration

1. According to Jainism, it is a class of *śruta-jñāna*. It is the stage of reconsidering the nature of a familiar phenomenon so that a new phenomenon which is known to be associated with it can be properly understood.

2. According to the Vais'eṣika school, it is a type of trait (*guṇa*) of *saṁskāras*. It is that quality of the self by which things are constantly practised, remembered, or recognized.

भावास्रव - *Bhāva-āsrava* - a Jaina term describing the state wherein an individual soul loses its resistence to the inflow of karmic particles

Vide *āsrava.*

भावात्मक - *Bhāvātmaka* - a type of attribute (*dharma*) in Jainism which indicates the form and condition of a thing

भावबन्ध - *Bhāva-bandha* - a Jaina term describing the state wherein there is a change in an individual's consciousness due to passions

Vide *bandha.*

भावकर्म - *Bhāva-karma* - actions of body, mind, and speech which produce subtle *karma* matter according to Jainism

भावकार्य - *Bhāva-kārya* - positive product

भावलेश्य - *Bhāva-leśya* - the feelings generated by the accumulation of *karma* matter according to Jainism Vide *leśya.*

भावलिङ्ग - *Bhāva-liṅga* - a form of the formless Śiva

Vide *liṅga-sthala.*

भावनिर्जरा - *Bhāva-nirjarā* - a Jaina term describing the stage of an individual soul wherein there is a partial disappearance of karmic particles

1. This stage is effected by a modification or change in the individual itself.

2. Vide *nirjarā.*

भावपदार्थ - *Bhāva-padārtha* - existent entities

भावप्रत्ययसमाधि - *Bhāva-pratyaya-samādhi* - a form of attributeless *samādhi* in which a trace of ignorance remains

1. In this stage the latent tendencies of an individual's passions remain. Thus, even after attaining this stage, one will have to return to the world again.

2. Vide *samādhi.*

भावरूप - *Bhāvarūpa* - positive in nature

An attribute of ignorance (*avidyā*) according to Advaita.

भावसंवर - *Bhāva-saṁvara* - a Jaina term describing the state of an individual wherein the susceptibility to the inflow of karmic particles is stopped

1. This state includes: *mahā-vrata*, *samiti*, *gupti*, *dharma*, *anuprekṣā*, *parīṣahajaya*, and *cāritra.*

2. Vide *saṁvara.*

भाव्य - *Bhāvya* - what-is-to-be-accomplished

भय - *Bhaya* - fear

भेद - *Bheda* - difference

1. A key-concept of Dvaita. According to Dvaita, it is fivefold: the difference between God and individuals; between different individuals;

between God and matter; between individuals and matter; and between matter and matter itself in its various forms.

2. It is of three types: *svagata-bheda* or internal difference; *sajātīya-bheda* or the difference which exists between two objects belonging to the same class; and *vijātīya-bheda* or the difference which exists between two objects belonging to different classes. Vide each *bheda* listed individually.

भेदाभाव - *Bhedābhāva* - absence of duality or difference

भेदाभेद - *Bhedābheda* - the relation of identity in difference; difference-cum-non-difference

A view held by the Bhāṭṭa Mīmāṁsākas, the Nimbārka school, and first made well-known by Bhartṛprapañca.

भेदाभेदवाद - *Bhedābheda-vāda* - the theory of non-difference in difference

Vide *bhedābheda*.

भेदादन्यः - *Bhedād-anyaḥ* - something other than difference

भेदाग्रहण - *Bhedāgrahaṇa* - non-apprehension of difference

भेदसहिष्णु - *Bheda-sahiṣṇu* - compatible with difference

भेदसंसर्ग - *Bheda-saṁsarga* - relation of duality

Vide *vākyārtha*.

भेदश्रुति - *Bheda-śruti* - Upaniṣadic texts which support the doctrine of duality and plurality

भेदविरोधि - *Bheda-virodhi* - what is opposed to difference

भिक्षु - *Bhikṣu* - Buddhist monk or mendicant; beggar

भिक्षुसूत्र - *Bhikṣu-sūtra* - 'the monk's scripture'

A name for the *Brahma-sūtra* since those who are most competent to study it are monks or renunciants.

भिन्न - *Bhinna* - differentiated

भिन्नविषय - *Bhinna-viṣaya* - difference in subject-matter

भोग - *Bhoga* - enjoyment; pleasure; experience

Enjoyment or unending bliss in the state of liberation, according to Dvaita.

भोगाङ्ग - *Bhogāṅga* - pleasure-seeking individual

Vide *ṣaṭ-sthala.*

भोगस्थान - *Bhoga-sthāna* - abode of enjoyment

भोगवस्तु - *Bhoga-vastu* - object of enjoyment

भोगोपभोगपरिमाण - *Bhogopabhoga-parimāṇa* - a Jaina ethical code of conduct dealing with establishing limits to the use of objects with a view to minimize attatchment

भोगोपकरण - *Bhogopakaraṇa* - means of enjoyment

भोग्य - *Bhogya* - object of experience

भोग्यकाण्ड - *Bhogya-kāṇḍa* - objects of enjoyment

According to Śaiva Siddhānta, *māyā* provides the individual with the means, locations, and objects of enjoyment.

भोक्ता - *Bhoktā* - enjoyer

भोक्तृ - *Bhoktṛ* - enjoyer

भ्रम - *Bhrama* - error

The cognition of an object not as it is.

भ्रान्ति - *Bhrānti* - delusion

भृत्याचार - *Bhṛtyācāra* - a code of conduct enjoining humility towards Śiva

Vide *pañcācāra.*

भूः - *Bhūḥ* - the earth; the material world

Vide *loka.*

भूमि - *Bhūmi* - the earth; stage; floor

भूत - *Bhūta* - element

भूतादि - *Bhūtādi* - the state where *tamas* preponderates over *sattva* and *rajas*

From this evolve the *tanmātras* according to Sāṅkhya.

भूतपञ्चक - *Bhūta-pañcaka* - the five elements

The five elements are: earth (*pṛthivī*), air (*vāyu*), fire (*tejas*), water (*ap*), and ether (*ākāśa*).

भूततथता - *Bhūta-tathatā* - 'that'-ness of elements

भूतत्व - *Bhūtatva* – elementness

भुवः - *Bhuvaḥ* - the mid-region; the world of becoming

Vide *loka.*

भुवन - *Bhuvana* - the universe; the world

भुवनसुन्दर - *Bhuvana-sundara* - God as cosmic beauty

भूयोदर्शन - *Bhūyo darśana* - repeated observation

बीजाङ्कुरन्याय - *Bījāṅkura-nyāya* - the analogy of the seed and the tree, each being the cause of the other

बिम्ब - *Bimba* - original, prototype

बिम्बप्रतिबिम्बवाद - *Bimba-pratibimba-vāda* - reflection theory

The reflection theory of the Advaita *Vivaraṇa* school in which consciousness is said to be reflected in the adventitious condition, *avidyā*. According to this view, the individual is a reflection of intelligence present in egoity. As there exists no difference between a reflection and the original, the *jīva* is non-different from Brahman.

बिम्बोपासन -*Bimbopāsana* - meditation on the reflection

1. Meditation on the position of the individual as a reflection of the Lord.

2. According to Dvaita, this is one step in the means of release for the individual.

बिन्दु - *Bindu* - drop

The cause of form (*rūpa*) in Kashmir Śaivism. It is a combination of the four subtle elements (*tanmātras*).

बोध - *Bodha* - consciousness; knowledge

बोधिचित्त - *Bodhicitta* - love; foundation of all good; attitude to serve all

It has two aspects according to Buddhism. The stage when the individual resolves to become a *bodhisattva* (*bodhi-praṇidhi-citta*) and actually entering the path and taking the journey *bodhi-prasthāna-citta*.

बोधिप्रणिधिचित्त - *Bodhi-praṇidhi-citta* - vide *bodhicitta*

बोधिप्रस्थानचित्त - *Bodhi-prasthāna-citta* - vide *bodhicitta*

बोधिसत्त्व - *Bodhisattva* - a being aspiring to enlightenment; one who has attained the essence of wisdom

1. They exist for the good and happiness of all. Their ideal is enlightenment for all sentient beings.

2. They are of two types: earthly and transcendent.

3. There are ten stages to perfect *bodhisattva*-hood: *pramuditā*, *vimalā*, *prabhākarī*, *arciṣmatī*, *sudurjayā*, *abhimukti*, *dūraṅgamā*, *acalā*, *sādhumatī*, and *dharma-megha*.

4. In its early usages, it referred to the career of Siddhārtha Gotama. It gradually became extended to refer to all one's previous lives in one's passage to *Buddha*-hood.

ब्रह्मभाव - *Brahma-bhāva* - the state of being Brahman

ब्रह्मचर्य - *Brahmacarya* - abstention from incontinence; celebacy; dwelling in Brahman

1. Literally 'the path that leads to Brahman.'

2. The first stage of life, i.e., studentship. Vide *āśrama*.

3. One of the abstentions in the Yoga system. Vide *yama*.

4. One of the great vows and one of the proper modes of conduct according to Jainism. Vide *mahāvrata* and *cāritra*.

ब्रह्मज्ञान - *Brahma-jñāna* - knowledge of the Absolute

ब्रह्मन् - *Brahman* - the ultimate Reality; the ground of the universe

1. It is not possible to explain Brahman in words. It transcends all concepts and ideas. It is declared to be the only Truth.

2. In the *Upaniṣads* it is conceived of in two modes: the Reality of which the universe is but an appearance (*niṣprapañca*) and the all-inclusive ground of the universe (*saprapañca*). It is described positively as existence (*sat*), knowledge (*cit*), bliss (*ānanda*), and infinite (*ananta*) and negatively as 'not this, not this' (*neti neti*). It has nothing similar to it and nothing different from it, and it has no empirical distinctions from the acosmic viewpoint. According to Advaita, Brahman is known in two forms: that as qualified by limiting conditions owing to the distinctions of 'name and form' and as what is free from all limiting conditions whatever. Both Viśiṣṭādvaita and Dvaita conceive of Brahman as endowed with auspicious qualities.

ब्राह्मण - *Brāhmaṇa* - a spiritual and intellectual being endowed with purity, who has understood Brahman, who fosters spirituality, and who helps others to know the Reality; the liturgical texts of the *Vedas*

1. One of the four castes whose duty it is to study and perpetuate the *Vedas*.

2. Vide *varṇa.*

3. Liturgical texts written in prose and explanatory of the significance of the different rituals found in the *saṁhitas.* They are the guide-books for performing sacrificial rites.

4. Vide *Veda.*

ब्रह्माण्ड - *Brahmāṇḍa* - the cosmic egg

1. One of the twenty Dvaita substances.

2. Vide *dravya* and chart no. 6.

ब्रह्मनिष्ठा - *Brahma-niṣthā* – remaining steadfast in Brahman

ब्रह्मप्राप्ति - *Brahma-prāpti* - attainment of liberation

ब्रह्मार्पण - *Brahmārpaṇa* - dedication to Brahman

ब्रह्मरन्ध्र - *Brahma-randhra* - the aperture in the crown of the head through which the individual soul is said to leave its body upon death

ब्रह्म सत्यं जगन्मिथ्या जीवो ब्रह्मैव नापरः - *Brahma satyaṁ jagan-mithyā jīvo brahmaiva nāparaḥ* - Brahman is real; the world is not real; the individual soul is non-different from Brahman

This verse gives the quintessence of the Advaita doctrine.

ब्रह्मसूत्र - *Brahma-sūtra* - brief aphorisms written by Bādarāyaṇa harmonizing the teachings of the *Upaniṣads*

1. It sets forth the teachings of the Vedānta in a logical order. Vide *prasthāna-traya.*

2. The Bhāṣyakāras or main commentators (exponents) of the *Brahma-sūtra* are: Śaṅkara, Bhāskara, Yādava, Nimbārka, Rāmānuja, Śrīkaṇṭha, Madhva, Vallabha, and Baladeva.

3. Other names for the *Brahma-sūtra* include: *Vedānta-sūtra*, *Śārīraka-sūtra*, *Bhikṣu-sūtra*, and *Uttara-mīmāṁsā-sūtra*.

4. It is divided into four chapters (*adhyāya*) with each chapter consisting of four parts (*pāda*) and each part being divided into a number of sections (*adhikaraṇa*). Each section contains one or more *sūtras* depending upon the interpretation of the Bhāṣyakāra thereof.

5. Its four chapters are entitled: harmony (*samanvaya*), bringing out the coherent import of the *Upaniṣads* by explaining apparently doubtful statements; non-conflict (*avirodha*), presenting the Vedāntic position philosophically with regard to other systems; the means (*sādhana*), outlining the spiritual pathway to liberation; and the fruit (*phala*), discussing the nature of the goal itself.

ब्रह्मविचार - *Brahma-vicāra* - enquiry into Brahman

ब्रह्मविहार - *Brahma-vihāra* - divine state

According to Buddhism, these are the characteristics of a perfectly enlightened individual (*bodhisattva*) who is in a divine state: compassion (*karuṇā*), love (*maitra*), equanimity (*upekṣā*), and joy (*muditā*).

बृहस्पतिसव - *Bṛhaspati-sava* - the name of a sacrifice by which, according to the *Taittirīya-brāhmaṇa*, the the priest who desired to become a *purohita* obtained that office

बृहत् - *Bṛhat* - the great; the large

In the *Veda*, the true, the right (*satyam*, *ṛtam*) is called the great (*bṛhat*).

बुभुक्षवः - *Bubhukṣavaḥ* - pleasure-seekers

Vide *jīva* and *Śāstra-vaśya*.

बुद्धि - *Buddhi* - intellect

1. The first evolute from *prakṛti*. It is the basis of the intelligence of the individual. It is the determinative faculty and by it one resolves upon a course of action.

2. According to Nyāya Vaiśeṣika, it is of two kinds: recollection (*smṛti*) and experience (*anubhava*).

C

चैतन्य - *Caitanya* -- consciousness; intelligence

चैत्त - *Caitta* – mental; mental process

1. In the Yogācāra system, it is what belongs to the mind. Vide *citta-samprayukta.*

2. Vide *saṁskṛta-dharma.*

चक्र - *Cakra* - wheel; plexus; center

1. The seven psychological centers in the subtle body located in places corresponding to positions along the spinal cord. The *sahasrāra*, thousand-petalled lotus, is on the top of the head; *ājñā*, middle of the forehead; *anāhata*, the heart center; *viśuddhi*, the throat center; *maṇipūra*, the navel center; *svādhiṣṭhāna*, the abdomen center; and *mūlādhāra*, the sex center located at the base of the spine.

2. Vide chart no. 13.

चक्रक - *Cakraka* - a type of hypothetical argument; circular argument

Vide *anyonya-āśraya*, *tarka*, *hetvābhāsa.*

चक्षुः - *Cakṣuḥ* - eye; visual sense

Vide *jñānendriya.*

चक्षुदर्शन - *Cakṣu-darśana* - seeing through the eye of the scripture

Vide *upayoga*.

चाक्षुष - *Cākṣuṣa* - ocular perception

चलन - *Calana* - motion

चरलिङ्ग - *Cara-liṅga* - moving form of *liṅga*
Vide *liṅga-sthala*.

चरमश्लोक - *Carama-śloka* - last verse; final passage; important stanza; vide *Gītā-caramaśloka* (*Gītā*, XVIII, 66)

चारित्र - *Cāritra* - right conduct; rules of conduct

1. According to Jainism, they are: *īryā*, *bhāṣā*, *īṣaṇa*, *dāna-samiti*, *utsarga-samiti*, *mano-gupti*, *vāg-gupti*, and *kāya-gupti*.
2. Vide *bhāva-saṁvara*.

चार्वाक - *Cārvāka* - the Indian Materialistic school

1. It is also known as Lokāyata.
2. It is traced to Bṛhaspati. Its central teaching is that matter is the only reality. The Cārvākas accept perception as the only *pramāṇa*. Sense-satisfaction is their goal.

चर्या - *Caryā* - a path of liberation in the Śaiva Siddhānta which consists of external acts of worship like cleaning the temple, gathering flowers for the deity, etc.

It is called the path of the servant (*dāsa-mārga*). Its fruit is residence in the realm of God (*sālokya*).

चर्यापाद - *Caryā-pāda* - that part of the *Āgamas* which describes the methods of worship

Vide *āgama*.

चतुःसूत्री - *Catuḥ-sūtrī* - four *sūtras*

1. The first four *sūtras* of the *Brahma-sūtra.* They are: *athāto brahma jijñāsā; janmādyasya yataḥ; śāstra-yonitvāt* and *tattu samanvayāt.* The first aphorism initiates the enquiry into *Brahman.* The second aphorism offers a definition of *Brahman.* The third aphorism concerns itself with the source of our knowledge of *Brahman.* And the fourth aphorism attempts to demonstrate the supreme value of the knowledge of *Brahman.*

2. Vācaspati's *Bhāmatī Catuḥ-sūtrī* is sometimes called the *Catuḥ-sūtrī.*

चतुर्थ - *Caturtha* - the fourth; the *turīya* state

Vide *avasthā* and *turīya.*

चत्वारि आर्यसत्यानि - *Catvāri ārya-satyāni* - four noble truths

The central teaching of the Buddha. They are: *Duḥkha* or suffering and pain, *Duḥkha-samudaya* or the cause and origin of suffering, *Duḥkha-nirodha* or the cessation of suffering, and *Duḥkha-nirodha-mārga* or the path to the cessation of suffering.

चेष्टा - *Ceṣṭā* – volitional activity; gesture; the tenth means of knowledge

Non-verbal body movements, facial expressions, etc., which convey certain ideas.

चेतन - *Cetana* - consciousness; volition; intelligence

Vide *cit.*

चेतोमुख - *Cetomukha* – gateway to cognition

It is used as a name for deep sleep (*suṣupti*).

छल - *Chala* - quibbling

1. One of the sixteen categories of the Nyāya school.

2. Vide *padārtha* and chart no. 6.

चिदाभास - *Cid-ābhāsa* - the reflection of intelligence which resides in the internal organ (intellect)

According to Advaita, this reflection of intelligence is needed in order to enable the psychosis (*vṛtti*) of the intellect to illumine an object. The intellect, by itself, is inert and non-intelligent, and thus unable to manifest any object.

चिदचित् - *Cid-acit* - sentient and insentient

According to Śaiva Siddhānta, the individual acts as *cit* as it unites with *cit*; and, the individual acts as *acit* as it unites with *acit*.

चिन्ता - *Cintā* - enquiry; thought; discussion

चित् - *Cit* - spirit; consciousness; the individual self

1. One of the three ultimate realities (*tattva-traya*) according to Viśiṣṭādvaita.

2. Vide *tattva*.

चित्र - *Citra* - variegated

चित्-शक्ति (चिच्छक्ति) - *Cit-śakti* (*cicchakti*) – the power of consciousness

Śaiva Siddhānta calls *Ātma-cit-śakti* as the sole valid means of knowledge (*pramāṇa*), with the other *pramāṇas* as its auxiliaries.

चित्त - *Citta* - consciousness; mind

1. In the Vaibhāṣika system, it is *saṁskṛta-dharmas* born out of the interaction of the senses with their objects. Vide *saṁskrta-dharma.*

2. In the Yogācāra system, it is the *mano-dharma.* It is the primary *dharma* and essentially the only *dharma.* Vide *citta-samprayukta.*

3. In the Yoga system, the intellect (*buddhi*), ego (*ahaṅkāra*), and the senses (*indriyas*) are often called *citta.*

4. According to the Sāṅkhya, the mind (*citta*) has five processes: *pramāṇa, viparyaya, vikalpa, nidrā*, and *smṛti.*

चित्तभूमि - *Citta-bhūmi* - stage of the mind

चित्तसम्प्रयुक्त - *Citta-samprayukta* - mental *dharmas* according to Yogācāra Buddhism

They are divided into those with form and those without form. The formless are again divided into mind (*citta*) and mental (*caitta*).

चित्तशुद्धि - *Citta-śuddhi* - purification of the mind

चित्तविमुक्त - *Citta-vimukta* – detatched from the mind

चित्तविप्रयुक्त - *Citta-viprayukta* - neutral *dharmas* according to Yogācāra Buddhism

They are *saṁskṛta-dharmas* which are neither physical (*rūpa*) nor mental (*caitta*). Vide *saṁskṛta-dharma.*

चित्तविप्रयुक्तसंस्कारधर्म - *Citta-viprayukta-saṁskāra-dharma* - non-mental composite things

चित्तवृत्तिनिरोध - *Citta-vṛtti-nirodha* - cessation of the activities of the mind

The goal of the Yoga school.

चोदना - *Codanā* - injunction; command

Cf. the *Mīmāṁsāsūtra* — '*codanā lakṣaṇārtho dharmaḥ.*'

D

दक्षिणा - *Dakṣiṇā* - gift; sacrificial fee

दम - *Dama* - self-control; control of the senses

Vide *sādhana-catuṣṭaya.*

डम्भ - *Ḍambha* - ostentation

दान - *Dāna* - gift; charity

दानपारमिता - *Dāna-pāramitā* - benevolence

दानसमिति - *Dāna-samiti* - avoiding all transgressions when taking or giving anything

Vide *cāritra.*

दण्ड - *Daṇḍa* - stick; staff

दण्डनीति - *Daṇḍanīti* – science of judicature

दर्प - *Darpa* - pride

दर्शन - *Darśana* - to have sight of; to see a great or holy individual, either human or divine; a philosophical school; sensation; apprehension

1. According to Jainism, that stage of knowledge where there is an awareness of sensations or sense-data. The specific characteristic of the objects are not noted however.

2. A stand-point in philosophy. Vide *ṣaḍ-darśana.*

दर्शनावरणीय - *Darśanāvaraṇīya* - apprehension-obscuring

According to Jainism, this is an obstructive type of *karma* which obscures one's apprehension. It is of nine types. The first four types pertain to obscuration in vision and apprehension, and the rest in producing various degrees and types of sleep.

दासः - *Dāsaḥ* - servant

दास्य - *Dāsya* – service; surrendering to the will of God

1. The relation of a servant to their master.
2. Vide *bhakti* and *śeṣa.*

दौर्मनस्य - *Daurmanasya* - feeling of wretchedness and miserableness

दया – *Dayā* - mercy; compassion; grace

देहात्मभाव - *Dehātmabhāva* - imagining the body to constitute the self

देहात्मवादिन् - *Dehātma-vādin* - a type of Cārvāka who considers the body as the individual

देश - *Deśa* - place

देशकालसम्बन्ध - *Deśa-kāla-sambandha* - the relation of time and place

देशापबन्ध - *Deśāpabandha* - limitation of place

One of the Jaina codes of conduct.

देशावधि - *Deśāvadhi* - a type of clairvoyance which is limited by time and space

Vide *avadhi.*

देशावकाशिक - *Deśāvakāśika* - a Jaina ethical code of conduct which fixes a limit on one's movement to a region limited by the boundaries of one's own village

This restriction assists the religious aspirant in observing non-violence.

देशित - *Deśita* - dictated

देव - *Deva* - god; celestial being

Vide *jaṅgama.*

देवयान - *deva-yāna* - the way of the gods

It is meant for those who cultivate faith and asceticism. At death, those individuals who attain *mokṣa* by *devā-yāna*, never return to the cycle of birth and death.

धम्म -*Dhamma* - (Pali) vide *dharma*

धारक - *Dhāraka* - sustenance; supporter

धारणा - *Dhāraṇā* - single-mindedness; concentration

1. The sixth limb of the Yoga discipline. It is the concentration of the mind (*citta*) on some object with fixed attention. Vide *aṣṭāṅga-yoga.*

2. According to Jainism, it is a stage in which the full knowledge about an object leaves an impression.

धर्म - *Dharma* - righteousness; merit; religious duty; medium of motion (Jainism); scriptural texts (Buddhism); quality (Buddhism); cause (Buddhism); unsubstantial and soulless (Buddhism); religious teaching (Buddhism); a goal of life (*puruṣārtha*)

1. Literally it means 'what holds together' and thus it is the basis of all order, whether social or moral. As an ethical or moral value, it is the instrumental value to liberation (except for the Mīmāṁsaka who considers it the supreme value).

2. *Varṇa-āśrama-dharma* is one's specific duty.

3. *Sanātana-dharma* is the eternal religion.

4. *Sva-dharma* is one's own individual duty.

5. *Āpad-dharma* is the *dharma* prescribed at the time of adversities.

6. *Yuga-dharma* is the law of time (aeon).

7. *Sādhāraṇa-dharma* is the general obligations or the common duties of each and every individual. It is comprised of virtues like self-control, kindness, truthfulness, and so on. This is based on the idea that individuals are born with a number of debts and these duties help to repay one's debts to humanity.

8. According to Jainism, it is the medium of motion and pervades the entire universe. It is one and eternal. It is neither active itself nor can it produce action in others. However, it makes the motion of all else possible by providing the movement-medium for them. Vide *ajīva*.

9. According to Buddhism, the chief definitions of this term include: cosmic order, the natural law,

the teachings of the Buddha, norms of conduct, things or facts, ideas, and factors of existence.

10. According to the Mīmāṁsā school, it is what is enjoined in the *Veda*. It is religious duty, the performance thereof bringing merit and its neglect bringing demerit.

11. Generally *dharma* is twofold: *sādhāraṇa-dharma*, which is common to everyone, and *varṇa-āśrama-dharma* which is specific to each class and stage of life.

12. Vide *puruṣārtha*.

13. According to Nyāya-Vaiśeṣika, *dharma* is a specific quality (*viśeṣa-guṇa*) that belongs to the self. However, *dharma* signifies merit (*puṇya*) rather than right. They believe that *dharma* is directly perceived, though it takes yogic power to do so. This is done by means of *alaukika-pratyakṣa*.

14. According to Sāṅkhya-Yoga, *dharma* is a mode of the intellect (*buddhi*). It is because of confusion that one believes that *dharma* belongs to the *puruṣa*. Thus morality belongs only to the empirical sphere, and good and evil do not ever touch the individual.

धर्मभूतज्ञान - *Dharma-bhūta-jñāna* - attributive consciousness

The key concept in Viśiṣṭādvaita. Knowledge is the attribute of God and individuals. It is a non-material, self-luminous, unconscious substance. It is both a substance and an attribute. It is a substance as the substratum of change through its states of expansion and contraction, and it is an attribute since it inheres in substances like *Īśvara* and individuals. It is eternal and all-pervasive in eternals (*Īśvara, nitya-sūris, muktas*), and it is obscured in the case of bound individuals. In the state of release it becomes all-pervasive. It has the power to reveal objects as well as itself, but not to know them. What it illumines is always for another. It functions through the mind in all knowing processes. Thus, all objective knowledge is a modification of it. In perception, it goes out to the object; takes on the object's form; and as a result the object becomes known to the perceiving subject. Its modes also include the internal states of the mind like desire and anger.

धर्मचक्रप्रवर्तन - *Dharma-cakra-pravartana* - the setting in motion of the wheel of the law

The title of the Buddha's first sermon after his enlightenment.

धर्मधातु - *Dharma-dhātu* – the core of Reality; the suchness or thus-ness of existence; the unity or oneness of all

According to the Buddhists, this is the highest Reality.

धर्मजिज्ञासा - *Dharma-jijñāsā* - an inquiry into *dharma*

The first *sūtra* of the *Mīmāṁsā-sūtra* of Jaimini is "*athāto dharmajijñāsā.*"

धर्मकाय - *Dharma-kāya*-the sheath of the law; the Reality; the Void; the Absolute; the embodied law

1. This is the reality of all beings and appearances, both immanent and transcendent. It refers to both the essence of worldly beings and to the

essence of the Buddhas. In the former, it means the reality or suchness or emptiness. In the latter, it refers to the Buddha-nature. It is the only one of the Three Bodies (*tri-kāya*) which all Buddhas have in common. While there are countless earthly and transcendent Buddhas, there is only one *dharma-kāya.*

2. Vide *trikāya.*

धर्ममेघ - *Dharma-megha* - cloud of the law

1. The final stage of the *Dodhisattva's* path to perfection. "He who rains down the law on earth."

2. Vide *bodhisattva.*

धर्मपरिणाम - *Dharma-pariṇāma* - changes of quality

धर्मास्तिकाय - *Dharmāstikāya* - the medium of motion (according to Jainism)

Vide *dharma* and *ajīva.*

धर्मस्वाख्याततभावना - *Dharma-svākhyātatā-bhāvanā* - the practice of the virtues which uphold the world order

धर्मि - *Dharmi* - subject; that which supports

धर्मिज्ञान - *Dharmi-jñāna* - substantive consciousness

Cf. *dharmabhūta-jñāna.*

धातु - *Dhātu* - the six sense-organs, the six sense-objects and the six sense-consciousnesses; element

1. According to Buddhism, these are the subtle elements whose groupings lead to the generation of knowledge.

2. According to Sāṅkhya (as given by Caraka) there are six elements: earth, air, fire, water, ether and *cetana* (consciousness), also called *puruṣa*.

धी - *Dhī* - mind; idea

धीर - *Dhīra* - steadfast

धृति - *Dhṛti* - attraction; sustaining effort

ध्रुव - *Dhruva* - permanent

धूमादिमार्ग - *Dhūmādi-mārga* - the way to heaven beginning with smoke

ध्वंसाभाव - *Dhvaṁsābhava* - (*pradhvaṁsa-abhāva*) - negation following the destruction of an object

Vide *abhāva*.

ध्वनि - *Dhvani* - word; suggested meaning; sound; noise According to the Ālaṅkārikas, it refers to the theory of poetic suggestion. It is said to be the soul of poetry. It is said to be of two main types: *avivakṣita-vācya* and *vivakṣitānyapara-vācya*. The former is sub-divided into: *atyantatiraskṛta-vācya* (where the literal sense is completely set aside) and *arthāntarasaṅkramita-vācya* (where the latter meaning is shifted). The latter (also known as *abhidhā-mūla*) is sub-divided into: *samlakṣyakrama-vyaṅgya* (where the stages of realizing the suggested sense from the expressed sense can be well perceived) and *asaṁlakṣyakrama-vyaṅgya* (where the stages in the realization of the suggested sense are imperceptible). *Saṁlakṣyakrama-vyaṅgya* is sub-divided into: *vastu-dhvani* (where a fact is suggested) and *alaṅkāra-dhvani* (where the suggested element is a figure of speech).

ध्यान - *Dhyāna* - medtation

1. The mind flowing in an unbroken current towards a particular object.

2. The seventh limb of *aṣṭāṅga-yoga.* Vide *aṣṭāṅga-yoga.*

3. One of the six *pāramitās* in Buddhism. Vide *pāramitā.*

ध्यानाग्निदग्धकर्म - *Dhyānāgnidagdhakarma* - one whose *karmas* have all been burnt by the fire of meditation

ध्याननियोगवादिन् - *Dhyāna-niyoga-vādin* - one who holds that meditation is a prescribed discipline to attain the knowledge of the Absolute

ध्यानपारमिता - *Dhyāna-pāramitā* - virtue of meditation

Vide *pāramitā.*

ध्यातृ - *Dhyātṛ* - meditator

ध्येय - *Dhyeya* - object of meditation

दिगम्बर - *Digambara* - sky-clad; clothed in space; naked

1. One of the two principal sects in Jainism. They hold an extremely puritan position. They differ from the *Śvetāmbaras* on certain tenets; i.e., they hold that: perfect saints live without food; a monk who owns property or wears clothes cannot attain liberation; women cannot attain liberation, etc.

2. Vide *Śvetāmbara.*

दिग्विरतिव्रत - *Digvirati-vrata* - one of the minor duties imposed upon householders, according to Jainism

It imposes a restricted area upon an individual in which to carry out one's activities. It is based on the principle of non-violence for it enables one to desist from injuring living beings in other areas where one is forbidden to go.

दिक् - *Dik* - space; spatial direction

A substance (*dravya*) according to Vaiśeṣika. It is that by virtue of which things are perceived as being on the right, left, up, down, etc. It is all-pervasive and is composed of eternal atoms.

दीक्षा - *Dīkṣā* - initiation; consecration

1. According to Vīra Śaivism, it is of three kinds: *vedhā*, which establishes the *bhāva-liṅga* in the causal body; *mantra*, which establishes the *prāṇa-liṅga* in the subtle body; and *kriyā*, which establishes the *iṣṭa-liṅga* in the gross body. The first eradicates *āṇava-mala*, the second eradicates *māyā-mala*, and the third eradicates *kārmika-mala*.

2. According to Śaiva Siddhānta, there are three stages in initiation: initial initiation into spiritual life (*samaya*); learning worship, rituals, etc., (*viśeṣa*); and when all bonds are broken (*nirvāṇa*). The first type is called *sādhāra* and is given to aspirants who are bound by *aṇavā-*, *karma-* and *māyā-malas*. The second and third types are called *nirā-dhāra* and are for aspirants with either *āṇava* and *karma* or only *āṇava-mala*.

3. Initiation is one of various kinds depending upon the qualifications of the individual. It may

be: by the teacher's mere sight, or touch, or word; by meditation techniques; by scriptural injunctions; by *yoga*, etc. Its purpose is to purify the individual.

दीर्घ - *Dīrgha* - long

दिशा - *Diśā* - quarter; direction

Vide *dik*.

दिवस - *Divasa* - day

A length of time. Vide *kāla*.

दिव्य - *Divya* – divine; celestial; divine nature

1. A type of perception caused by the grace of the Lord. It is independent of the senses. Vide *pratyakṣa*.

2. One of the four kinds of fire. Vide *tejas*.

दिव्यप्रबन्ध - *Divya-prabandha* - the divine composition (of poems or verses)

1. The collection of the hymns of the *Āḻvārs* which were composed in the Tamil language. It consists of four parts, each numbering a thousand hymns. Its main purport is devotion to God. It is said to constitute the Tamil *Veda* and is held by Viśiṣṭādvaitins to be as authoratative as the works of the *prasthāna-traya*. For this reason Viśiṣṭādvaita is referred to as *Ubhaya-vedānta*.

2. Vide *āḻvār* and *ubhaya-vedānta*.

दोष - *Doṣa* - defect

According to Buddhism, one of the afflictions (*kleśa*).

द्रष्टा - *Draṣṭā* - the pure consciousness comprehending all objects

द्रवत्व - *Dravatva* - liquidity; fluidity

According to Vaiśeṣika, a quality belonging to a genus, is called fluidity. It is the non-intimate cause of the first flow of a fluid substance. It is found in earth, water and fire. It is of two kinds: natural and artificial. Natural fluidity is found in water and artificial fluidity is found in earth and fire.

द्रव्य - *Dravya* - substance

1. It is the principal category according to the Vaiśeṣika school. It includes in it all living and non-living entities. It is defined as the substrate of qualities and activity, and as the inherent cause of a product. It is of nine types: earth, water, fire, air, ether, time, space, individuals, and mind. See chart no. 7.

2. According to Jainism, it is constituted of the six real and independent categories. These are: individuals (*jīva*), matter (*pudgala*), principle of motion (*dharma*), principle of rest (*adharma*), space (*ākāśa*), and time (*kāla*). Except for time, they are all extended reals (*astikāya*). Except for matter, they are all immaterial. Vide chart no. 8.

3. According to Viśiṣṭādvaita, it is one of the two fundamental categories. There are six substances: primeval matter (*prakṛti*), time (*kāla*), pure matter (*śuddha-sattva* or *nitya-vibhūti*), attributive consciousness (*dharmabhūta-jñāna*), individual soul (*jīva*), and God (*Īśvara*). The first two are material (*jaḍa*)

and the others are nonmaterial (*ajaḍa*). By substance is meant, "what has modes." Except God, all the substances are dependent. Vide chart no. 6.

3. According to Dvaita, it is one of the ten categories. It is the most important category as all the others are dependent upon it. The substances are twenty in number: God (*Paramātman*), consort of God (*Lakṣmī*), individual souls (*jīva*), unmanifested ether (*avyākṛtākāśa*), primordial matter (*prakṛti*), the three qualities (*guṇa-traya*), the 'great' (which is a product of the three *guṇas*) (*mahat*), egoity (*ahaṅkāra*), intellect (*buddhi*), mind (which is of two forms — the substantive and the non-substantive) (*manas*), sense-organs (*indriya*), subtle essences of the elements (*tanmātra*), elements (*māha-bhūta*), cosmic egg (*brahmāṇḍa*), ignorance (*avidyā*), letters (*varṇa*), darkness (*timira*), mental impressions (*vāsanā*), time (*kāla*), and reflection (*pratibimba*). The first three are sentient (*cetana*) and the others are insentient (*acetana*). God is independent and the other 19 *dravyas* are dependent upon Him. Vide chart no. 6.

4. Both of the Pūrva-mīmāṁsā schools call substance a category. Vide chart no. 6.

द्रव्यार्थिकनय - *Dravyārithika-naya* - substance-viewpoint

1. According to Jainism, this is the consideration of an object in the light of its substance. It includes three standpoints: universal-particular standpoint (*naigāma-naya*); class viewpoint (*saṅgraha-naya*); and the standpoint of the particular (*vyavahāra-naya*).

2. Vide *naya.*

द्रव्यास्रव - *Dravya-āsrava* - the stage of the actual inflow of karmic particles into the individual

1. According to Jainism, it affects the individual in eight different ways.

2. Vide *āsrava.*

द्रव्यबन्ध - *Dravya-bandha* - the actual contact of karmic particles with the individual

1. It produces bondage according to Jainism.

2. Vide *bandha.*

द्रव्यकर्म - *Dravya-karma* – actions of body, speech and mind which have actually transformed themselves into subtle matter and stick to the individual

A type of action according to Jainism. Vide *karma.*

द्रव्यलेश्य - *Dravya-leśya* - the actual coloration of the individual by *karma* matter

According to Jainism, as good or bad matter sticks to the individual, the individual itself gets coloured as either golden, lotus-pink, white or black, blue and grey. Vide *leśya.*

द्रव्यनय - *Dravya-naya* - substance-viewpoint

Vide *dravyārthika-naya.*

द्रव्यनिर्जरा - *Dravya-nirjarā* - the stage of the actual destruction of binding *karma* particles

1. According to Jainism, it is either by the reaping of their fruits or by penances done before their

time of fruition that *karma* particles can be destroyed.

2. Vide *nirjarā.*

द्रव्यपरमाणु - *Dravya-paramāṇu* - simple atoms

According to Buddhism, it is the subtlest form of matter. It is a unit possessing the fourfold substratum of colour, smell, taste and contact, though it is invisible, inaudible, untastable, and intangible. Seven such *paramāṇus* combine to form an *aṇu*, and in this combined form they become perceptible.

द्रव्यसंवर - *Dravya-saṁvara* - the stage of the actual stoppage of the inflow of *karma* particles according to Jainism

Vide *saṁvara.*

द्रव्यत्व - *Dravyatva* - substanceness; thingness

The characteristic of a substance. Substance is defined, according to the Nyāya school, as that which has the characteristic of a substance.

दृक् - *Dṛk* - seer; perceiver; consciousensss

Vide *draṣṭā.*

दृक्छक्ति - *Dṛkchakti* - power of manifestation; capacity to know

दृष्ट - *Dṛṣṭa* - perceived resemblance

1. A class of inference in which a previously known case and the inferred case are exactly the same, according to Praśastapāda.

2. Vide *sāmānyatodṛṣṭa.*

दृष्टान्त - *Dṛṣṭānta* - typical instance; illustration; example

1. One of the sixteen categories of the Nyāya school. Vide *padārtha* and chart no. 6.

2. It is the third member of a five-membered syllogism: e.g., "Wherever there is smoke there is fire, such as in a hearth." Nyāya defines it as that on which both the common man and the expert hold the same opinion.

3. The Vaiśeṣika refers to this as '*nidarśana*'.

दृष्टान्ताभास - *Dṛṣṭāntābhāsa* - fallacious example

दृष्टार्थ - *Dṛṣṭārtha* - perceptible result

दृष्टार्थापत्ति - *Dṛṣṭa-arthāpatti* – postulation from what is seen

Vide *arthāpatti.*

दृष्टफल - *Dṛṣṭa-phala* – perceptible result

दृष्टि - *Dṛṣṭi* - seeing; inner sight; vision; speculative standpoint

According to Buddhism, it means belief, dogma, or false theory.

दृष्टिसृष्टिवाद - *Dṛṣṭi-sṛṣṭi-vāda*-the theory that "Perception is creation"

According to Advaita, a theory that regards the entire world as the fabrication of the individual's intellect. Before the objects of experience are perceived, they are held to be nonexistent. The world is created by an imaginer who imagines it.

दृश्य - *Dṛśya* - visible; object seen; objects of consciousness; perceived

दृश्यत्व - *Dṛśyatva* - objectivity

The notion of objectivity carries with it the idea of materiality.

दुःख - *Duḥkha* - pain; suffering

1. The first noble truth of the Buddha.
2. Vide *catvāri ārya-satyāni.*

दुःखनिरोध - *Duḥkha-nirodha* – the cessation of suffering

1. The third noble truth of the Buddha.
2. Vide *catvāri ārya-satyāni.*

दुःखनिरोधमार्ग - *Duḥkha-nirodha-mārga* - the path to the cessation of suffering

1. The fourth noble truth of the Buddha.
2. Vide *catvāri ārya-satyāni.*
3. From this truth came the eightfold path to enlightenment. Vide *ārya-aṣṭāṅga-mārga.*

दुःखानुव्यवसाय - *Duḥkha-anuvyavasāya* - apperception of sorrow

दुःखसमुदय - *Duḥkha-samudaya* - the cause and origin of suffering

1. The second noble truth of the Buddha.
2. Vide *catvāri ārya-satyāni.*
3. From this truth is expounded the causal chain of existence. Vide *pratītyasamutpāda.*

दुरागम - *Durāgama* - bad scripture

दूरङ्गम - *Dūraṅgama* - the far-going

One of the stages of *bodhisattva*-hood. Vide *bodhisattva.*

दुर्नीति - *Durnīti* - knowledge which views part of an object as the whole

According to Jainism, a particular standpoint. Vide *naya.*

दूषण - *Dūṣaṇa* - refutation; objection

दुष्टहेतु - *Duṣṭa-hetu* - defective reason

A defect in the inferential process.

द्वादशाङ्ग – *Dvādaśāṅga* - the twelve interdependent links in the causal chain of existence

Vide *pratītya-samutpāda.*

द्वैत - *Dvaita* - dual; duality; dualism

The name given to Madhvācārya's system of philosophy. It is a school of Vedānta which teaches that God, the individual souls, and the world of matter are eternally separate and real.

द्वन्द्व - *Dvandva* - pairs of opposites in nature

E.g., pleasure and pain, hot and cold, light and darkness, gain and loss, victory and defeat, love and hatred, etc.

द्वन्द्वमोह - *Dvandva-moha* - the delusion of the pairs of opposites in nature, such as pain and pleasure

द्वापरयुग - *Dvāpara-yuga* - the third *yuga* among 4 *yugas*; the bronze age

1. The age where truth is said to stand on only two of its legs. The path to liberation in this age is said to be worship of the deity.

2. Vide *yuga*.

द्वेष – *Dveṣa* - antipathy; hatred; aversion

1. One of the five types of false knowledge according to Sāṅkhya.

2. Vide *kleśa*.

द्विप्रदेश - *Dvipradeśa* - the combination of two atoms

द्वित्व - *Dvitva* - twoness

The concept of numbers greater than one is due to a relative oscillatory state of the mind, according to Vaiśeṣika.

द्व्यणुक - *Dvyaṇuka* - dyad; a binary molecule

Two atoms combine to generate a dyad and three dyads form a triad, which is the smallest visible substance. Vide *Paramāṇu*.

E

एक - *Eka* - one; unique

एकाग्र - *Ekāgra* - one-pointed; close attention

1. The one-pointed mind is that which is devoted to a single object. It is a mind filled with *sattva*.

2. According to Buddhism, one of the five elements which comprise meditation.

3. According to the Yoga school, it is a stage of the mind (*citta*) in which one concentrates steadily on an object for a long time.

एकजीव - *Eka-jīva* - a single self or individual

एकजीववाद - *Eka-jīva-vāda* - the theory that there is only one self or individual

A theory within Advaita which posits that there is but one *jīva* and one material body. The manifold world is erroneously imagined by the ignorance of the one individual while the one personal consciousness is real. This one *jīva*, *viz. Hiraṇyagarbha*, is a reflection of Brahman, and all other individuals are mere semblances of individuals and to these semblances pertain bondage and liberation.

एकम्-एव-अद्वितीयम् - *Ekam-eva-advitīyam* - one only without a second

A great saying, *mahāvākya* which occurs in the *Chāndogya Upaniṣad* of the *Sāma Veda.* It denotes Brahman.

एकान्त - *Ekānta* - a false belief unknowingly accepted and uncritically followed

It is one of the five kinds of delusion according to Jainism. The others are: *viparīta*, *vinaya*, *saṁśaya* and *ajñāna.*

एकान्तभाव - *Ekānta-bhāva* - one-pointedness; aloofness

An aspect of devotion according to Dvaita.

एकपृथक्त्व - *Eka-pṛthaktva* - distinctive separateness

एकात्मप्रत्ययसार - *Ekātma-pratyaya-sāra* - the essence as oneness with the Self

एकत्वभावना - *Ekatva-bhāvanā* - meditation on the uniqueness of each individual

एकत्वान्यत्व - *Ekatvānyatva* - either this or that

एकवाक्यता - *Eka-vākyatā* – one meaning; syntactic unity

Syntactic unity is based on a twofold relation: that of a word to a sentence (*padaikavākyatā*) and that of a sentence to another sentence (*vākyaika-vākyatā*).

एकविषय - *Ekaviṣaya* - the same subject

एकायन - *Ekāyana* - a name of Dvaita system

एकीभाव - *Ekībhāva* - oneness with the Absolute

एवम्भूतनय - *Evambhūtanaya* - the such-like standpoint

According to Jainism, the standpoint which is concerned with the performance of an actual function suggested by the etymology of a word. Thus, if one is called '*Bhīma*', he can be referred to by this name only when he is actually displaying strength (*bhīma*). The word must be entirely true in meaning and sense to fulfil this standpoint's requirements.

G

गगनोपमम् - *Gaganopamam* - similar to vacuous sky

गमक - *Gamaka* - pervaded; indicative

गमन - *Gamana* – locomotion; action

Vide *karma.*

गम्य - *Gamya* - pervader

गण - *Gaṇa* - group

गणाचार - *Gaṇācāra* - striving for the upliftment of all

An ethical code of conduct in Vīra Śaivism. Vide *pañcācāra.*

गणधर - *Gaṇadhara* - the leader of a group (*gaṇa*) of disciples

According to Jaina legend, the eleven leader-disciples of Mahāvīra who composed the eleven *Aṅgas.*

गन्ध – *Gandha* - smell

Vide *tanmātra.*

गान्धर्वशास्त्र - *Gāndharva-śāstra* - the scripture expounding the science of music

One of the *Upa-vedas.*

गाथा - *Gāthā* - verse; stanza

गति - *Gati* - path; motion; result

गतिचिन्तन - *Gati-cintana* - meditation on the path to the world of *Brahman*

Name of a chapter in the *Rahasyatrayasāra* of Vedāntadeśika.

गौः - *Gauḥ* - cow

गौण - *Gauṇa* - secondary; implied

गौणी - *Gauṇī* - an aspect of the secondary meaning of words

1. This type of meaning is illustrated by such sentences as: "The boy is a lion." The relation between the word 'lion' and its meaning is indirect. It is based on the similarity of the actual intended sense with the original primary sense.

2. Vide *aupacārika-vṛtti.*

गौतम - *Gautama* -- the founder of the Nyāya school and the author of the *Nyāya-sūtra*; also called Akṣapāda

गवय - *Gavaya* -wild ox

Traditionally used in Indian philosophy as an example in demonstrating *upamāna* or comparison.

गायत्री - *Gāyatrī* - Vedic *mantra*; Vedic metre of twenty-four syllables

Sage Viśvāmitra is the seer of the *mantra.* This is held to be the most sacred *mantra* of the

Vedas. It is: *om bhūr-bhuvaḥ suvaḥ tat saviturvareṇi-yam-bhargo devasya dhīmahi dhiyo yo naḥ pracodayāt.*

घट - *Ghaṭa* - pot

घटाकाश - *Ghaṭākāśa* - the ether enclosed in a pot

घटकश्रुति - *Ghaṭaka-śruti* - mediatory text

Cf. *abhedaśruti* and *bheda-śruti.*

घातिकर्म - *Ghāti-karma* - obstructive *karma*

1. According to Jainism, there are four types of obstructive *karmas*: comprehension - obscuring (*jñānāvaraṇa*); apprehension-obscuring (*darśanā-varaṇa*); feeling-producing (*vedinīya*); and deluding (*mohanīya*).

2. Vide *karma.*

घ्राण - *Ghrāṇa* - sense of smell

Vide *jñānendriya.*

घ्राणज - *Ghrāṇaja* - olfactory perception

गोचर - *Gocara* - object; place

गोप्तृत्ववरण - *Goptṛtva-varaṇa* - to seek *Īśvara* alone as the protector

Vide *prapatti.*

गोत्र - *Gotra* - clan; family; lineage

1. According to Jainism, one of the eight kinds of *karma.* Vide *dravya-āsrava.*

2. The patriarchal family to which an individual belongs.

गोत्व - *Gotva* - cowness

ग्रहण - *Grahaṇa* - apprehension

ग्राह्य - *Grāhya* – object of knowledge

ग्रन्थ - *Grantha* - treatise; work; book

ग्रन्थि - *Granthi* - knot

गृहस्थ - *Gṛhastha* - householder

1. The second stage in the Indian social order.
2. Vide *āśrama*.

गुल्म – *Gulma* - shrubs

Vide *sthāvara*.

गुण - *Guṇa* - quality; attribute; characteristic; excellence; rope; constituent; subsidiary

1. It is either composed of, or constituted of (depending on individual school's interpretations) the three aspects: *sattva*, which is buoyant, light, illuminating, knowledge, and happiness; *rajas*, which is stimulating, mobile, pain, and action; and *tamas*, which is heavy, enveloping, indifferent, and laziness.

2. According to Nyāya, it is that which has substance for its substratum, has no further qualities, and is not the cause of, or concerned with conjunction or disjunction. There are twenty-four qualities, some being material and others being mental: colour (*rūpa*), taste (*rasa*), odour (*gandha*), touch (*sparśa*), sound (*śabda*), number (*saṅkhyā*), measure (*parimiti*), mutual difference (*pṛthaktva*), connection (*saṁyoga*), separation

(*vibhāga*), perception of long time (*paratva*), perception of short time (*aparatva*), heaviness (*gurutva*), fluidity (*dravatva*), viscidity (*sneha*), knowledge (*buddhi*), happiness (*sukha*), sorrow (*duḥkha*), will (*icchā*), hatred (*dveṣa*), effort (*yatna*), *saṁskāra* (which is of three types: *vega*, *sthiti-sthāpaka*, and *bhāvanā*), *dharma* and *adharma*.

3. According to Dvaita, it is the first product of *prakṛti*. It always resides in a substance. There are infinite number of qualities, mental as well as physical. Insentient entities have physical qualities while sentient beings have both physical and mental qualities.

4. According to Advaita and Viśiṣṭādvaita, it is an attribute of *prakṛti* and is threefold. However, the two schools differ as to the ontological status of the *guṇas*.

5. According to Sāṅkhya, guṇas, being the three constituents of *prakṛti* (composed of *sattva*, *rajas*, and *tamas*), are like a rope in that they bind the individual and they are subsidiary in that they provide enjoyment for the individuals and also serve to liberate them. They are the subtle substances or cosmic constituents which evolve into all the various categories of existence. Vide chart no. 12.

गुणाश्रय -*Guṇa-āśraya* - locus of qualities

गुणगणनिधिः - *Guṇagaṇanidhiḥ* - the store-house of all innumerable auspicious qualities

गुणाष्टक - *Guṇāṣṭaka* - the eightfold divine qualities of *Īśvara* and *jīvas*

A person possessing the above qualities is *apahatapāpmā, vijaraḥ, vimṛtyuḥ, viśokaḥ, vijighatsaḥ, apipāsaḥ, satyakāmaḥ*, and *satyasaṅkalpaḥ*.

गुणस्थान - *Guṇasthāna* - states of excellence

According to Jainism, there are fourteen stages through which an individual soul passes on its journey to spiritual perfection. They are: *mithyā-dṛṣṭi-, sāsādana-samyagdṛṣṭi-, miśra-, avirata-samyagdṛṣṭi-, deśavirata-samyagdṛṣṭi-, pramatta-saṁyata-, apramatta-saṁyata-, nivṛtti-bādara-samparāya-, anivṛtti-bādara-samparāya-, sūkṣma-bādara-samparāya-, upaśānta-kaṣāyavītarāga-chadmastha-, kṣīṇa-kaṣāya-vītarāga-chadmastha-, sayogi-kevali-*, and *ayogi-kevali-guṇasthāna*.

गुणव्रत - *Guṇa-vrata* - ethical code of conduct

According to Jainism, it is comprised of *digvrata* and *deśāvakāśika anrthadaṇḍavrata*.

गुणवृत्ति - *Guṇa-vṛtti* - implied meaning through similarity

Vide *lakṣaṇā*.

गुप्ति - *Gupti* - restraints; moderations

The endeavour of an individual to attain the threefold control over himself. According to Jainism this is control over the body, mind, and speech. Vide *bhāva-saṁvara*.

गुरु - *Guru* - teacher; preceptor; great

One who removes the darkness of ignorance.

गुरुकुलवास - *Gurukulavāsa* - remaining at the house of the teacher

गुरुलिङ्ग - *Guru-liṅga* - a form of the formless Śiva
Vide *liṅga-sthala.*

गुरुपरम्परा - *Guru-paramparā* - line of teachers
The Advaita lineage *śloka* is:

nārāyaṇam padma-bhuvaṁ vaśiṣṭhaṁ śaktiṁ ca tatputra-parāśarañca

vyāsaṁ śukaṁ gauḍapadaṁ mahāntaṁ govinda-yogīndram athāsya śiṣyam

śrī śaṅkarācāryam-athāsya padmapādañca hastāmalakañca śiṣyam

taṁ toṭakaṁ vārttikakāram-anyān-asmad-gurūn santatam-ānato'smi.

गुरूपसत्ति - *Gurūpasatti* – devotion to the preceptor

गुरुत्व - *Gurutva* - heaviness; weight; greatness
According to Nyāya-Vaiśeṣika, it is the non-intimate cause of the first downward motion of a falling substance. It is found in earth and water.

H

हैतुक - *Haituka* - name of Naiyāyika

हर्ष - *Harṣa* - joy

हेतु - *Hetu* - reason; probans; middle term

1. It is the reason or mark on the strength of which something is inferred. It must fulfil five conditions in a valid inferential process: there must exist the knowledge of the universal and invariable concomitance between the middle term and the major term; it must be observed as being necessarily and unconditionally present in the minor term; it must not be found where the major term is not found; it must not be related to something absurd; and it must not be contradicted by an equally strong middle term.

2. Nyāya holds the middle term to be of three kinds: positive and negative (*anvaya-vyatireka*); merely positive (*kevalānvaya*); and merely negative (*kevala-vyatireka*). Advaita only accepts merely positive middle term.

3. Vide *vyāpti* and *pakṣa-dharmatā-jñāna*.

हेतूपनिबन्ध - *Hetūpanibandha* - antecedent reason

हेतुवाद - *Hetu-vāda* - the science of logic

A name of the Nyāya school.

हेतुविभक्ति - *Hetu-vibhakti* - one of the limbs in a ten-membered syllogism

Vide *anumāna.*

हेत्वाभास - *Hetvābhāsa* - pseudo-probans; semblance of reason; fallacious reasoning

1. The Nyāya school enumerates five types of fallacious reasoning due to a defective probans (*hetu*). These are: the reason is inconsistent or the reason strays away (*savyabhicāra* or *anaikāntika*); the reason is contradictory or an adverse reason (*viruddha*); the reason is contradicted by a counter inference or opposite reason (*prakaraṇasama* or *satpratipakṣa*); the reason is unproved or an unestablished reason (*sādhyasama* or *asiddha*); and the reason is mistimed or inopportune (*kālātīta* or *bādhita*).

2. An inconsistent or straying reason is of three kinds: common (*sādhāraṇa*), uncommon (*asādhāraṇa*), and non-conclusive (*anupasaṁhārin*). A common strayer is that reason which is present in a place where the subject is not present. The uncommon strayer is that reason which is present only in the subject and not present in any similar example or counter example. The non-conclusive strayer is that reason which has no affirmative or negative example.

3. The unestablished reason is of three kinds, *viz.*, unestablished in respect of locus or abode (*āśrayāsiddha*); unestablished in respect of itself (*svarūpāsiddha*); and unestablished in respect of its concomitance (*vyāpyatvāsiddha*).

हेत्वसिद्ध - *Hetvasiddha* - a logical fallacy involving the non-establishment of the reason (*hetu*)

Vide *hetvābhāsa.*

हेयोज्झित - *Heyojjhita* - devoid of all inauspicious qualities

An essential feature of Brahman according to the theistic systems.

हिंसा - *Himsā* - injury; violence

हिंसोपकारिदान - *Himsopakāridāna* - desisting from giving implements of agriculture to individuals which will lead to the killing of insects

A limb of the Jaina ethical code called *anartha-daṇḍavrata.*

हीनयान - *Hīnayāna* - the small vehicle

A term referring to the Theravāda Buddhist schools. The two main representatives are the Sautrāntika and the Vaibhāṣika. It is called such because its disciplines are meant for the few and stresses individual enlightenment. It may be termed a realistic school. In this school one frees oneself from bondage by one's own efforts. The *Hīnayāna* is prevalent in Śrī Laṅkā, Burma and Thailand.

हिरण्यगर्भ - *Hiraṇyagarbha* - the golden egg; the cosmic form of the self; cosmic womb; creator of the subtle universe

It is the thread-self or the subtle vesture. It is the form of all the individuals together or the only individual (vide *eka-jīva-vāda*). It is the seed of the universe. It is also known as *sūtrātman*. The *Ṛg Veda* (X. 121) says: "*Hiraṇyagarbha* arose in the beginning; born, he was the one lord of things existing."

हित - *Hita* - means to the end

Viśiṣṭādvaita refers to three main aspects of philosophy: *tattva* (reality), *hita* (means), and *puruṣārtha* (goal of life).

ह्रस्व - *Hrasva* - small; short

The name given to two atoms when they generate a dyad.

ह्री - *Hrī* - modesty

One of the three consorts of Lord Viṣṇu, according to Viśiṣṭādvaita.

I

इच्छा - *Icchā* - desire; will

The will of *Īśvara* not only brings about creation and dissolution, but also is the sustainer and disposer of merit and demerit.

इच्छाशक्ति - *Icchā-śakti* - the power of desire

According to Śivādvaita, *parā-śakti* is the form of the Lord. Through his *icchā-śakti*, he desired "May I become many." By his *jñāna-śakti* he considered the means and instruments necessary for creation. By his *kriyā-śakti* he created the universe, which is like a picture painted on the wall of *icchā-śakti*.

इदम् - *Idam* - this

The *Veda* often uses this term to refer to the manifested universe.

Advaita uses this term to refer to the *adhiṣṭhāna* of illusions. The 'this' in the perception of a snake superimposed upon a rope, is the rope which is the basis of the illusion of the snake.

ईह - *Īha* - a stage in *mati* knowledge in which the location of cognition is sought

1. According to Jainism, the individual appreciates of a visible object in this stage.

2. Vide *mati.*

इज्या - *Ijyā* - the principal worship at mid-day (as ordained in the school of Pāñcarātra *Āgama*).

इन्द्रिय - *Indriya* - sense organ

1. According to the Buddhists the senses are but orbs.

2. According to the Mīmāṁsakas, the senses are the capacities of the orbs.

3. According to Advaita, the senses are the instruments of perception.

4. According to Dvaita, the senses are: the five external senses, the mind (*manas*), and the witness consciousness (*sākṣin*).

5. The five organs of knowledge are: the ear (*śrotra*), skin (*tvak*), eye (*cakṣus*), tongue (*jihvā*), and nose (*ghrāṇa*). Vide *jñānendriya.*

6. The five organs of action are the voice (*vāk*), hand (*pāṇi*), foot (*pāda*), organ of excretion (*pāyu*) and the organ of generation (*upastha*). Vide *karmendriya.*

7. According to Nyāya, a sense-organ is the seat of such contact with the mind which causes a cognition.

इन्द्रियानपेक्ष - *Indriya-anapekṣa* - a type of perception independent of the senses

1. It is of two kinds: *svayaṁsiddha* and *divya.*

2. Vide *pratyakṣa* and *arvācīna.*

इन्द्रियनिग्रह - *Indriyanigraha* - sense-control

इन्द्रियार्थ - *Indriyārtha* - sense-objects

इन्द्रियार्थसन्निकर्ष - *Indriyārtha-sannikarṣa* - contact of the sense organs with objects

Vide *sannikarṣa.*

इन्द्रियात्मवादिन् - *Indriyātma-vādin* - a type of Cārvāka who considers the senses as the individual

इन्द्रियसापेक्ष - *Indriya-sāpekṣa* - a type of perception dependent on the senses

Vide *pratyakṣa* and *arvācīna.*

इरुविनैयोप्पु - *Iruviṉai-oppu* (Tamil) - equanimity

1. The state of the individual in which it takes an attitude of perfect equanimity towards both righteous and sinful deeds.

2. It is called *karma-sāmya* in Sanskrit.

ईर्या - *Īryā* - an external rule of conduct in Jainism

1. To go by well-established paths so as not to kill living entities which might be lying on the way.

2. Vide *cāritra* and *samiti.*

ईश - *Īśa* - Lord; master

ईषण - *Īṣaṇa* - to beg alms in the proper monastic order.

1. According to Jainism, one of the external rules of conduct.

2. Vide *cāritra.*

ईशित्व - *Īśitva* - the power of absolute mastery over all physical objects

1. One of the eight powers (*siddhi*).
2. Vide *aṣṭa-aiśvarya.*

इष्टदेवता - *Iṣṭa-devatā* - one's chosen deity; tutelary deity

इष्टलिङ्ग – *Iṣṭa-liṅga* - a form of the formless Śiva

Vide *liṅga-sthala.*

इष्टापूर्त - *Iṣṭā-pūrta* - the sacrifices and digging of wells and tanks

A forerunner of the idea of *karma.* The term occurs in the *Ṛg-veda*

ईश्वर - *Īśvara* - Lord; God

1. The Divine with form (*saguṇa-brahman*)

2. According to Viśiṣṭādvaita, He is the Supreme Ruler and Controller. He is full of auspicious qualities. He is both transcendent and immanent. The world of animate and inanimate entities emerge from His body. He is omnipresent, omnipotent, and omniscient. He is all-merciful and by His grace, individual souls attain liberation. He is the author of the universe, both as its material and efficient causes. He manifests himself in five forms as: transcendent (*para*); emanations (*vyūha*); incarnations (*vibhava*); indweller (*antaryāmin*); and sacred icons (*arcā*). As *para,* He possesses six divine qualities: knowledge (*jñāna*), strength (*bala*), lordship (*aiśvarya*), potency (*śakti*), virility (*vīrya*), and splendour (*tejas*).

3. According to Advaita, *Īśvara* is *Brahman* as conditioned by *māyā.* The Absolute knows no

distinctions; yet in relation to the world, the Godhead becomes its source and ground. *Īśvara* is both the material and efficient cause of the world. The *saguṇa-brahman* is said to be omnipotent, omniscient, and the creator, etc.

ईश्वरप्रणिधान - *Īśvara-praṇidhāna* - devotion to God

1. The cultivation of a spirit of absolute self-surrender to God in whatever one does. It has also been represented as a means of attaining *samādhi* and, through *samādhi*, *kaivalya*.

इति - *Iti* - thus

Iti is used at the end of a work to denote its conclusion.

J

जड - *Jaḍa* - inert; unconscious

According to Viśiṣṭādvaita, it is a substance devoid of pure *sattva*. It is of two types: *prakṛti* and *ākāśa*.

जगत् - *Jagat* - the world

In Indian philosophy the world origin is traced either to a plurality of ultimate reals which are simple and atomic (as in Nyāya-Vaiśeṣika) or it may be derived from a single substance which is assumed to be complex and all-pervasive (as in Sāṅkhya-Yoga).

जगत्प्रपञ्च - *Jagat-prapañca* - world appearance

जाग्रत् - *Jāgrat* - the waking state

Vide *avasthā*.

जहदजहल्लक्षणा - *Jahad-ajahal-lakṣaṇā* - exclusive-non-exclusive implication

1. A type of secondary implication in which part of the primary meaning of a word is given up and part of it is retained. In an identity statement, 'This is that Devadatta,' the meaning of the word 'this' means Devadatta as qualified by present time, place, etc., and the sense of the word 'that' is this same Devadatta as qualified by past

time, place, etc. In this type of judgment, part of the meaning of the words 'that' and 'this' viz. 'qualified by present time' and 'qualified by past time', are rejected.

2. This method is used by the Advaitins to obtain the meaning of identity-statements, *mahāvākyas*, etc.

3. Vide *lakṣaṇā*.

जहल्लक्षणा - *Jahal-lakṣaṇā* - exclusive implication

1. The implication of a sentence's meaning which is other than the primary sense as indicated by the words, but which is related to them while the primary meaning is completely given up. In the phrase, 'the village on the river', the primary meaning of the word 'river' is given up and the 'bank' which is related to the river, is implied and accepted.

2. Vide *lakṣaṇā*.

जैमिनी - *Jaimini* – founder of the Pūrva-mīmāṁsā school and author of the *Pūrva-mīmāmsā-sūtra*

जल- *Jala* - water

जल्प - *Jalpa* - arguing constructively as well as destructively for victory in a debate; sophistry

1. One of the sixteen categories of the Nyāya school.

2. Vide *padārtha*, *vitaṇḍā*, and chart no. 6.

जनः - *Janaḥ* - the world of delight; the world of the great gods; man

Vide *loka*.

जङ्गम - *Jaṅgama* - moving bodies

1. They are of four types: celestial beings (*deva*), human beings (*manuṣya*), animal beings (*tiryak*), and hell-beings (*nāraki*).

2. According to Vīra Śaivism, it denotes a person, endowed with knowledge, who moves from place to place preaching Vīra Śaivite ideals and guiding the devotees of Lord Śiva.

जन्म - *Janma* - birth

जन्मादि अस्य यतः - *Janmādi asya yataḥ* - that (is *Brahman*) from which (are derived) the origin, etc. of this (universe)

The second *sūtra* of the *Brahmasūtra*.

जन्य - *Janya* - producible thing

जन्यबुद्धि - *Janya-buddhi* - created intellect

जन्यकृति - *Janya-kṛti* - originated volition

जप - *Japa* - the repetition of the name of God

जरामरण - *Jarā-maraṇa* - old age, decay, and death

1. According to Buddhism, twelfth link in the wheel of empirical existence. Birth is its cause.

2. Vide *pratītya-samutpāda*.

जरायुज - *Jarāyuja* - womb-born beings

जातक - *Jātaka* - birth stories

The stories of the various lives of the Buddha on earth. It is written in Pali and forms part of the orthodox Hīnayāna canon, the *Sutta-piṭaka*.

जाति - *Jāti* - birth; class; class notions; futilities; specious and unavailing objections; part; generality; universal

1. One of the links in the wheel of empirical existence according to Buddhism. Vide *pratītya-samutpāda.*

2. One of the sixteen categories of the Nyāya school. In this context, it refers to specious and unavailing objections. Vide *padārtha* and chart no. 6.

3. According to Nyāya, the meaning of words is said to refer to class-notions. Class is defined as that which produces the notion of sameness.

4. According to Mīmāṁsā, class-character has no separate existence apart from individuals (unlike the Nyāya position which claims it does).

5. The Mīmāṁsakas, the Vedāntins, and the Grammarians say that a word primarily refers to a universal.

6. The highest genus is being (*sattā*) according to the Nyāya school. It is called *parajāti* or the highest universal. The lower universals are called *aparajāti.*

7. It consists in the drawing of contradictory conclusion and the raising of false issues with a deliberate intention of defeating an opponent.

जय - *Jaya* - Victory

झान - *Jhāna* - (Pali) meditation

Vide *dhyāna.*

जिह्वा - *Jihvā* - tongue

जिज्ञासा - *Jijñāsā* - enquiry; desire to know

जिन - *Jina* - conquering one; victor

The title given to the twentyfour teachers (*tīrthaṅkaras*) of the Jaina tradition. More specifically it refers to Mahāvīra, the 24th *tīrthaṅkara.* Disciples of a *Jina* are called Jainas.

जीव - *Jīva* - individual soul

1. According to Jainism, the individual soul is characterized by consciousness, life, immateriality, and extension in space. Consciousness is its characteristic mark and consists in knowledge, insight, bliss and power. The size of the individual (soul) is the same as that of the body that it occupies; expanding and contracting as the case may necessitate. It is held that there is plurality of individuals. They are of two basic kinds: stationary and mobile.

2. According to Buddhism, there is no individual (soul) apart from a cluster of factors. The individual is a mere name for a complex of changing constituents.

3. According to Nyāya, it is a non-composite, partless, pervasive, eternal substance. There is an infinite number of individual souls.

4. According to Vaiśeṣika, it is an eternal, imperceptible, all-pervading, spiritual substance. There is an infinite number of individual souls.

5. According to Sāṅkhya, *puruṣa* is an eternal, immutable, conscious entity. It is non-active and has neither birth nor death. What is subject to experience and empirical changes is the phenomenal self which is a blend of *puruṣa* and

mind. There is an infinite number of individual souls.

6. According to Viśiṣṭādvaita, individual souls are real, eternal, unborn, spiritual, have knowledge and are of the nature of knowledge. They are atomic in size and infinite in number. They are an inseparable part of God and dependent thereupon. They are of three types: those eternally free (*nitya*), those liberated (*mukta*), and those bound (*baddha*). The individual soul as knowledge does not change; but bound soul's knowledge changes. The soul's knowledge is eternal and in the state of liberation is all-knowing, but on account of empirical limitations this knowledge is diminished. The souls are both agent and enjoyer. They are a part or mode of God. Their relation is one of inseparability, with the individual soul related to and dependent upon God.

7. According to Dvaita, individual souls are atomic in size and infinite in number. They are eternal and no two are alike. They are similar to *Brahman* in kind, but not in degree. They are active agents dependent upon God's will. They are of three grades: the ever-free (*nitya*), those having attained freedom (*mukta*), and those bound (*baddha*). Among the liberated souls there is an intrinsic gradation; and among the bound souls, there are three types: those fit for release (*mukti-yogya*), those eternally within the cycle of birth and death (*nitya-saṁsārin*), and those fit only for hell (*tamo-yogya*).

8. According to Advaita, it is a blend of the Self and the not-Self with a wrong identification of

each as the other. It is a complex entity consisting of the mind-body organism. It is a complex of the substrate-intelligence plus the subtle body plus a reflection of consciousness therein. It is consciousness, inseparably qualified by the internal organs. It is a reflection of the consciousness (*cid-ābhāsa*) in impure *sattva*-predominant ignorance. It is the phenomenal, empirical ego. Intrinsically individuals are one, but phenomenally they are many; they are held to be all-pervading in size.

9. According to Vīra Śaivism, individual souls are in three stages of spiritual maturity: *vīra*, *puruṣa*, and *aṅga*. They are a part of Lord Śiva, eternal and essentially pure and perfect. They are also distinct from Śiva in that, though they share his essence, they do not possess his attributes of omnipotence, omniscience, omnipresence, etc. Their powers of knowledge and action are limited due to impurities. Thus they are both identical and different from Lord Śiva. This relation is called difference-cum-non-difference (*bhedābheda*).

10. According to Śaiva Siddhānta, individual souls are infinite in number, all-pervasive, and omniscient by nature, though veiled by the three impurities (*mala*). They are dependent upon God. They are of four types: those completely liberated (*para-mukta*), those liberated while living (*jīvan-mukta*), those craving power (*adhikāra-mukta*), and those failing to understand (*apara-mukta*). Individual souls are also of three classes: those subject to the three *malas* (*sakala*), those subject only to *āṇava-* and *karma-malas* (*pralayā-kala*), and those subject only to *āṇava-mala*

(*vijñānākala*). Individual souls are related to Lord Śiva as the body is related to the individual soul. That is, they are different, but they are not separate. In nature they are similar, but in essence as an entity they are different. Even in release this distinctiveness remains.

11. According to Kashmir Śaivism, individual souls are called *paśu* due to limitations caused by impurities. Individual souls are eternal, real, identical with Lord Śiva, and essentially unlimited, all-pervading, ever-conscious luminosity. Liberation comes by recognition of their real nature as being identical with Śiva. They are of four types: bound (*paśu*), peaceful (*śānta*), conceited and devoid of knowledge (*pralaya-kevalin*), and liberated (*vijñāna-kevalin*). The individual soul passes through the five *tattvas* of the pure creation in a reverse order on its way to liberation. These stages are called: *mantra*, *mantreśa*, *mantra-maheśa*, *śaktija*, and *śāmbhava*. Liberation comes when the soul remembers its identity with Lord Śiva.

12. According to Śivādvaita, individuals are a part of *Brahman*, eternal, atomic in size, infinite in number, dependent, and bound by their impurities (*mala*), though in essence they are pure and perfect. Liberation is being similar to, but not identical with, Lord Śiva. It is the realization of one's own essential nature. This is achieved through contemplation of Lord Śiva.

13. According to Mīmāṁsā, the individual soul is one of the substances. It is eternal and distinct from the mind-body complex. It is an agent of

action and the enjoyer of the fruits thereof. There is a plurality of individual souls.

14. According to the Yoga school, the individual soul is a changeless, eternal, omnipresent, conscious entity. It is entirely passive. Liberation comes when the individual soul roots out ignorance and stills the modifications of the mind.

15. The word *'jīva'* is derived from the root *'jīv'*, which means 'to continue breathing'. Other names for it include *'bhoktā'* (experient) and *'kartā'* (agent). It is also described as *'puruṣa'*, which is explained as *puri-śaya* or 'what lies in the citadel of the body'.

जीव-ब्रह्म-ऐक्य - *Jīva-brahma aikya* - the oneness of the individual soul with the Absolute

The central teaching of Advaita.

जीवन्मुक्त - *Jīvanmukta* - liberated while living

1. A doctrine admitted by Sāṅkhya, Advaita, and Śaiva Siddhānta, though with variations according to each system. The doctrine posits that an individual may be liberated even while living in a physical body.

2. According to Sāṅkhya, it occurs the moment there is an essential, experiential discrimination between the *puruṣa* and *prakṛti*. The physical body continues due to past *karma* which has brought it about in the first place. When this *karma* subsides, through experience thereof, the physical body falls and one is then released without the body (*videha-mukti*).

3. According to Advaita, liberation occurs with the destruction of ignorance (*avidyā*). The continuance of the physical body is in no way incompatible to liberation. Before liberation, one thinks of oneself as the body. After liberation, one realises that the physical body is only an illusory appearance. If the body were real, liberation could occur only after its destruction. However, liberation is a change of perspective. Since the physical body is not real, its continued appearance or disappearance is of no consequence. Thus the *Jīvanmukta* is one who lives in the world, but is not of it. Whether such an individual has a body or not is of no difference.

4. According to Śaiva Siddhānta, it is an individual soul which is freed from *āṇava-*, *māyā-*, and *karma-malas* and their operations. The individual enjoys bliss even while living in an embodied state.

जीवन्मुक्ति - *Jīvanmukti* - liberation while living

Vide *jīvanmukta.*

जीवन्योनि - *Jīvanyoni* - the activity of procreation

जीवात्मन् - *Jīvātman* - the individual self

Vide *jīva.*

ज्ञान - *Jñāna* - knowledge; wisdom; comprehension

1. According to Jainism, it is the knowledge of details.

2. According to Śaiva Siddhānta, it is a path to liberation. It is the direct means and takes the individual straight to God. Its goal is union with God (*sāyujya*).

3. According to Advaita, it is the ultimate means to liberation. Since it is the only thing which is opposed to ignorance (*avidyā*), it is the only means to release.

4. According to Nyāya-Vais'eṣika, knowledge is not only about objects but also about itself.

5. According to Mīmāṁsā, knowledge is a mode of the self. It is described as an act (*kriyā*) or process (*vyāpāra*). It is supersensible and though knowable, it is known only indirectly through inference and not directly through introspection as Nyāya-Vais'eṣika posits. It may be either mediate or immediate.

6. According to Advaita, it is a blend of a *vṛtti* as inspired by the *sākṣin*. The *vṛtti* element is contingent and the element of consciousness is eternal. It is divided into *sākṣi-jñāna* and *vṛtti-jñāna*. (Vide both listed separately). It may be either mediate or immediate. The 'that' of an object is known in mediate knowledge. In immediate kowledge, the 'what' is also revealed. Immediate knowledge takes place when the following conditions are fulfilled: The objec tmust be directly knowable (*yogya*); the object must be existent at the time; there should be established a certain intimate relation between the subject and the object.

7. According to Vis'iṣṭādvaita, knowledge is able to manifest itself and other objects unaided, but what it manifests is never for itself but always for another. Thus it can only show and cannot know. It is like light in that it exists for another

and not for itself. It pertains to either individual soul (*jīva*) or to God (*Īśvara*).

ज्ञान-आभास - *Jñāna-ābhāsa* - erroneous cognition

ज्ञान-अभाव - *Jñāna-abhāva* - absence of knowledge; negation of knowledge; non-cognition

ज्ञान-आश्रय - *Jñāna-āśraya* - locus of knowledge

ज्ञान-काण्ड - *Jñāna-kāṇḍa* - the parts of the *Veda* dealing with the knowledge of *Brahman*

Vide *karma-kāṇḍa*.

ज्ञान-कर्म-समुच्चय - *Jñāna-karma-samuccaya* - the combination of knowledge and action

1. Brahmadatta, Maṇḍana, and others held the view that the knowledge-cum-action is the means to liberation. Advaitins like Sureśvara strongly opposed this combination view as a possible means for liberation because knowledge and action are opposed to each other in three essential respects. Per their source: the former arises from a valid means of knowledge (*pramāṇa*) while the latter arises from ignorance (*avidyā*). Per their nature: the former illumines while the latter conceals. And per their effect: knowledge destroys ignorance, while action's results are either origination, attainment, modification or purification.

2. Generally it may be said that Pūrva-mīmāṁsā takes the position that *karma* is primary and knowledge is subsidiary; the Bhedābheda-vādins take the position that the two means are of equal importance; and Maṇḍana takes the position that knowledge is primary and actions are subsidiary.

ज्ञान-लक्षण - *Jñāna-lakṣaṇa* - super-normal sense contact

1. The contact (*sannikarṣa*) through the cognition of an object revived in memory. It is the relation characterized by previous knowledge and it is responsible for all cases of acquired perception; e.g., the sight of sandalwood is an occasion for the perception of fragrant sandal, even though there is no physical contact between the sandalwood and one's sense of smell. This is due to one's past associations with it. It is perception by complication because it is based upon past experience. It is extra-ordinary perception because generally one sense organ does not perceive sensation of a different nature which usually stimulates some other sense organ.

2. Vide *alaukika-pratyakṣa*.

ज्ञान-निवर्त्य - *Jñāna-nivartya* - removable by right knowledge

Vide *avidyā*.

ज्ञान-प्रागभाव - *Jñāna-prāgabhava* - prior non-existence of of knowledge

Vide *abhāva*.

ज्ञान-शक्ति - *Jñāna-śakti* - the potency or power of knowledge

1. According to Śivādvaita, the power of knowledge is the instrument by which the Lord considered the means and instruments necessary for creation.

2. According to Kashmir Śaivism, the power of knowledge is that by virtue of which the objects

of creation are brought together and held together in consciousness.

ज्ञान-स्वरूप - *Jñāna-svarūpa* - the knowledge as essence

According to Advaita, one's true nature is *jñāna-svarūpa.*

ज्ञानता - *Jñānatā* - consciousness

ज्ञानावरणीय - *Jnānāvaraṇīya* - knowledge-obscuring; comprehension-obscuring

1. According to Jainism, these are obstructive (*ghāti*) *karma* particles which obscure right knowledge. They limit the individual's capacity to acquire direct knowledge (***kevala-jñāna***).

2. Since knowledge is of five types, there are, corresponding to them, five types of knowledge-obscuring *karmas.*

ज्ञानेन्द्रिय - *Jñānendriya* - organs of knowledge

1. The five cognitive sense organs are the organs of knowledge. They are: the organs of hearing (***śrotra***), touch (***tvak***), sight (***cakṣus***), taste (***rasana***), and smell (***ghrāṇa***).

2. The Sāṅkhya school also includes the mind (***manas***) as one of the sense organs. The Nyāya-Vaiśeṣika also includes mind as one of the ***indriyas.***

3. They are also referred to as the 'internal senses' as they impart knowledge from inside.

ज्ञप्ति - *Jñapti* - knowledge; cognition

ज्ञाता - *Jñātā* (*jñātṛ*) - knower

ज्ञात-ज्ञापन - *Jñāta-jñāpana* - knowing what is already known

ज्ञातता - *Jñātatā* - state of being known; cognizedness

ज्ञातृत्व - *Jñātṛtva* - being the knower

ज्ञेय - *Jñeya* - knowable thing; the known object of knowledge

ज्योतिः - *Jyotiḥ* - light

ज्योतिषां ज्योतिः - *Jyotiṣām-jyotiḥ* - light of lights

ज्योतिष्टोम - *Jyotiṣṭoma* - name of a Vedic sacrifice

A variety of the *agniṣṭoma.*

K

कैंकर्य - *Kaiṅkarya* – spiritual service

कैवल्य - *Kaivalya* - aloofness; alone-ness; isolation

According to Sāṅkhya and Yoga, the state of liberation. It is complete detatchment from matter and from transmigration. Yoga defines it as 'when the purity of contemplation equals the purity of the individual, there is isolation...' Sāṅkhya sees it as an aloofness from *prakṛti* and all its transformations. There is no pain in this state, but there is no pleasure either. The immediate cause for this aloofness is discriminating knowledge (*viveka*).

कैवल्यपर - *Kaivalya-para* - a seeker of liberation who is desirous of the bliss of the self (*ātman*) or of the bliss of meditation

Vide *mumukṣutva.*

कला - *Kalā* - a unit of time; limited agency; part

1. It is made of thirty *kāṣṭhās*. Vide *kāla*.
2. One of the five constrictors. Vide *kañcuka*.
3. One of the five sheaths. Vide *pañca-kañcuka*.

काल - *Kāla* - time

1. According to Jainism, it is a non-individual category (*ajīva-dravya*). It has no parts (*anasti-*

kāya), is beginningless, and is immaterial. It is real and the auxiliary cause of change. It is of two types: absolute time (*dravya-kāla*) and relative time (*vyavahāra-kāla* or *samaya*).

2. According to Sāṅkhya, the existance of any real time is denied. Sāṅkhya considers time as the duration taken by an atom to traverse its own unit of space. Time has no existance separate from atoms and their movements.

3. According to the Nyāya and Vaiśeṣika schools, time is an all-pervading, partless substance which exists by itself. It appears as many due to its association with changes which are related to it.

4. According to Viśiṣṭādvaita, time is an inert substance devoid of the three *guṇas*. It is eternal and all-pervasive. It is divided into past, present, and future. It is designated as simultaneous, immediate, long, the winking of an eye, etc. It is co-ordinate of *prakṛti* and is comprised in *Brahman*, and dependent thereon.

5. According to Dvaita, it is one of the substances (*dravya*). It always has a beginning and it is subject to destruction. It consists of ever-flowing time-units.

6. According to the Śaiva schools, it is one of the *tattvas*.

7. According to Advaita, time is the relation between the real *Brahman* and the non-real *māyā*. Thus time is phenomenal.

8. Vide charts no. 6, 7, 8, 9, and 10.

कालातीत - *Kālātīta* - mis-timed reason or probans

1. A type of fallacious reasoning in which the reason is mis-timed or inopportune, e.g., 'sound is eternal because it is manifested through conjunction, like colour.' This inference is unsound because the reason does not coincide with the example given in the point of time.

2. Vide *hetvābhāsa.*

कालात्ययापदिष्ट - *Kālātyayāpadiṣṭa* - a type of fallacious inferential reasoning same as *kālātīta*

कलि - *Kali* - the last of the four *yugas*

Vide *kaliyuga* and *yuga.*

कालिक-सम्बन्ध - *Kālika-sambandha* - time relation

कालिक-विशेषणता - *Kālika-viśeṣaṇatā* - temporal attributiveness

According to the Nyāya school, time is infinite and single, yet to explain such common empirical notions as minutes, hours, days, etc., all things are posited to exist in temporal time through the relation of temporal attributiveness.

कलियुग - *Kali-yuga* - the dark age; the iron age

The age in which truth is said to stand on only one of its four legs. The means to liberation in this age is said to be the repetition of the names of God, *nāmasaṅkīrtana*. Vide *yuga.*

कल्प - *Kalpa* - a cycle of time of an extremely long duration; way; method

1. One of the six limbs of the *Vedas.* Vide *vedāṅgas.*

2. It is a 'day' of *Brahmā* and is divided into a number of lesser periods called *manvantara.*

4 *yugas* makes a *mahā-yuga* (or *manvantara*) and 1000 *mahā-yugas* make a half-*kalpa* or 4,320,000,000 years, which is the duration of one day or one night of *Brahmā*. Two half-*kalpas* make a *kalpa* which is One Day of *Brahmā* (i.e., a day and a night).

कल्पना - *Kalpanā* - the association of name and permanance to objects; imagination; presumptive knowledge; assumption; creation

Also called *abhilāpa*.

कल्पित - *Kalpita* - imaginary

कल्पितसंवृति - *Kalpita-saṁvṛti* - imaginary relative point of view

कल्याण - *Kalyāṇa* - excellence

Vide *sādhana-saptaka*.

कल्याणगुण - *Kalyāṇa-guṇa* - auspicious quality

काम - *Kāma* - desire; pleasure

1. One of the four values of life. It is the hedonistic or the psychological value of life.

2. Vide *puruṣārtha*.

कामिक - *Kāmika* - given to lust; a Śaiva *Āgama*

काम्यकर्म - *Kāmya-karma* - desire-prompted actions; optional rites

Positively enjoined ritual actions prescribed for one who wishes to obtain a certain result, i.e., increase in wealth or heavan, etc.

कणाद् - *Kaṇāda* - atom-eater

A name given to the founder of the Vaiśeṣika school and the author of the *Vaiśeṣikasūtras.*

कञ्चुक - *Kañcuka* - constrictor

The categories of *kāla, niyati, rāga, vidyā,* and *kalā.* They envelop an individual soul and constitute the limitations imposed upon it. *Kāla* is temporal limitation; *niyati* is spatial limitation; *rāga* is attachment; *vidyā* is limited knowledge; and *kalā* is limited agency. According to Kashmir Śaivism, these five envelop the individual soul and thus make for its finitude.

काण्ड - *Kāṇḍa* - section; part; chapter

कपिल - *Kapila* - brown; the red one

The name of the sage who is the author of the *Sāṅkhya-śāstra* and the founder of the Sāṅkhya school. It is also an epithet of the Sun.

कारकव्यापार - *Kārakavyāpāra* - causal operation

करण - *Karaṇa* - the best cause; reason; origin

कारण - *Kāraṇa* - instrument; the efficient or instrumental cause

1. The unique or special cause through the action of which a particular effect is produced. The adherents of *satkāraṇa-vāda* hold that the cause alone exists and all effects are illusory appearances of the cause.

2. *Sādhāraṇa-kāraṇas* are common causes.

3. *Asādhāraṇa-kāraṇas* are specific causes.

4. *Samavāyi-kāraṇa* is the material cause.

5. *Asamavāyi-kāraṇa* is that which produces its characteristics in the effect through the medium of the material cause.

6. Nyāya-Vaiśeṣika, unlike the other systems which posit that all positive effects have two sets of causes (the material cause - *upādāna-kāraṇa* and the efficient cause - *nimitta-kāraṇa*), says that besides the efficient cause, the material cause is taken by two causes known as *samavāyi* - and *asamavāyi-kāraṇas*. The *samavāyi-kāraṇa* is invariably a *dravya* and the *asamavāyi-kāraṇa* is a *guṇa* or *karma*.

कारण-चित्त - *Kāraṇa-citta* - the causal mind; the cosmic mind

According to the Yoga school, the causal-mind is all-pervading like ether.

कारण-दोषज्ञान - *Kāraṇa-doṣajñāna* - knowledge which is known to be faulty and defective

कारणानुपलब्धि - *Kāraṇānupalabdhi* - non-perception of the cause

A type of non-perception; e.g , "there is no smoke here, since there is no fire."

कारण-शरीर - *Kāraṇa-śarīra* - causal body

1. The sheath of bliss enveloped in ignorance, according to Advaita.

2. It is also called *ānandamayakośa.*

3. Vide *śarīra.*

कारणविरुद्धकार्योपलब्धि - *Kāraṇaviruddhakāryopalabdhi* presence of effects of opposite causes

A type of non-perception; e.g., "this place is not occupied by individuals of shivering sensations for it is full of smoke."

कारणविरुद्धोपलब्धि - *Kāraṇaviruddhopalabdhi* - presence of opposite causes

A type of non-perception; e.g., A person says: "there is no shivering through cold here," since he is near the fire.

कारिका - *Kārikā* - verse

Independent treatises which try to summarize the main topics of a system in a succinct manner.

कर्म - *Karma* - action; rite; deed

1. The accumulated effect of deeds in lives, past and present.

2. All the Indian systems except the Cārvāka school accept the theory of *karma* in one form or the other. They agree that "As one sows, so shall one reap." That is, an action done by an individual leaves behind it some sort of potency which has the power to cause either joy or sorrow in the future according to its nature.

3. According to Jainism, it means an aggregate of extremely fine matter which is imperceptible to the senses. This matter consists of eight main types: comprehension-obscuring (*jñānāvaraṇa*), apprehension-obscuring (*darśanāvaraṇa*), feeling-producing (*vedanīya*), deluding (*mohanīya*), age-determining (*āyus*), personality-making (*nāma*),

status-determining (*gotra*), and power-obscuring (*antarāya*). The first four are obstructive (*ghāti*) and the rest are non-obstructive (*aghāti*).

4. According to Buddhism, it is the correlation between cause and consequence and the effect is conditional upon circumstances. According to the Buddha, one of the three factors viz., external stimuli, conscious motives, and unconscious motives determines *karma.* Though the Buddhists deny identity, they do not deny continuity. Their doctrine of *karma* is based on the doctrine of dependent origination.

5. According to the Yoga school, it is divided into four classes: white (*śukla*) actions which produce happiness; black (*kṛṣṇa*) actions which produce sorrow; white-black (*śukla-kṛṣṇa*) actions which produce partly happiness and partly sorrow; and neither white nor black (*aśukla-kṛṣṇa*) actions which are devoid of any pleasure or pain.

6. According to Mīmāṁsā, the *Veda* has action as its purport. The aim of the *Veda* is to prescribe certain actions and to prohibit others. Liberation or release is said to be gained through actions alone. There are obligatory actions (*nitya-karma*); occasional rites (*naimittika-karma*), and optional rites (*kāmya-karma*). One is enjoined to perform the first two types of actions and to refrain from the optional rites. One should also refrain from prohibited actions (*pratiṣiddha-karma*). By these actions one will balance one's *karma* and at the end of one's life, there will be no more *saṁsāra* for that person. Release requires what-

is-to-be-accomplished and the latter requires action for its accomplishment.

7. According to Advaita, the entire *Veda* does not have its purport in ritualistic action and action is not the means to release. Action is for the purification of the mind and is thus a remote auxiliary to liberation.

8. *Vihita-karmas* are the actions prescribed by the *Veda*

9. *Sañcita-karma* is residue produced by acts performed either in this life or in a previous one, but which remains latent during this present life.

10. *Āgāmi-karma* is the result of acts performed during this present life which will mature in the normal course of events.

11. *Prārabdha-karma* is the residue of acts that is working itself out during the present life.

12. *Prāyaścitta-karma* is expiatory action. It is performed to purify oneself because one has failed to do certain prescribed acts either in this life or in past lives.

13. According to the Vaiśeṣika school, it means physical motion. It is defined as: "That which resides in only one substance, is devoid of qualities, and is the direct and immediate cause of both conjunction and disjunction." Motion is of five kinds: upward (*utkṣepaṇa*), downward (*avakṣepaṇa*), contraction (*ākuñcana*), expansion (*prasāraṇa*), and locomotion (*gamana*).

कर्मकाण्ड - *Karma-kāṇḍa* - ritual portion of the *Veda*

The section of the *Veda* dealing with actions. Also known as *Pūrvakāṇḍa*.

कर्मकृत - *Karma-kṛta* - action-born bodies

These are non-eternal bodies and of five types: born out of the earth (*udbhijja*), sweat-born (*svedaja*), egg-born (*aṇḍaja*), womb-born (*jarāyuja*), and those whose origin is unknown (*ayonija*).

कर्मलकार - *Karma-lakāra* - verbal suffix of the object in a sentence

कर्ममल - *Karma-mala* - impurity of action

कर्मसाम्य - *Karmasāmya* - Vide *iruviṉai-oppu*

कर्मशरीर - *Karma-śarīra* - the *karma* matter which has accumulated around the individual self during its numberless past lives.

Vide *karma* according to Jainism.

कर्मेन्द्रिय - *Karmendriya* - organs of action

The five conative sense organs. They are the organs of speech (*vāk*), prehension (*pāṇi*), movement (*pāda*), excretion (*pāyu*), and generation (*upastha*).

कार्पण्य - *Kārpaṇya* - meekness

Also known as *ākiñcanya*. Vide *prapatti*.

कर्ता - *Kartā* - agent; doer

कर्तृलकार - *Kartṛ-lakāra* - verbal suffix of agency

करुणा - *Karuṇā* - compassion

1. A type of meditation in Buddhism. One should sympathize with the sorrows of one's friends and foes alike.

2. An inherent principle embraced and protected by all Buddhas and Bodhisattvas.

कार्य - *Kārya* - effect; product

कार्यब्रह्मन् - *Kārya-brahman* - *Hiraṇyagarbha*; effected *Brahman*

कार्यचित्त - *Kārya-citta* - the effect mind

According to the Yoga school, as the mind associates with an individual self, it expands or contracts in accordance with the space of the body in question. Thus it is subject to modifications and afflictions.

कार्यकाल - *Kārya-kāla* - divisible time

Time as human beings experience in their ordinary empirical lives. It is changing and non-eternal. Vide *kāla*.

कार्यकारणभाव - *Kārya-kāraṇa-bhāva* - cause and effect relation.

Unconditionality and invariability are indispensable for the cause-effect relationship.

कार्यानुपलब्धि - *Kāryānupalabdhi* - non-perception of the effects

For example, "there are not the causes of smoke here, for there is no smoke." Vide *anupalabdhi*.

कार्यपरवाक्य - *Kāryaparavākya* - proposition which conveys what has to be done.

कार्यतावच्छेदक - *Kāryatāvacchedaka* - determinant of effect

कार्यतावच्छेदकसंसर्ग - *Kāryatāvacchedaka-saṁsarga* - relation determining the effect

कार्यविरुद्धोपलब्धि - *Kāyaviruddhopalabdhi* - opposition of effect

A type of non-perception; e.g., "there is not here the causes which can give cold since there is fire." Vide *anupalabdhi.*

कषाय - *Kaṣāya* – astringent; passions

One of the five *bhāva-āsravas.*

काष्ठा – *Kāṣṭhā* - a unit of time

1. It is fifteen *nimeṣas* (winking of an eye).
2. Vide *kāla.*

कतिपयदृष्टि - *Katipaya-dṛṣṭi* - partial cognition

An object is only seen incompletely and at most, one at a time.

कायक्लेश - *Kāya-kleśa* - an exrernal penance in Jainism

An absolute steadiness and fixity of the body.

काययोग - *Kāyayoga* - the sensation of *karma* particles through actions

A type of *āsrava* according to Jainism. Vide *āsrava.*

केवल - *Kevala* - oneness; absolute; alone; uncompounded; perfect

केवलाधिकरण - *Kevalādhikaraṇa* - mere container

केवलज्ञान - *Kevala-jnāna* - direct knowledge; immediate perception; omniscience

According to Jainism, it is omniscience. It is the height of wisdom — pure, perfect, and absolute. It transcends all spatial and temporal categories. It manifests itself in the individual once all of the limiting obstructions have been removed. It is independent of the senses. It is uncontaminated by doubt, error, or delusion.

केवलकर्मकृत - *Kevala-karma-kṛta* - purely action-made bodies

According to Viśiṣṭādvaita, these are bodies of bound individuals made out of latent predispositions. Vide *baddhajīva.*

केवलान्वयि - *Kevalānvayi* - only co-presence

1. A type of inference in which the middle term (*hetu*) is only co-present with the major term (*sādhya*); e.g., whatever is knowable is nameable. There is no negative instance possible to illustrate such a statement.

2. Vide *anumāna.*

केवलप्रमाण - *Kevala-pramāṇa* - knowledge of an object as it is (*yathārtha-jñānam kevalam*)

1. It is the form of valid knowledge in Dvaita. Corresponding to every source of knowledge, there is a mode of knowledge. *Kevala-pramāṇa*

is the means by which is effected direct intuition of the objects of cognition. They reveal an object directly. It is generated by the means of valid knowledge (*anupramāṇa*), and has three forms corresponding to the three means (perception, inference, and verbal testimony).

2. It is the means by which is effected direet intuitions which are of four kinds: of ordinary persons; of Yogins; of *Lakṣmī*; and of God.

केवलव्यतिरेकि - *Kevala-vyatireki* - only co-absence

1. A type of inference in which the middle term (*hetu*) is only co-absent with the major terms (*sādhya*), there being no positive instance possible to illustrate such a statement; e.g., all beings that possess animal functions have souls, can be proved only by negative examples such as chairs, tables, etc., which have no animal functions and therefore no souls.

2. Vide *anumāna*.

खण्ड - *Khaṇḍa* - continent

There are nine continents in Hindu cosmology. They are: *Bhārata*, *Kimpuruṣa*, *Hari*, *Ramyaka*, *Hiraṇyaka*, *Kuru*, *Bhadrāśva*, *Ketumāla* and *Ilāvarta*. These nine constitute the *Jambū-dvīpa*.

खन्ध - *Khandha* - (Pāli) vide *skandha*

ख्याति - *Khyāti* - apprehension; discernment; knowledge

ख्यातिवाद - *Khyāti-vāda* - theory of error

There are three types of theories of error: theories where the object of error is real (*sat-khyāti-vāda*), theories where the object of error is unreal (*asat-khyāti-vāda*), and the theory where the object of error is neither real nor unreal (*anirvacanīyakhyāti-vāda*). Under the first group comes Yogācāra's *ātma-khyāti,* Nyāya's *anyathā-khyāti*, Sāṅkhya's and Prābhāhara's *a-khyāti*, Bhāṭṭa's *Viparīta-khyāti*, and Rāmānuja's *sat-khyati* (or *yāthārtha-khyāti*). Under the second group comes the Mādhyamika's *asat-khyāti* and Madhva's *abhinava-anyathā-khyāti.* Under the last group comes Advaita's *anirvacanīya-khyāti.*

किञ्चिज्ज्ञ - *Kiñcijjña* - knowing only in parts; parviscient

कीर्तन - *Kīrtana* - singing the praises of the Lord

1. One of the nine forms of devotion.

2. Vide *bhakti.*

क्लेश - *Kleśa* - affliction; passion

1. The afflictions of the body, mind, and speech.

2. Afflictions are of five types: ignorance (*avidyā*), egoism (*asmitā*), attatchment (*rāga*), aversion (*dveṣa*), and the will-to-live (*abhiniveśa*).

क्लिष्ट - *Kliṣṭa* - afflicted

When the states of the mind lead one toward passions and their satisfaction, the *citta* is afflicted.

क्लिष्टमन - *Kliṣṭa-mana* - the seed of all thought and experience; afflicted mind

The afflicted mind is ignorance's first expression. The subject-object distinction is born. It is the individuation of the strorehouse consciousness (*ālaya-vijñāna*) according to Yogācāra Buddhism.

कोश - *Kośa* - sheath; subtle body

The individual self is enveloped within five subtle bodies: physical (*annamaya*), vital (*prāṇamaya*), mental (*manomaya*), consciousness (*vijñānamaya*), and bliss (*ānandamaya*). Each sheath is within the the previous one and thus they become subtler and subtler, one within the next. Vide each *kośa* listed separately.

क्रम - *Krama* - sequential; order

क्रमभाव - *Krama-bhāva*- invariable antecedent

One of the ways in which the reason is connected with the probandum in an inferential statement.

क्रमदृष्टि - *Krama-dṛṣṭi* - seeing in succession

क्रममुक्ति - *Krama-mukti* - attainment of liberation in stages; gradual liberation

Gradual liberation in stages in which an individual goes first to the world of *Brahmā*, gains knowledge of *Brahman* there, and is liberated at the destruction of that world at the time of the great dissolution. The means prescribed for this ascent is meditation on the *praṇava-mantra* (*om*).

क्रमसमुच्चय - *Krama-samuccaya* - sequential combination.

Vide *samuccaya* and *jñāna-samuccaya.*

क्रिया - *Kriyā* - action

A path or preparatory stage to liberation in Śaiva Siddhānta which is characterized by acts of intimate service to God. It is called the path of the good son (*satputra-mārga*). Its goal is to attain nearness to God (*sāmīpya*).

क्रियापाद् - *Kriyā-pāda* - action-denoting word

1. According to the Mīmāṁsākas, the central element in the scripture (*Veda*) is verb signifying action. A sentence is meaningless without a verb and the function of a verb is to signify an action to be done.

2. That section of the *Āgamas* which contains directions for the building of temples and the making of idols.

क्रियाशक्ति - *Kriyā-śakti* - power of action

1. Lord Śiva created the universe with this power, according to Śivādvaita.

2. According to Kashmir Śaivism, the principle (*tattva*) which is predominant in the *sad-vidyā-tattva* and functions as its dominating influence. In this stage there is activity and movement of thought. It is responsible for the actual manifestation of objects and their relations.

क्रोध - *Krodha* - anger

One of the four *kaṣāyas*.

कृष्ण - *Kṛṣṇa* - black; ninth descent of Viṣṇu

According to the Yoga school, a class of *karma*.

कृत - *Kṛta* - action

कृतकत्व - *Kṛtakatva* - producibility; artificiality

कृतयुग - *Kṛta-yuga* - the golden age

1. The age when truth is said to stand on all of its four legs. The means to liberation in this age is meditation (*dhyāna*).

2. It is also known as the *Satya-yuga*. Vide *yuga*.

कृति - *Kṛti* - volitional effort

क्षण - *Kṣaṇa* – moment; an extremely small portion of time

According to Sāṅkhya, the time taken by an atom to move its own measure of space.

क्षणिक - *Kṣaṇika* - existing only for one moment

क्षणिकवाद - *Kṣaṇika-vāda* - the theory of momentariness

The Buddhist theory that nothing continues the same for even two consecutive moments. All things not only change, but everything exists only for a moment of time.

क्षणिकविज्ञान - *Kṣanika-vijñāna* - momentary consciousness

क्षान्ति - *Kṣānti* - patience

1. One of the ten virtues (*dharmas*) of Jainism.

2. In Buddhism, one of the virtues (*pāramitā*).

क्षायिक - *Kṣāyika* - the state of the individual self wherein *karma* is not only prevented from operating, but is annihilated

According to Jainism, from this state liberation is attained. Vide *guṇa-sthāna*.

क्षेत्रज्ञ - *Kṣetrajña*-knower of the field; the individual self

क्षिप्र - *Kṣipra*- immediate

1. An aspect of designate time.
2. Vide *kāla.*

क्षिप्रता - *Kṣipratā* - quickness

क्षिप्त - *Kṣipta* - restless

A condition of the mind when it is tossed about by objects. In this state there is an excess of *rajas* in the mind.

क्षीराब्धि - *Kṣīrābdhi* - ocean of milk; the abode of Viṣṇu (of *vyūha* form)

क्षिति - *Kṣiti*- earth

कुमति - *Kumati* - a type of perception in Jainism

1. According to Jainism, it is a fallacious form of *mati* (knowledge).
2. Vide *mati.*

कुम्भक - *Kumbhaka* - retention (of the breath)

Vide *prāṇāyāma.*

कुश - *Kuśa* - one of the varieties of sacred grass (*dar bha*) which is used in religious rites

कुश्रुत - *Kuśruta* – a type of perception in Jainism

1. According to Jainism, it is a fallacious form of *śruta* knowledge.
2. Vide *śruta-jñāna.*

कूटस्थ - *Kūṭastha* - immutable; not subject to change Literally, "the on the summit or on the anvil".

L

लब्धि - *Labdhi* – the power of comparing or conceiving

According to Jainism, it is one of the four classes of *śruta-jñāna*. It stands for the stage of explanation which needs reference to a phenomenon with which the one under consideration is associated.

लाभ - *Lābha* - gain

लाघव - *Lāghava* - principle of parsimony or logical economy

लघिमा - *Laghimā* - lightness; becoming buoyant

1. One of the eight powers which enables one to rise up in the air (on the rays of the sun).

2. Vide *siddhi.*

लघु - *Laghu* - simple

लक्षण - *Lakṣaṇa* - definition

लक्षणा - *Lakṣaṇā* - secondary meaning of a word; implied meaning

1. When the primary meaning of a word does not fit in with the context, the word must be interpreted in a secondary sense. This is classified in two ways: bare implication (*kevala-lakṣaṇā*) and implication by the implied (*lakṣita-lakṣaṇā*). Bare

implication stands in direct relation to the expressed sense as in the expression, 'the hamlet on the river.' For the word 'river' there is bare implication of the 'bank' which is in direct relation to the river. Implied implication has no direct relation to the expressed sense, as in the example, 'the boy is a lion'; the *gauṇī* type of implied implication refers to his strength.

2. A second classification of implication is divided into three kinds: exclusive implication (*jahal-lakṣaṇā*), non-exclusive implication (*ajahal-lakṣaṇā*), and exclusive-cum-non-exclusive implication (*jahad-ajahal-lakṣaṇā*). *Jahal-lakṣaṇā* is where the original meaning is altogether given up and a quite new meaning is acquired. A meaning is implied other than the sense primarily implied, but which is related to the primary meaning while the primary meaning is totally rejected. In the phrase, 'the village on the river,' the primary meaning of the word 'river' is rejected and the bank which is related to it, is implied. *Ajahal-lakṣaṇā* cognizes another sense even while including the expressed sense. The entire original meaning is preserved in total. 'The red runs' means the 'red horse runs'. The entire original meaning of 'red' is retained and the implied meaning 'horse' is added to it. *Jahad-ajahal-lakṣaṇā* preserves a part of the original meaning and rejects the rest. In the phrase, 'this is that Devadatta', 'this' and 'that' as they relate to Devadatta (the substrate) are accepted and as they relate to time and place, they are relinquised. (Vide each term listed separately.)

3. There are three essential conditions necessary in a *lakṣaṇā*: in the context, the primary meaning must be inapplicable; there must exist some relation between the primary and the actual referent of the word; and either popular usage must sanction the implied sense or else there must be a definite motive justifying the transfer of meaning.

4. Besides the primary and the secondary meaning of a word, some Grammarians also accept a suggested meaning (*vyaṅgyārtha*).

लक्षणावृत्ति - *Lakṣaṇā-vṛtti* - implied meaning

Vide *lakṣaṇā* and *lakṣyārtha*.

लक्ष्मीः - *Lakṣmīḥ* - the consort of Lord *Viṣṇu*

1. According to Dvaita, one of the twenty substances (*dravya*). While all substances are dependent upon the independent Lord, *Lakṣmī* is the foremost of the dependents. She is the personification of the Lord's creative energy. She is eternally free from *saṁsāra* and is untainted by sorrow.

2. According to Viśiṣṭādvaita, she is the creative energy of the Lord and the divine mother of the universe. She intercedes with God on behalf of a weak and erring humanity.

3. Vide *Śrīḥ*.

लक्ष्य - *Lakṣya* - secondary

लक्ष्यलक्षणसम्बन्धज्ञान - *Lakṣya-lakṣaṇa-sambandha-jñāna* - indirect indication

Knowledge of the relation between the primary meaning and the secondary meaning.

लक्ष्यार्थ - *Lakṣyārtha* - secondary meaning of a word

1. It is necessarily related to the primary meaning of a word.

2. Vide *lakṣaṇā.*

लता - *Latā* - creeper; vine

Vide *sthāvara.*

लौकिक - *Laukika* - secular; worldly; normal

लौकिकवाक्य - *Laukika-vākya* - everyday language

Sentences about empirical discourse.

लौकिकसाक्षात्कार - *Laukika-sākṣātkāra* - normal immediate apprehension

लौकिकविषयता - *Laukika-viṣayatā* - normal objectness

लय - *Laya* - dissolution

It is release or liberation proper according to Dvaita.

लेश्या- *Leśyā* - colouration

It is produced by *karma* particles which make the character of the individual self according to Jainism.

लीला - *Līlā* - play; sport

1. The cosmic play. The idea is that creation is a play of the divine, existing for no other reason than for the mere joy of it.

2. According to some of the Vedānta schools, it is the motive of creation. Some Nyāya-Vaiśeṣikas and Tantrics also hold this view.

लीलाविभूति - *Līlā-vibhūti* - the cosmic sport of *Īśvara*

1. For God, the creation of the universe is mere play. Thus the act of creation is a drama undertaken by the Lord at his own sweet will. It implies a certain joy, freedom, and disinterestedness as well as implying the absolute independence of God.

2. Vide *nityavibhūti.*

लिङ्ग - *Liṅga* - mark; indication

1. The outward symbol of the formless Reality. The merging of the form with the formless is materially sombolized thus. It is a 'mark' of Lord *Siva.* Vide *liṅga-sthala.*

2. According to Vīra Śaivism, its followers (*Lingāyats*) wear a *liṅga* on their person. It represents Lord *Śiva* and is the object of worship or adoration.

3. Vide *aṅgatva-bodhaka-pramāṇa*

लिङ्गाचार - *Liṅgācāra* - one of the five ethical codes of conduct per Vīra Śaivism

Vide *pañcācāra.*

लिङ्गाङ्गसामरस्य - *Liṅgāṅgasāmarasya* - identity in essence between the Lord (*liṅga*) and the individual self (*aṅga*)

The final stage of liberation according to Vīra Śaivism. In this stage there is unity (*aikya*) between the individual self and *Para Śiva,* wherein the individual enjoys unexcellable bliss.

लिङ्गपरामर्श - *Liṅga-parāmarśa* - subsumptive reflection

Parāmarśa is the ratiocinative process which makes known the fact that the mark (*liṅga*), which is universally concomitant with the inferred character, is present in the subject. There is a correlation of a particular case with the universal which pervades it. The presence of fire on the hill is inferred when the particular (smoke) is observed on the hill and subsumed under the generalization involving the universal pervasion of smoke by fire.

लिङ्गशरीर - *Liṅga-śarīra* - subtle body

1. According to Sāṅkhya-Yoga, what transmigrates is the subtle body consisting of the eleven organs of sense together with the intellect, egoity, and the five subtle essence of the elements.

2. Vide *sūkṣma-śarīra.*

लिङ्गस्थल - *Liṅga-sthala* - the worshipped form of the formless *Śiva*

1. According to Vīra Śaivism, it is *Śiva* or *Rudra,* and is the object of worship/adoration. It manifests itself in six forms divided into three types: a manifestation of *Śiva's* Being (*sat*) which is called *bhāva-liṅga.* This is the infinite divine and is of two types: *mahā-liṅga* and *prasāda-liṅga.* A manifestation of *Śiva's* consciousness (*cit*) is called *prāṇa-liṅga.* This is the universal divine and is of two types: *cara-liṅga* and *śiva-liṅga.* And lastly there is a manifestation of *Śiva's* bliss (*ānanda*) which is called *iṣṭa-liṅga.* This is the individual divine and is of two types: *guru-liṅga* and *acārā-liṅgā. Bhāva-liṅga* is located in the causal body and is perceived by faith. *Prāṇa-liṅga* is located in the subtle body and is perceived by the mind. *Iṣṭa-linga* is located in the physical body and is perceived by the eye. There

is a similar sixfold manifestation of *aṅga-sthala* which proceeds along similar lines. It is this correspondence which shows the essential identity between the individual soul and God and assists the individual soul in realizing this identity.

2. Vide chart no. 14 and *aṅga-sthala.*

लिङ्गायत - *Liṅgāyata* - a general term used to denote the community which follows the principles of Vīra Śaivism

लोभ - *Lobha* - greed; covetousness

1. According to Buddhism, one of the *kleśas.*

2. According to Jainism, one of the four *kaṣāyas.*

लोक - *Loka* - world; universe; plane

1. There are seven planes according to Indian lore: *bhū-*, *bhuvar-*, *svar-*, *mahar-*, *jano-*, *tapo-*, and *satya-loka.* These planes represent the heavens or the places of vastness, light, and becoming. They are said to be located in the human body respectively as: in the feet, genitals, navel, heart, throat, between the eyebrows, and on the crest of the head. Vide *cakra.*

2. According to Jainism, the universe has three parts: where the gods reside (*ūrdhva-loka*), earth (*madhya-loka*), and hell (*adho-loka*). It is that place in which happiness and misery are experienced as results of virtue and vice. The perfected individual goes beyond the *ūrdhva-loka*, to the top of *lokākāśa* and remains motionless there.

3. Another list of planes includes: *Brahma-loka*, the abode of *Brahmā*; *Tapoloka*, the abode of

Virāj; *Janaloka*, the abode of certain of *Brahmā's* sons; *Mahar-loka*, the abode of certain Prajāpatis; *Svar-loka*, the paradise of *Viṣṇu*, *Siva*, *Indra*, and *Kṛṣṇa*; *Bhuvar-loka*, the atmospheric sphere, and abode of the *pitṛs*; and *Bhū-loka*, the earth.

4. Vide *tala*.

लोकसङ्ग्रहव्यापार - *Loka-saṅgraha-vyāpāra* - action in the interest of world-welfare

लोकायत - *Lokāyata* - 'restricted to the world of common experience'

A name for the Cārvāka school.

M

मद् - *Mada* - pride; conceit

मधुर - *Madhura* - sweet

One of the emotions (*bhāva*) representing the relationship of love towards God by the devotee.

मध्य - *Madhya* - middle

According to Jainism, it is the earth region. Vide *loka*.

माध्यमक - *Mādhyamaka* - middle doctrine

मध्यमपरिमाण - *Madhyama-parimāṇa* - the size of the individual (soul) in Jainism; middling size

According to Jainism, the individual occupies the whole of the body in which it dwells, shrinking or growing accordingly as the size of the body alters. Thus, unlike other systems which hold the individual to be either atomic or all-pervasive, Jainism holds the individual to be of middling size.

मध्यमाप्रतिपद् - *Madhyamā-pratipad* - the middle path

1. Tho eightfold path which serves as the central foundation of Buddhist ethics. It may be cryptically expressed as: faith (*śraddhā*), insight (*darśana*), and contemplation (*bhāvanā*).

2. It consists of: right views, right motivation, right speech, right action, right livelihood, right endeavour, right mindfulness, and right concentration.

3. This path avoids the extremes of self-indulgence and self-mortification. The eight disciplines constituting the path are not successive steps for they are to be cultivated together. When followed, this path leads to *nirvāṇa*, here and now.

4. Vide *ārya-aṣṭāṅga-mārga*.

माध्यमिक - *Mādhyamika* - a school of Mahāyāna Buddhism which holds that all is void (*Śūnya*)

1. This school owes its foundation to Nāgārjuna. Its name is derived from the Middle Way which the Buddha taught. Nāgārjuṇa rejected the alternative standpoints of 'is' and their conjunction and disjunction. It is also known as '*Śūnya-vāda*' because voidness is the ultimate reality.

2. This school excludes all conceivable predicates to reality, whether they be of existence, of non-existence, of neither existence nor non-existence, or of both existence and non-existence. Starting from the Buddha's silence over metaphysical questions, Nāgārjuna demonstrated that every possible speculative standpoint is guilty of self-contradiction.

3. The school holds that all is void, without essence. Since all phenomena are embedded in the one absolute emptiness, which itself is without essence, it follows that the world of phenomena and the absolute emptiness are identical. And

since nothing can be said about this emptiness without self-contradiction, the realization of this fact constitutes liberation.

मध्यस्थ - *Madhyastha* - one who is impartial

महाबाह्याकाश - *Mahā-bāhyākāśa* - unlimited external ether

महाभूत - *Mahā-bhūta* - the five great elements

1. They are: ether (*ākāśa*), which emerges from sound (*śabda*), air (*vāyu*) which emerges from touch (*sparśa*), fire (*tejas*) which emerges from colour (*rūpa*), water (*ap*) which emerges from taste (*rasa*), and earth (*pṛthivī*) which emerges from smell (*gandha*). These five gross elements emerge from the subtle essences of the elements (*tanmātras*).

2. Vide chart no. 12.

महादेव - *Mahādeva* - great God

A name for Lord *Śiva*.

महः - *Mahaḥ* - heaven; the world of vastness

Vide *loka*.

महाकाल - *Mahākāla* - undivided time

महाकालिकविशेषणता - *Mahākālika-viśeṣaṇatā* - (relation of) temporal attributiveness

महालिङ्ग - *Mahā-liṅga* - a worshipped form of the formless *Śiva*

Vide *liṅga-sthala*.

महान् - *Mahān* - great

महाप्रलय - *Mahā-pralaya* - final cosmic dissolution

The end of a world-age or *manvantara.* The end of a cosmic age or *kalpa.* It is usually used to designate the dissolution of a cosmic age.

महासामान्य - *Mahā-sāmānya* - grand generality; the *summum genus*

महासङ्घिक - *Mahā-saṅghika* - the great community

At the Second Council, the Buddhist community split into two groups: the Theravādins and the Mahā-saṅghikas. The later were more liberal and wanted a more esoteric interpretation of the doctrine. Eventually they led to the formation of the Mahāyāna school.

महत् - *Mahat* - the Great; intellect

The first evolute of *prakṛti.* It is the cosmic aspect of the intellect; and along with the intellect, ego and mind, it is the cause of the entire creation. It is also called *buddhi* which is the psychological aspect of the intellect in individuals. It is both eternal and non-eternal. Its special function is determination. From it evolves egoity (*ahaṅkāra*). Vide chart no. 12.

महातल - *Mahātala* - hell; great plane

1. The nether pole of *bhuvar-loka.* It is a region of darkness.

2. Vide *tala* and *loka*.

माहात्म्यज्ञान - *Māhātmya-jñāna* - knowledge of God's greatness

According to Dvaita, it is one of the steps leading to liberation. Here the individual turns towards God and begins to study scriptures.

महत्त्व - *Mahattva* - largeness; medium dimension

महावाक्य - *Mahāvākya* - great saying

1. They are the great sayings of the *Upaniṣads*. Traditionally they are four in number: '*prajñānam brahma*' which occurs in the *Aitareya Upaniṣad* of the *Ṛg Veda*; '*ayam ātmā brahma*' which occurs in the *Māṇḍūkya Upaniṣad* of the *Atharva Veda*; '*tat tvam asi*' which occurs in the *Chāndogya Upaniṣad* of the *Sāma Veda*; and '*aham brahmāsmi*' which occurs in the *Bṛhadāraṇyaka Upaniṣad* of the *Yajur Veda*. Vide each listed separately.

2. Advaita says that the *mahāvākyas* posit the essential identity between the individual and the Absolute. Some Advaitins say that this knowledge by itself can cause direct understanding while others hold that it is only by meditating on the meaning of the *mahāvākya* that causes the cognition (and not the mere hearing).

3. Viśiṣṭādvaita also says that the *mahāvākyas*' import is to affirm the identity of the individual with *Brahman*. However, unlike Advaita, the unity means that individual souls are eternal with God and not external to God. The souls and the world are real and distinct, but they are included as parts within the one Absolute. Distinction is not denied, but at the same time, the organic unity of the whole is affirmed.

महाव्रत - *Mahā-vrata* - great vow

1. According to Jainism, there are five vows which are meant for asceticsm. They pave the way for the liberation of the individual from the bondage of *karma.* They include: non-killing (*ahiṁsā*), truthfulness (*satya*), non-stealing (*asteya*), celibacy (*brahmacarya*), and non-possession (*aparigraha*).

2. Compare with *yama.*

महायान - *Mahāyāna* - great vehicle

The school of Buddhism which stresses universal enlightenment. Its two main branches are the Mādhyamika and the Yogācāra. They are both idealistic schools. Unlike the Hināyāna which is atheistic and conceived of Buddha as a human being, the Mahāyāna gradually came to deify him and even developed ways to worship him as a means to liberation.

महेश्वर - *Maheśvara* - great God

1. A name for Lord *Śiva.*

2. A stage of consciousness in Vīra Śaivism.

Vide *sthala.*

महिमा - *Mahimā* - extensive magnitude; miracle

1. One of the eight super-normal powers.

2. Vide *siddhi.*

मैत्री - *Maitrī* - friendliness; love

One of the inherent principles cultivated and protected by all Buddhas and Bodhisattvas.

मल - *Mala* - taint; the impurity of ignorance

1. It is of three kinds according Śaiva Siddhānta: *āṇava*, *māyika*, and *karma*. They bind the individual soul and limit its inherent qualities. They are the cause of the individual's transmigration from birth to death and death to birth. *Pāśa* means a rope and these three are said to be its three strands. *Āṇava* is the *mūla-mala* and the main constraint on the individual. *Karma* follows the individual through births and death. *Māyā* is the material source for the body, instruments, world and objects of enjoyment. *Āṇava* is *pratibandha*. *Karma* is *anubandha*. *Māyā* is *sambandha*.

2. Śivādvaita also speaks of the three impurities that envelop the individual soul.

3. Kashmir Śaivism says that the individual soul is covered with three impurities: *āṇava*, *karma*, and *māyika-malas*. *Āṇava* is the innate impurity of ignorance and the root cause of bondage. It is beginningless but can be destroyed. *Karma-mala* is the result of *āṇava*. *Māyika-mala* is caused by *karma-mala* and is the impurity of transmigratory existence.

4. Vide *pāśa*.

मलपरिपाक - *Mala-paripāka* - the individual's attainment of the stage wherein the three impurities are rendered powerless and ripe for removal

मान - *Māna* - vanity; pride

1. One of the four *kaṣāyas* according to Jainism.

2. One of the *kleśas* according to Buddhism.

मनः - *Manaḥ* - mind; one of the aspects of the internal organ

1. Mind emerges from the *sattva* aspect of egoity (*ahaṅkāra*).

2. Mind stimulates the other senses to attend to their respective objects. Thus it is an organ of cognition and of action. It is the door-keeper to the senses. Its specific function is to explicate.

3. According Nyāya-Vaiśeṣika, it is atomic and eternal. It is an instrument of knowing and is inert as any other sense. Its co-operation is necessary for all knowledge. It exercises a double-function: it helps the self to acquire knowledge and it narrows its field to a single object or group of objects. Association with the mind is the basic cause of bondage.

4. According to Jainism, it is not a sense organ, but the organ of cognition of all objects of all the senses. It is of two types: psychical mind (*bhāva*) which performs the mental functions proper, and material mind (*dravya*) which is subtle matter compounded into the physical mind.

5. According to Dvaita and Sāṅkhya, the mind is considered as one of the sense organs (*indriya*).

6. According to Mīmāṁsā, different cognitions are explained by a type of atom called *manas*. The mind alone brings about cognitions, aversions, efforts, etc., but by itself it is devoid of any qualities such as colour, smell, etc. Thus it needs the aid of the other organs to cognize these qualities.

मनःपर्याय - *Manaḥ-paryāya* - telepathy; thought-reading

1. According to Jainism, it is one of the five types of knowledge. Vide chart no. 11. It is

possible for saints only, as it is a refined and subtle type of knowledge. It stands for the individual's capacity to directly apprehend the modes of other minds. It is a type of *vikala* knowledge.

2. It is of two kinds: *ṛju-mati* and *vipula-mati*, which vary only in degree.

मनःशुद्धि - *Manaḥ - śuddhi* - purity of the mind

According to Jainism, when the *kaṣāyas* are removed, there is purity of the mind.

मान - *Māna* - same as *pramāṇa*

Vide *pramāṇa*.

मनन - *Manana* - reflection; consideration

1. According to Advaita, it removes the doubt of an aspirant regarding the nature of the object (*prameya*) to be contemplated, i.e., Brahman. Reflection is to be employed so as to get an intellectual conviction of the truth. It is the constant thinking of Brahman.

2. According to Advaita, the path of knowledge consists of three steps: study (*śravaṇa*), reflection (*manana*), and contemplation (*nididhyāsana*). Reflection is discovering how and why the teachings are true. The truth has been discovered by study, but now any doubts (*asambhāvanā*) are to be removed so that what has been received on trust can be made one's own. This reveals a unique feature of Advaita which posits and recognizes the value of analytical reflection.

3. Vide *mukhya-antaraṅga-sādhana*.

मानसप्रत्यक्ष - *Mānasa-pratyakṣa* - mental perception

मानसिक - *Mānasika* - mental action

मानित्व - *Mānitva* - pride

मनोगुप्ति - *Mano-gupti* - equanimity of the mind

1. According to Jainism, it is one of the external rules of conduct. Vide *cāritra*. It enables one to remove all false thoughts, to remain satisfied within one-self, and to hold all people to be the same.

2. Vide *gupti*.

मनोजन्य - *Mano-janya* - according to Jainism, the mind can function without the help of the sense organs

Vide *kevala-jñāna*.

मनोमयकोश - *Manomaya-kośa* - the sheath of the mind; the mental sheath

1. It is part of the subtle sheath (*sūkṣma-śarīra*), with its patterns of desires, motives, etc., which form the complex called mind. It is the third sheath of the body composed of thought.

2. Vide *kośa*.

मनोवर्गण - *Mano-vargaṇa* - peculiar material molecules According to Jainism, the material mind is made of subtle particles of matter.

मनोविज्ञान - *Manovijñāna* - ego consciousness; mental perception

1. A type of perception which refers to sensual knowledge in the form of parallel concepts formed after the acquisition of knowledge through the

senses. This knowledge is a mental modification born of both the object as well as the consciousness.

2. According to Buddhism, the *manovijñāna* possesses actual discrimination as present, past and future as well as reminiscent discrimination referring only to the past. It is the ignorant mind which clings to the conception of I and not-I.

मनोयोग - *Mano-yoga* - sensation of *karma* particles through the mind

1. According to Jainism, it is a type of *āsrava*. Before the *karma* particles enter the individual soul, the latter feels a sort of sensation which is due to either the mind, the body or speech.

2. Vide *kāya-yoga*, *vāg-yoga* and *āsrava*.

मन्तव्य - *Mantavya* - what should be reflected upon

मन्त्र - *Mantra* - a sacred word or phrase of spiritual significance and power; hymns; ' that which saves the one who reflects '

1. Along with the *Brāhmaṇas*, as hymns they constitute the ritual section of the *Veda* (*karma-kāṇḍa*).

2. They are classified according to their metres: *gāyatrī* has twenty-four syllables with nine sub-divisions; *uṣṇik* has twenty-eight syllables with eight sub-divisions; *anuṣṭup* has thirty-two syllables with seven sub-divisions; *prakṛti* has forty syllables with eight sub-divisions; *bṛhatī* has thirty-six syllables with nine sub-divisions; *triṣṭup* has forty-four syllables with ten sub-divisions; *jagatī* has

forty-eight syllables with three sub-divisions; *atijagatī* has fifty-two syllables; *śakvarī* has fifty-six syllables; *atiśakvarī* has sixty syllables; *aṣṭi* has sixty-four syllables; *dhṛti* has seventy-two syllables; and *atidhṛti* has seventy-six syllables.

3. The *mantras* are preserved chiefly in the *Ṛk-* and *Atharva-saṁhitās.*

4. According to Śākta philosophy, a *mantra* is so called because it saves one who meditates on its significance. Each *mantra* has a deity (*devatā*). For instance, the *mantra* of *Kālī* is *krīṁ*; of *Māyā* is *hrīṁ*, etc.

5. *Mantras* are of two classes: *kaṇṭhika* or those given expression to by the voice, and *ajapa* or those non-uttered *mantras* which are not spoken but repeated internally.

मन्त्रद्रष्टारः - *Mantra-draṣṭāraḥ* - seers of the Vedic hymns intuiting the Vedic truths

मन्त्रमहेश्वर - *Mantra-maheśvara* - one of the seven stages of the individual soul in Kashmir Śaivism

Vide *sapta-pramātṛ.*

मनुष्य - *Manuṣya* - human being

Vide *jaṅgama.*

मन्वन्तर - *Manvantara* - epoch

1. One of the five topics which a *Purāṇa* should deal with. An age of Manu. Within a *kalpa* or cosmic age there are fourteen *manvantaras.*

2. Vide *purāṇa.*

मरण - *Maraṇa* - death

Vide *pratītyasamutpāda.*

मार्ग - *Mārga* - way; path

According to Śaiva Siddhānta, there are four paths: the way of the servant (*dāsa-mārga* with *caryā* as the means and *sālokya* as the goal); the way of the son (*putra-mārga* with *kriyā* as the as the means and *sāmīpya* as the goal); the way of the friend (*sakhā-mārga* with *yoga* as the means and *sārūpya* as the goal); and beyond a path (*san-mārga* with *jñāna* as the means and *sāyujya* as the goal). These four paths are supposed to attune the body, the sense organs, and the mind to worship and union.

मास - *Māsa* - month

Vide *kāla*.

मति - *Mati* - perceptual knowledge; mind; thought

According to Jainism, it is a type of direct, practical knowledge. It is perceptual, being caused by the senses and/or the mind. It occurs in the following order: cognition of sense data (*avagraha*), speculation (*īha*), perceptual judgment (*avāya*), and then retention (*dhāraṇā*).

मात्रा - *Mātrā* - mode; measure; prosodial instant

1. The *Oṁkāra* is composed of the three modes, *A U M* and a fourth, *a-mātrā*, silence (*turīya*). Vide *avasthā-traya-vicāra*.

2. It is the length of time required for pronouncing a short vowel.

मात्सर्य - *Mātsarya* - envy; jealousy

मौन - *Mauna* - silence

मौनी - *Maunī* - one who silently meditates on the Self

माया - *Māyā* - the principle of appearance; illusion; marvellous power of creation

1. The principle which shows the attributeless Absolute as having attributes.

2. According to Advaita, it is the indeterminable principle which brings about the illusory manifestation of the universe. It is the principle of illusion. It is the key concept of Advaita (vide *avidyā*). It is not ultimately real, nor can it function without *Brahman/Ātman* as its locus. It is the device by which the Advaitin explains how the one reality appears as many. It is the power which brings about error and has significance only at the empirical or relative level. It has six facets: it is beginningless (*anādi*); it is terminated by right knowledge (*jñāna-nivartya*); it veils and projects (*āvaraṇa* and *vikṣepa*); it is indefinable (*anirvacanīya*); it is of the nature of a positive existence (*bhāvarūpa*); and it is located either in the *jīva* or in *Brahman.* Śaṅkara uses the term *māyā* as interchangeble with *avidyā.*

3. According to Dvaita, it is God's power.

4. According to Viśiṣṭādvaita; it is the mysterious power of God. Vide *sapta-vidha-anupapatti* for Rāmānuja's major objections to the Advaita concept of *avidyā/māyā.*

5. According to Śaiva Śiddhānta, it is the material cause of the world. It is non-conscious. It

is twofold as: pure (*śuddha*) and impure (*aśuddha*). It is both a bond (*pāśa*) of the individual soul and that which provides the individual souls with the means, locations, and objects of enjoyment. It requires the guidance of *Śiva* to function, though *Siva* does not directly operate on *māyā*, but only through his *cit-śakti*.

6. According to Vīra Śaivism, it is the name of *śakti* or *mūla-prakṛti*. It evolves into the phenomenal universe.

7. According to Kashmir Śaivism, it is the power of obscuration. Its purpose is to limit the experience as regards both the experiencer and what is experienced. It is a restrictor (*mala*) which is the impurity of transmigratory existence. It is real and a creation of the Lord. It is divided into *śuddha*- and *aśuddha-māyā*.

मायाध्वन् - *Māyādhvan* - impure way

1. The impure creation (the latter thirty-one categories of Kashmir Śaivism).

2. Vide chart no. 9.

मायिकमल - *Māyika-mala* - the impurity of transmigratory existence

Vide *mala*.

मेघ - *Megha* - cloud

1. The feeling that one need not hurry towards salvation as it will come in its own time.

2. Vide *tuṣṭi*.

मीमांसा - *Mīmāṁsā* - literally it means 'enquiry'; investigation

1. It is short for Pūrva-mīmāṁsā, one of the *ṣaḍ-darśanas*.

2. It is one of the six orthodox *āstika* schools and it primarily investigates the Vedic rites and their uses. Its main objective is to establish the authority of the *Veda*.

3. Jaimini is the founder and the author of the *Mīmāṁsā-sūtra* which is the foundational work of the school, and the longest of the *sūtra* works.

4. The aphorisms commented on by Śabarasvāmin gave rise to two main schools of interpretation: Prabhākara's and Kumārila Bhaṭṭa's.

मीमांसक - *Mīmāṁsaka* - a follower of the Pūrva-mīmāṁsā school of Jaimini

मिश्र - *Miśra (sṛṣṭi)* - pure and impure (creation)

Vide *śuddhāśuddha-māyā*.

मिश्रसत्त्व - *Miśra-sattva* - matter in which all three *guṇas* exist

मिथ्या - *Mithyā* - not real; neither real nor unreal; illusory

According to Advaita, it has a special status as it is not the real (*sat*), for it is sublatable; and it is not the unreal (*asat*), because it is perceived (unlike a barren woman's son or a square circle).

मिथ्यादृष्टि - *Mithyā-dṛṣṭi* - wrong views

मिथ्याज्ञान - *Mithyā-jñāna* - false knowledge; false cognition

मिथ्याज्ञानवासना - *Mithyā-jñāna-vāsanā* - impression of false knowledge

मिथ्यात्व - *Mithyātva* - delusion

मिथ्योपाधि - *Mithyopādhi* - false limitation

म्लेच्छ - *Mleccha* - foreigner; an alien

मोह - *Moha* - infatuation; delusion

1. The power to delude. A power of *māyā*.
2. One of the *kleśas* according to Buddhism.
3. One of the five types of false knowledge (*viparyyaya*) according to Sāṅkhya.

मोहमूल - *Moha-mūla* - rooted in delusion

मोहनीय - *Mohanīya* - delusion-producing *karma*

According to Jainism, they are a type of obscuring *karma* (*ghāti*). They are *karmas* which obscure the right attitude of the individual towards right faith and right conduct. The individual is so infatuated that it does not know right from wrong. Vide *karma* and *ghāti*.

मोक्ष - *Mokṣa* - liberation; spiritual freedom; release; the final goal of human life

1. There are two views in the *Upaniṣads* towards liberation. Some say it is attainable in this very life and others say that it is attainable only atfer death. Vide *jīvan-mukta*.

2. Mīmāṁsā says that it is achieved through *karma* and Vedic rites alone. It is release from

action, both in the sense of action and in the sense of the fruits of one's actions.

3. Advaita says that knowledge (*jñāna*) is the ultimate means to release. Truly speaking release is the eternal nature of the Self (*ātman*) and manifests itself once ignorance is removed. It is not a new acquisition, but the realization of what eternally is.

4. Viśiṣṭādvaita says that devotion (*bhakti*) is the ultimate means to release. *Karma-yoga* and *jñāna-yoga* are aids to devotion (*bhakti-yoga*). Liberation is living in *Vaikuṇṭha* with a non-physical body enjoying omniscience and bliss and dwelling in the presence of God. Viśiṣṭādvaita also recognizes total surrender (*prapatti*) as a means of release.

5. Dvaita says that God's grace (*prasāda*) is the ultimate means to release. Leading to ultimate release, the individual soul practises knowledge, dispassion, action, devotion, and a loving meditation of God, regarding oneself as His reflection. In the state of release, the individual soul remains separate from God though similar and dependent. Its personality remains in one of the four levels of graded release which Dvaita posits. Vide *ānanda-tāratamya*.

6. Jainism says that release is the highest state of isolation in which the individual is freed from all fetters of *karma* particles. The means to release are right faith, right knowledge, and right conduct (vide *tri-ratna*). Aids to these include the *mahā-vratas*.

7. Buddhism says that release (*nirvāṇa*) is the eradication of all craving and an overcoming of

the wheel of birth and death. The means to it is the eightfold path.

8. Nyāya-Vaiśeṣika says that release (*apavarga*) is a separation from all qualities. There is no pleasure, happiness, or pain, or any experience whatsoever in release. It is achieved by cultivating ethical virtues and obtaining an insight into the nature of the categories.

9. Sāṅkhya says that release (*kaivalya*) is aloofness from all matter. There is neither pleasure nor pain, though there is an undisturbable peace. It is achieved once the individual is able to discriminate between spirit (*puruṣa*) and matter (*prakṛti*).

10. Yoga says that the cultivation of the eight-limbed yogic path is the way to *kaivalya* or a state of superconscious *samādhi* in which the individual is left totally alone.

11. Śaiva Siddhānta says that the path to release consists in *caryā*, *kriyā*, *yoga*, and *jñāna*. In release, the soul retains its individuality. It becomes similar to God and thus release is a unity-in-duality. The soul enjoys God's nature, though it is not identical with God.

12. Vīra Śaivism says that release is identity in essence between *Śiva* and the individual soul (*liṅgāṅga-sāmarasya*). The individual soul is a part of *Śiva* though it is also different. Release is a unity (*aikya*) of the individual soul with *Śiva*, wherein the individual soul enjoys unexcellable bliss. The path to release is devotion as aided by the eight aids (*aṣṭāvaraṇa*).

13. Śivādvaita says that release is freedom from bondage and an attainment of bliss. Release is attained through realization of one's own nature. Contemplation of Lord *Śiva* is the means to release.

14. Kashmir Śaivism says that release is the recognition of the individual's identity with the ultimate Reality. It is a return to one's original state of perfection and purity. It is gained by the four steps of: *āṇavopāya*, *śāktopāya*, *śāmbhavopāya*, and *anupāya*, culminating in the grace of the Divine Will.

15. Vide *puruṣārtha*.

मोक्षपर - *Mokṣa-para* - a seeker of liberation

According to Viśiṣṭādvaita, they are of two kinds: lovers of God (*bhakta*) and those who have completely resigned themselves to God (*prapanna*).

मूढ - *Mūḍha* - blinded; delusive

When there is an excess of *tamas* in the mind, one becomes a victim to sleep.

मुदित - *Mudita* - joy; happiness

मुहूर्त - *Muhūrta* - a unit of time

Thirty *kalās*. Vide *kāla*.

मुख्य - *Mukhya* - primary; important; main; principal

मुख्यान्तरङ्गसाधन - *Mukhya-antaraṅga-sādhana* - the principal proximate aid to liberation

1. According to Advaita, the main proximate aid to liberation consists in hearing (*śravaṇa*), reflection (*manana*), and meditation (*nididhyāsana*). After an

aspirant becomes qualified (vide *sādhana-catuṣṭaya*), he should hear the Upaniṣadic texts from a qualified teacher, reflect on their truth, and contemplate upon their purport.

2. Vide *śravaṇa*, *manana* and *nididhyāsana*.

मुख्यार्थ - *Mukhyārtha* - primary meaning; *abhidhā* or *vācyārtha*

मुख्यवृत्ति - *Mukhya-vṛtti* - primary meaning of words

मुक्त - *Mukta* - liberated; freed

One who is liberated from bondage.

मुक्तजीव - *Mukta-jīva* - liberated individual soul

One of the three types of individual soul according to Viśiṣṭādvaita. Vide *jīva*.

मुक्ति - *Mukti* - liberation

Vide *mokṣa*.

मुक्तियोग्य - *Mukti-yogya* - individuals who are eligible for release according to Viśiṣṭādvaita

These are *sattva*-dominant individual souls which include celestial beings, sages, and advanced human beings. Vide *svarūpa-traividhya*.

मूल - *Mūla* - original; primary; text

मूलमल - *Mūla-mala* - the main constraint on the individual which is called 'impurity of ignorance'; the primary impurity

The Śaiva schools speak of *āṇava* as the *mūla-mala*.

मूलप्रकृति - *Mūla-prakṛti* - the primordial matter; root-nature

The original germ out of which matter and all forms arose and evolved. The primary cause. It is not an evolute itself, but that from which all else evolves.

मूलाविद्या - *Mulāvidyā* - primordial nescience

According to Advaita, the root-cause of everything in the world.

मुमुक्षु - *Mumukṣu* - a seeker with a burning desire for liberation

According to Viśiṣṭādvaita, they are of two kinds: votaries of self-realization (*kaivalya*) and votaries of liberation (*mokṣa*). Vide *kaivalya-para* and *mokṣa-para.*

मुमुक्षुत्व - *Mumukṣutva* - A burning desire for liberation.

It is one of the four qualifications for a spiritual aspirant. Vide *sādhana-catuṣṭaya.*

मुनि - *Muni* - sage; ascetic

मुनिधर्म - *Muni-dharma* - the duties of an ascetic

According to Jainism, these duties include a strict observance of the great vows (*mahā-vrata*), complete control over one's body, mind, and speech (*gupti*), and moderation (*samiti*).

मूर्त - *Mūrta* - form; body

N

नाद् - *Nāda* - sound

According to Śākta philosophy, the first movement of *śabda* is called *nāda-tattva.* Along with *bindu,* they are the complements of the ultimate potency of creation. From these arise the *tri-bindu* or *kāma-kalā*, which is the root of all *mantras.*

नैगमनय - *Naigama-naya* - the universal-particular (or teleological) standpoint

1. According to Jainism, a *naya* is a particular view-point or opinion. In this case, the view-point considers both the universal and the specific aspects of an entity. It signifies that the particular aspect must consider the universal aspect and vice-versa. Thus a synthesis of the two aspects is enjoined. With this, is averted asserting either absolute identity or absolute distinction.

2. Another interpretation of this standpoint is that it relates to the purpose of a given action or actions. Thus one says, " I am cooking " instead of saying, " I am cutting the vegetables, heating the water, etc." All the individual acts are controlled by a single purpose, i.e., cooking food.

नैमित्तिक - *Naimittika*-occasional

नैमित्तिककर्म - *Naimittika-karma* - occasional duties to be performed on special occasions like the full moon, new moon days, etc.

Vide *karma*.

नैरात्म्य - *Nairātmya* - non-soul; no substance in anything

नैरात्म्यवाद - *Nairātmya-vāda* - the doctrine of no self according to Buddhism

The term '*nairātmya*' is negative and tells what an object is not. Thus, there is no self-sustaining substance apart from the attributes or sense-data of any object, conscious or non-conscious.

नैष्कर्म्य - *Naiṣkarmya* - freedom from *karma* (action) and its influence

According to Advaita, disinterested and dedicated action which serves to purify the mind and thus serve as an auxiliary to liberation.

नैष्ठिकब्रह्मचारिन् - *Naiṣṭhika-brahmacārin* - one vowed to celibacy

नाम - *Nāma* - name

1. According to Jainism, it is one of the eight main types of *karma*. In itself it is of one hundred and three types. They all have to do with personality-making. They are sub-divided into four groups: collective types (*piṇḍa-prakṛti*); individual types (*pratyeya-prakṛti*); self-movable body (*trāsa-daśaka*); and immovable body (*sthāvara-daśaka*).

2. According to Buddhism, one of the names for the four elements (because they are objects of name).

नामधेय - *Nāmadheya* - a portion of the *Veda* whose words have the appearance of a name of an action and yet are capable of another interpretation

नामरूप – *Namārūpa* - name and form

1. According to Buddhism, one link of the causal chain of dependent origination. It provides the support for the six fields of contact (*āyatana*) and in turn is dependent itself on consciousness (*vijñāna*). 'Name' is said to be the three groups (sensation, perception, and predisposition); and 'form' is the four elements and forms derived from the four elements.

2. In the *Upaniṣads*, the term is used in the sense of determinate forms and names as distinguished from the indeterminate indefinable reality.

3. Advaita uses the term to indicate the phenomenally existent (*vyāvahārika*) universe.

4. Vide *pratītyasamutpāda.*

नानाजीववाद - *Nānājīva-vāda* - the theory of the plurality of selves

नर - *Nara* - man

नरक - *Naraka* - hell

There are various hells: *put* - the childless hell; *avīci* - hell for those awaiting reincarnation; *saṁhāta* - for general evil-doers; *tāmisra* - where the real gloom of hell begins; *ṛjīṣa* - where torments attack; *kuḍmala* - the worst hell for those who will be reincarnated; *talātala* - the bottomless pit, the eternal hell of indescribable tortures and pain for those who have no hope of reincarnation. Vide *loka* and *tala*.

नारकि - *Nāraki* - hell-being

Vide *jaṅgama*.

नाश - *Nāśa* - annihilation

नास्तिक - *Nāstika* - atheist

1. Those systems of Indian philosophy (Jainism, Buddhism, and Cārvāka) which neither regard the *Vedas* as infallible nor try to establish their own system's validity on their authority. Sometimes it is said that there are six heterodox systems in contrast to the six orthodox systems. These six *nāstika* systems include the Cārvāka and Jainism and Buddhism is split into its four main schools, Vaibhāṣika, Sautrāntika, Yogācāra, and Mādhyamika.

2. Vide *āstika*.

नास्तिकाय - *Nāstikaya* – non-extended real

1. According to Jainism, time is the only substance which has no body.

2. Vide *astikāya* and *kāla*.

नवविधा भक्ति - *Navavidhā bhakti* - the nine forms of devotion

These are: listening to God's glory (*śravaṇa*), singing God's praise (*kīrtana*), contemplating the Lord (*smaraṇa*), worshipping the Lord's feet (*pāda-sevana*), worshipping the Lord (as in a image) (*arcana*), doing obeisance to the Lord (*vandana*), waiting on the Lord as a servant (*dāsya*), fellowship with the Lord (*sakhya*), and offering oneself totally to the Lord (*ātma-nivedana*).

नय - *Naya* - standpoint; opinion

According to Jainism, a particular opinion or view-point which does not rule out other (different) view-points is called *naya*. Each stand-point is a partial truth about an entity. It is the knowledge of a thing in a particular context or relationship. It may be divided into two kinds: *artha-naya*, and *śabda-naya*. *Artha-naya* concerned with the meaning of objects, is further sub-divided into *naigama*, *saṅgraha*, *vyavahāra*, and *ṛjusūtra*. *Śabda-naya*, concerned with the meaning of words is further sub-divided into *śabda*, *samābhiruddha*, and *evambhūta*. (Vide each term listed separately.) *Naya* has also been divided into two categories: *dravya-artha*, which considers an object from the standpoint of substance, and *paryāyārthika-naya* which considers an object from the standpoint of its modifications and conditions. The former views the manifold qualities and characteristics of an object as a unified whole, e.g., 'a book', while the latter views these aspects separately, e.g., 'paper, ink, binding, etc.'

नयाभास - *Nayābhāsa* - fallacy of view-point; false standpoint

1. According to Jainism, any one view-point which regards itself as absolutely true to the exclusion of all other view-points is fallacious. The Jainas regard any one view-point as but one of an infinite number of ways to view a thing. Any one view-point is true in a limited sense and

under limited conditions. This idea led to the Jaina doctrine of *syād-vāda.*

2. Vide *naya* and *syād-vāda.*

नायन्मार् - *Nāyaṉmār* - the sixty-three Śaivite saints (or Nāyaṉārs)

Also known as *aḍiyār,* these saints lived and demonstrated the way of devotion to *Śiva.* Foremost among them were: Tirujñāṉa-sambandhar, Tirunāvukkarasar, and Sundaramūrtti Nāyaṉār.

नयनिश्चय - *Naya-niścaya* - perfect vision or knowledge of a thing in a particular context

According to Jainism, it is of two types: *aśuddha-niścaya* or the knowledge of an object minus its attributes and *śuddha-niścaya* or the knowledge of an object in its conditional stages.

नयवाद - *Naya-vāda* - the theory of relative pluralism in Jainism

Vide *naya* and *nayābhāsa.*

नेति नेति - *Neti-neti* - 'not this, not this' (not such, not such)

1. Yājñavalkya said, "The *ātman* is not this, not this" (*Bṛhadāraṇyaka Upaniṣad,* IV, v, 15).

2. The ultimate Reality cannot be described by any positive means, according to Advaita, because conceptual thought is always limited to the finite. Thus, the most appropriate way to indicate it is to say, 'not this, not this'.

निबन्ध - *Nibandha* - bondage; composition

निदान - *Nidāna* - cause of disease

The method of the cause and effect relation.

निदर्शन - *Nidarśana* - exemplification; application

One of the members of a five-membered syllogism. Vide *udāharaṇa*.

निदर्शनाभास - *Nidarśanābhāsa* - fallacy of the example

निदिध्यासन - *Nididhyāsana* - meditation; contemplation

1. According to Advaita, it removes the contrarywise tendencies of the mind. It is one of the principal aids to liberation (vide *mukhya-antaraṅga-sādhana*).

2. It is a continuous, unbroken stream of ideas of the same kind as those of *Brahman.*

निदिध्यासितव्य - *Nididhyāsitavya* - that should be meditated upon (Brahman)

निद्रा - *Nidrā* - sleep

According to the Yoga school, sleep is the modification of the mind (*citta*) which is the substratum of the knowledge of absence of any thing. Due to a preponderance of *tamas* in its *vṛtti*, there is no modification of waking or dreaming. However, the state is still a modification, for upon waking, one has the consciousness that he had slept well.

निगमन - *Nigamana* - conclusion

1. The last member of a five-membered syllogism. It states the original thesis as having been proved; e.g. 'therefore, the hill has fire.'

2. Vide *anumāna.*

निगन्थ - *Nigantha* - vide *nirgrantha*

निघण्टु - *Nighaṇṭu* - a vocabulary

निग्रहस्थान - *Nigraha-sthāna* - refutations; vulnerable points

1. A term relating to debates and one of the sixteen categories of the Nyāya system. It means the exposure of the opponent's argument as involving self-contradiction, inconsistency, etc. by which the opponent is conclusively defeated.

2. Vide *padārtha* and chart no. 6.

निःसम्बोध - *Niḥsambodha* - indeterminate consciousness

निःश्रेयस - *Niḥśreyasa* - release; freedom from *karma* salvation; highest good

1. A Vaiśeṣika term for liberation. (Vide *mokṣa.*) It is attained through *dharma.*

2. According to Nyāya, it is the highest good which is attained through a knowledge of the sixteen categories.

नीज - *Nīja* - perception without sense organs

1. According to Jainism, it is of two types: (i) imperfect(*vikala*) *avadhi* and *manaḥparyāya jñāna*; and (ii) perfect (*sakala*) or *kevala-jñāna.*

2. Vide *pratyakṣa* per Jainism.

निकाय - *Nikāya* - collection; heap

The collection of the Buddhist *sūtras* are named thus. Vide chart no. 2.

निक्षेप - *Nikṣepa* - the study of words to see their implications

According to Jainism, its function is to analyse and understand the exact content of words in terms of meaning and usage. It has four aspects: primary (*pradhāna*), secondary (*apradhāna*), imagined (*kalpita*), and unimagined (*akalpita*). It is of four types: that which refers to proper names (*nāma-nikṣepa*), that which refers to the meaning of an object with reference to time (*dravya-nikṣepa*), that which refers to the meaning of a word (*sthāpana-nikṣepa*), and that which refers to the meaning of the nature of an object (*bhāva-nikṣepa*).

Also means *śaraṇāgati*. Vide *nyāsa*

नील - *Nīla* - blue

नीळा - *Nīḷā* – one among the three consorts of Lord Viṣṇu

निमेष - *Nimeṣa* - twinkling of an eye

A unit of time. Vide *kāla*.

निमित्त - *Nimitta* - concomitant; instrumental; efficient

निमित्तकारण - *Nimitta-kāraṇa* - the instrumental cause; the efficient cause

E.g., the loom is the instrumental cause of the cloth. Vide *kāraṇa*.

निराकार - *Nirākāra* - without form

निराकार उपयोगज्ञान - *Nirākāra-upayoga-jñāna* - apprehension

According to Jainism, it is one of the two types of understanding. Vide *upayoga*.

निरालम्बन - *Nirālambana* - without support

निरञ्जन - *Nirañjana* - without blemish

निरपेक्ष - *Nirapekṣa* - independent; free from desire

निरतिशय - *Niratiśaya* - unsurpassed

निरवधिकैश्वर्य - *Niravadhikaiśvarya* - infinite glory

निरवद्य - *Niravadya* - faultless

निरवयव - *Niravayava* - partless

निर्बीज - *Nirbīja* - attributeless

निर्देश - *Nirdeśa* - definition; discrimination

Discrimination is of three kinds: *svabhāva-nirdeśa* (natural perceptual discrimination); *prayoga-nirdeśa* (actual discrimination as present, past, and future); *anusmṛti-nirdeśa* (reminiscent discrimination referring only to the past). The senses only possess the first type, while the mind performs the latter two types of discrimination.

निर्ग्रन्थ - *Nirgrantha* - those who have been freed from fetters

1. A name for the Jainas in early Sanskrit classical literature.

2. The Pali classics of Buddhism called the Jainas '*Nirgranthas*'.

निर्गुण - *Nirguṇa* - attributeless; devoid of qualities

निर्गुणोपासना - *Nirguṇopāsanā* - meditation on the attributeless *Brahman*

निर्हेतुककटाक्ष - *Nirhetuka-kaṭākṣa* - unconditioned or operative grace

Cf. *sahetukakṛpā* (*kaṭākṣa*).

निर्जरा - *Nirjarā* - the destruction of *karma* particles

According to Jainism, there are two stages in the shedding of *karma* particles from the individual. *Bhāva-nirjarā* refers to the modifications caused in the individual as a consequence of which there is a partial disappearance of *karma* particles. This is also of two types: *avipāka* or *akāma-bhāva-nirjarā*, wherein the particles are automatically destroyed after enjoyment, and *vipāka* or *sakāma-bhāva-nirjarā*, wherein the particles are destroyed even before enjoyment is finished. *Dravya-nirjarā* refers to the actual destruction of *karma* particles residing in the individual.

निर्माणकाय - *Nirmāṇa-kāya* - vide *trikāya*

निर्माणशक्ति - *Nirmāṇa-śakti* - the power to project

A power belonging to *māyā*.

निर्णय - *Nirṇaya* - decisive knowledge; conclusion; ascertainment

1. One of the sixteen categories of the Nyāya system. It is the conclusion which one arrives at as a result of deliberation (*tarka*).

2. Vide *padārtha* and chart no. 6.

निरोध - *Nirodha* - negation; cessation

1. According to Buddhism, it is of two types: space (*ākāśa*) and *nirvāṇa*.

2. According to Sāṅkhya, immediately before liberation occurs, the mind (*citta*) is in a state of cessation (*nirodha*).

निरुद्ध - *Niruddha* - restricted

निरुक्त - *Nirukta* - definition; etymology; the work of Sage Yāska.

One of the *Vedāṅgas.* It consists of the science of etymology.

निरुपाधिक - *Nirupādhika* - unconditioned

In the theistic systems, God is called *nirupādhika-bandhu* (an unconditioned relative).

निरुपाधिप्रतिबिम्ब - *Nirupādhi-pratibimba* - reflection where there is no medium

The reflection theory of the Dvaita school.

निरुपाधिशेष - *Nirūpādhi-śeṣa* - a state of *nirvāṇa* in which there is complete extinction of all impressions

निरूपक - *Nirūpaka* - correlating; correlated

निरूपितस्वरूपधर्म - *Nirūpita-svarūpa-dharma* - qualities which abide in the Lord

According to Viśiṣṭādvaita, they are six in number: knowledge (*jñāna*), strength (*bala*), dominion (*aiśvarya*), might (*śakti*), energy (*vīrya*), and splendour (*tejas*). Cf. *svarūpa-nirūpaka-dharma.*

निरूप्यनिरूपकसम्बन्ध - *Nirūpya-nirūpaka-sambandha* - the relation between the determined and the determinent

निर्वचन - *Nirvacana* - definite predication; explanation; elucidation; etymological derivation

निर्वाण - *Nirvāṇa* - extinction; perfection; the Great Peace

1. According to Buddhism, it is the goal of life.

2. According to Theravāda Buddhism, it is non-conditional *dharma* (*asaṁskṛta-dharma*).

3. According the Hīnayāna, it is the eradication of the craving that causes rebirth. It is an overcoming of *saṁsāra* (the wheel of birth and death), and a final exit from the world of becoming.

4. According to the Mahāyāna, it is becoming conscious of one's own suchness. In this school, *nirvāṇa* equals *saṁsāra*. Its four characteristics are: bliss, permanence, freedom, and purity.

5. In the Hīnayāna interpretation, *nirvāṇa* must be created, while according to the Mahāyāna, it is one's very essence.

6. The Mahāyāna divides *nirvāṇa* into active (*apratiṣṭhita*) and static (*pratiṣṭhita*).

7. It is a state of peace and the Buddha said that it is unknown, unique, uncreated, and uncultured.

8. Its two divisions; *nirvāṇa* in which some impressions remain due to rebirth (*sopādhi-śeṣa*) and *nirvāṇa* in which there is complete extinction of all impressions (*nirupādhi-śeṣa*).

9. The Yoga describes it as '*citta-vṛtti-nirodha*' or the cessation of all mental activities.

10. It has been called: unborn, absolute freedom, unconditional, *tathātā* or suchness, unchangeable, indescribable, *Dharma-kāya*, non-attatchment to either being or non-being.

निर्वेद - *Nirveda* - regret and repentance

There is a section, "*Nirvedakārikāḥ*" in the beginning of the *Āhnikakārikāḥ* of Vaṅgi Vaṁśeśvara (Viśiṣṭādvaita).

निर्विचार - *Nirvicāra* - without enquiry

1. When the mind concentrates on the subtle essence of the elements (*tanmātra*) and is one with them without any notion of their qualities, it is called this. It is a state of concentration according to the Yoga school.

2. Vide *vicāra*.

निर्विकल्प - *Nirvikalpa* – indeterminate

1. A type of unifying concentration (*samādhi*).

2. A type of perception (*pratyakṣa*).

निर्विकल्पकप्रत्यक्ष - *Nirvikalpaka-pratyakṣa* - indeterminate perception; or cognition of the object for the first time

1. According to Nyāya-Vaiśeṣika, it is perception of an object isolated and altogether uncharacterized. It is a preliminary cognition which is only logically deduced from a fundamental postulate of the system. All complex things are explained as the putting together of simples constituting them. However, such simples, cannot be directly cognized.

2. According to Mīmāṁsā, the knowledge which one first gains in perception is quite vague and indefinite. However, unlike the Nyāya-Vaiśeṣika conception, this knowledge is not a theoretical supposition. It is part of the perception process

itself and serves a purpose and can even be acted upon.

3. According to Viśiṣṭādvaita, perceptual experience is called *nirvikalpaka* when an object is experienced for the first time. According to it, all experience involves judgement and it is merely a case of primary presentation or subsequent apprehension.

4. According to the Buddhists, indeterminate perception is the only kind of perception. An object, when it is perceived, is unique and any name, universal, etc., which is added to this perception is added by the mind.

5. According to the Advaitins, indeterminate perception is knowledge which does not apprehend any relatedness of the substantive and its qualifying attribute. Thus it is not necessarily the first or initial perception, but any perception which is indeterminate.

निर्विकार - *Nirvikāra* - without transformation or change

निर्विशेष - *Nirviśeṣa* - without difference; attributeless; undifferentiated

निर्वितर्क - *Nirvitarka* - a concentration on objects without any notion of their names and qualities
According to the Yoga school, it is a state of concentration.

निसर्गज - *Nisargaja* - natural

निश्चय - *Niścaya* - determination; resolve

निश्चयज्ञान - *Niścayajñāna* - determinate knowledge

निषेध - *Niṣedha* - negative command; prohibition

According to Mīmāṁsā, it is an injunction stating what one should not do. By avoiding such actions, an individual can purify himself and become elgible for the attainment of heavenly bliss.

निष्कल - *Niṣkala* - partless; undivided

निष्कामकर्म - *Niṣkāma-karma* - dedicated action; disinterested action; desireless action

1. Action dedicated to the divine without any personal desire for the fruits of one's labour. It purifies the mind and is a remote auxiliary to the path of knowledge (according to Advaita). It is activity engaged in as dedication and worship.

2. Some aver that it is the central teaching of the *Bhagavad-gītā*. It is to act according to God's will; to be a successful instrument in the divine hands through complete identity with the divine. In doing action thus, one relinquishes the desire for any fruits of such action.

निष्कम्पप्रवृत्ति - *Niṣkampa-pravṛtti* - unfaltering effort

निष्क्रिय - *Niṣkriya* - actionless

निष्फल - *Niṣphala* - fruitless

निष्प्रपञ्च - *Niṣprapañca* - trans-phenomenal; acosmic view of the Absolute

निष्प्रपञ्चीकरण-नियोगवादिन् - *Niṣprapañci-karaṇa-niyoga-vādin* - one who believes in the theory of liberation as cosmic dissolution

निष्वभावता - *Niṣvabhāvatā* - devoid of nature; devoid of existence

According to Buddhism, *dharmas* are devoid of nature.

नित्य - *Nitya* - permanent; eternal; unchanging

According to Nyāya-Vaiśeṣika, the size of the atoms, ether, time, space, mind, and the self (*ātman*) is eternal.

नित्यधर्म - *Nitya-dharma*-eternal attributes (of a substance)

नित्यदोष - *Nitya-doṣa* - permanent defect

According to Nyāya-Vāiśeṣika, there is a distinction between permanent defect (a defect, which, when rightly detected, always vitiates the probans) and occasional defect (*anitya-doṣa*) (a defect, which, when rightly detected, vitiates the probans only under certain circumstances).

नित्यगुण - *Nitya-guṇa* - eternal quality

नित्यकर्म - *Nitya-karma* - obligatory Vedic duties; categorical imperative

According to the Mīmāṁsākas, they produce no specific fruits, though if these actions are not performed, they produce demerit or sin. This theory is denied by the Advaitins. The Advaitins claim that omission of these actions does not produce sin. *Nitya-karmas* are the regular rites which are to be performed daily, e.g., the daily fire-sacrifice (*agni-hotra*), etc.

नित्यनैमित्तिककर्म - *Nitya-naimittika-karma* - obligatory and occasional rites

These are two of the positive commands in the *Veda*. Obligatory duties are to be performed daily and do not depend upon the option of an individual. Occasional rites are rituals which should be observed on certain occasions, e.g., the ceremonial bath to be taken during eclipses. The performance of these two types of rites does not lead to any merit; but according to the Mīmāṁsakas, their non-performance will result in demerit.

नित्यप्राप्त - *Nitya-prāpta* - eternally realized

नित्यसंसारिन् - *Nitya-saṁsārin* - eternally transmigrating individual

1. According to Dvaita, these are individuals who are tied down to the cycle of birth and death forever. They are *rajas*-dominated and can never obtain liberation.

2. Vide *svarūpa-traividhyā.*

नित्यशरीर - *Nitya-śarīra* - eternal body

According to Viśiṣṭādvaita, these are the bodies of God and of eternally liberated individuals

नित्यसूरि - *Nitya-sūri* - ever-free; eternal individual

1. According to Viśiṣṭādvaita and Dvaita, these are individuals which are ever-free.

2. Vide *jīva.*

नित्यविभूति - *Nitya-vibhūti* - eternal manifestation

According to Viśiṣṭādvaita, this is the eternal, self-luminous, immaterial, infinite realm beyond *prakṛti* and its three *guṇas*. It is the 'material' out of which the bodies of *Īśvara*, eternals, and liberated beings are made. The five powers (*śakti*) of *sarva*, *nivṛtti*, *viśva*, *puruṣa*, and *parameṣṭhin* comprise its nature. With the aid of *śuddhasattva* which has only *sattva* characterizing it, *nitya-vibhūti* is a type of super-nature. It is matter without the latter's mutability.

निवर्तकानुपपत्ति - *Nivartaka-anupapatti* - the untenability of that which removes (i.e., knowledge)

1. One of the seven untenables of Rāmānuja in his criticism of the Advaita concept of *avidyā*.

2. Vide *sapta-vidha-anupapatti*.

निवर्तकज्ञान - *Nivartaka-jñāna* - knowledge which removes error

निवृत्ति - *Nivṛtti* - negation; the path of turning away from activity; involution

1. An infolding or a flowing back, inwards of that which is outwardly manifested.

2. According to the Vaiśeṣika school, it is the effort to get rid of something.

3. According to the *Bhagavad-gītā*, duty (*dharma*) as taught in the *Veda* is two-fold: of the form of active involvement in the world (*pravṛtti*) and the form of turning away from activity (*nivṛtti*). It is by the latter or renunciation that one will gain liberation.

4. Vide *nitya-vibhūti*.

निवृत्ति-अनुपपत्ति - *Nivṛtti-anupapatti* - the untenability against release

1. One of the seven untenables of Rāmānuja in his criticism of the Advita concept of *avidyā.*

2. Vide *sapta-vidha-anupapatti.*

नियम - *Niyama* - observance; discipline

1. The second limb of *rāja-yaga* which comprises five positive virtues. These are: purity (*śauca*), contentment (*santoṣa*), austerity (*tapas*), study (*svādhyāya*), and devotion to God (*Īśara-praṇidhāna*).

2. Vide *aṣṭāṅga-yoga.*

नियमविधि - *Niyama-vidhi* - restrictive injunction

1. This is an injunction where, when a thing could have been done in a number of ways, an order is given by the *Veda* restricting one to follow some definite alternative. For instance, though the chaff from the corn could be separated even by the nails, the order that 'corn should be threshed' restricts one to threshing ast he only acceptable action.

2. Vide *vidhi.*

नियमेन-आधेयत्व - *Niyamena-ādheyatva* - the body is defined as that which the individual (soul) controls

This is an example given to illustrate the concept of *apṛthak-siddhi* according to Viśiṣṭādvaita.

नियमेन-प्रकार - *Niyamena-prakāra* - invariable mode

नियमेनशेषत्व - *Niyamena-śeṣatva* - the body is defined as that which the individual (soul) utilizes for its own ends

This is an example given to illustrate the concept of *aprthak-siddhi* according to Viśiṣṭādvaita.

नियमेन-विधेयत्व - *Niyamena-vidheyatva* - the body is defined as that which the individual (soul) supports

This is an example given to illustrate the concept of *aprthak-siddhi* according to Viśiṣṭādvaita.

नियाम्य - *Niyāmya* - controlled

नियन्ता - *Niyantā* - the controller

नियन्तृ - *Niyantṛ* - ruler; controller

नियत - *Niyata* - invariable

नियतपूर्ववृत्ति - *Niyata-pūrva-vṛtti* - invariable antecedent

नियति - *Niyati* - restriction (as regards to space)

1. According to Kashmir Śaivism, this is one of the impure *tattvas* which envelop the individual and make for its finitude.
2. Vide *pañca-kañcuka.*

नियोगकार्य - *Niyogakārya* - what-is-to-be-accomplished as per an injunction

According to Mīmāṁsā, the *Veda* has *niyoga* as its sole purport. Advaita denies and attempts to refute this claim.

नोदन - *Nodana* - push; upward or side motion

न्यास - *Nyāsa* - renunciation

न्याय - *Nyāya* - logic; axiom; logical reasoning

1. An *āstika* school of Indian philosophy. Its founder was Gautama; its *vārttika-kāra* was Uddyotakara; and its *bhāṣya-kāra* was Vātsyāyana. It is primarily a school of logic and epistemology. It has been defined as a critique of the categories through means of valid knowledge. It is also referred to by the names, *ānvīkṣikī* and *tarka*.

2. The school holds a philosophy of logical realism. The distinctive contribution of this school was its fashioning of the tools of enquiry and its formulation of the technique of argumentation.

न्यायप्रस्थान - *Nyāya-prasthāna* - the *Brahma-sūtra*

It is so called because it sets forth the teachings of the Vedānta in a logical order.

न्यायावयव - *Nyāyāvayava* - component of a syllogism

O

ओजः - *Ojaḥ* - vitality; lustre; splendour

ओम् - *Om* - the Word; the *praṇava*; the Eternal

1. All words are said to be but various forms of the one sound, *om*, according to the *Upaniṣads*. It represents the divine and the power of God. It is the sound-symbol for the ultimate Reality.

2. The three *mātrās* of A, U, M represent the outer, the inner, and the superconscient states of consciousness and the waking, dream and deep sleep states respectively. And beyond these, is the modeless fourth (*a-mātrā*), which is the Self, according to Advaita.

ओषधि - *Oṣadhi* - medicinal plant

P

पाद - *Pāda* - part; chapter; a type of significatory power of words; foot

1. *Vaiśvānara*, *taijasa*, *prajñā*, and *turīya* are the four *pādas* of the Self as described in the *Māṇḍūkya Upaniṣad.* The first three are parts and the fourth is the whole.

2. It means 'a quarter', as originally it referred to the four feet of an animal. Thus, there are four parts to the Self or four parts to a verse, etc.

3. Sometimes it is used as an honorific ending, applied to form titles of individuals; e.g. Pūjyapāda.

4. Vide *karmendriya.*

पदैकवाक्यता - *Padaikavākyatā* - the syntactic unity of a word to a sentence

Vide *eka-vākyatā.*

पदार्थ - *Padārtha* - category

1. According to Jainism, there are two main categories: individual soul (*jīva*) and non-soul (*ajīva*). The individual soul is an extended, conscious, immaterial substance. The non-soul is divided into time (*kāla*), space (*ākāśa*), medium of motion (*dharma*), medium of rest (*adharma*), and matter (*pudgala*). All these except time are

extended, non-conscious substances. Time has no parts and thus is not extended.

2. According to Nyāya, there are sixteen categories: means of valid knowledge (*pramāṇa*), objects of valid knowledge (*prameya*), doubt (*saṁśaya*), purpose (*prayojana*), instances (*dṛṣṭānta*), established conclusion (*siddhānta*), members of a syllogism (*avayava*), *reductio ad absurdum* (*tarka*), arguing (*jalpa*), decisive knowledge (*nirṇaya*), arguing for truth (*vāda*), mere destructive argument (*vitaṇḍā*), fallacious reasons (*hetvābhāsa*), quibbling (*chala*), specious and unavailing objections (*jāti*), and vulnerable points (*nigraha-sthāna*).

3. According to Vaiśeṣika, there are seven categories: substance (*dravya*), quality (*guṇa*), activity (*karma*), generality (*sāmānya*), particularity (*viśeṣa*), inherence (*samavāya*), and non-existence (*abhāva*). These are defined as: what can be known (*jñeya*), validly cognized (*prameya*), and named (*abhidheya*).

4. According to Sāṅkhya, there are two basic categories: spirit (*puruṣa*) and matter (*prakṛti*). The former is conscious, non-active, unchanging, pure, and many. The latter is non-conscious, active, ever-changing, and one.

5. According to Prābhākara Mīmāṁsā, there are eight categories; substance (*dravya*), quality (*guṇa*), action (*karma*), generality (*sāmānya*), dependence (*paratantratā*), potency (*śakti*), similarity (*śādṛśya*), and number (*saṅkhyā*).

6. According to Bhāṭṭa Mīmāṁsā, there are five categories: substance (*dravya*), quality (*guṇa*),

action (*karma*), generality (*sāmānya*), and non-existence (*abhāva*).

7. According to Viśiṣṭādvaita, there are two categories: substance (*dravya*) and non-substance (*adravya*). The substances are six: primal matter (*prakṛti*), time (*kāla*), pure matter (*śuddha-sattva* or *nitya-vibhūti*), attributive consciousness (*dharma-bhūta-jñāna*), individual soul (*jīva*), and God (*Īśvara*). The non-substances are ten: the five qualities of the elements — sound, touch, colour, taste, and smell; the three *guṇas* of *prakṛti* (*sattva*, *rajas*, and *tamas*); potency (*śakti*); and conjunction (*saṁyoga*).

8. According to Dvaita there are ten categories; substance (*dravya*), quality (*guṇa*), action (*karma*), generality (*sāmānya*), particularity (*viśeṣa*), qualified (*viśiṣṭa*), whole (*aṁśīn*), power (*śakti*), similarity (*sādṛśya*), and non-existence (*abhāva*).

9. According to Śaiva Siddhānta, the main categories are three: God (*pati*), individual soul (*paśu*), and bonds (*pāśa*).

10. According to Advaita, there are two empirical categories: spirit (*cit*) and non-spirit (*acit*). From the Absolute standpoint, there is only *Brahman*.

11. According to Kashmir Śaivism, there are thirty-six categories: *Śiva*, *Śakti*, *Sadāśiva* or *Sādākhya*, *Īśvara*, *Ṣaḍ-vidyā*, the power of obscuration (*māyā*), time (*kāla*), spatial restriction (*niyati*), attachment (*rāga*), knowledge (*vidyā*), agency (*kāla*), individual soul (*puruṣa*), nature (*prakṛti*), intellect (*buddhi*), individuation (*ahaṅkāra*), mind (*manas*),

the five organs of knowledge (*jñānendriya*), the five organs of action (*karmendriya*), and the five gross elements (*mahā-bhūta*).

12. Vide charts No. 6–9.

पादसेवन - *Pādasevana* - worship of the Lord's feet

Vide *bhakti*.

पादोदक - *Pādōdaka* - drinking the water used to clean the *guru's* or the *jaṅgama's* feet

1. According to Vīra Śaivism, it is the taking of the water which is used to clean either the *guru's* or a *jaṅgama's* feet or the water which is used to worship the *liṅga* and drinking it as sacred *prasāda*.

It is said to purify the threefold body of a spiritual aspirant.

2. Vide *aṣṭa-āvaraṇa*.

पाक - *Pāka* - heat; cooking; ripening; baking

पक्ष - *Pakṣa* - minor term; subject; probandum

1. It is that in which the presence of the probandum is not known for certain and is yet to be proved; e.g., the mountain is the probandum when smoke is the probans. It is the subject where the character is inferred, e.g., fire (the character) is inferred on the hill (the subject).

2. It is of two kinds: *sapakṣa*, a similar instance in which the probandum is known for certain, and *vipakṣa*, a counter-example in which the non-existence of the probandum is known for certain.

3. It is one of the two factors essential in an inferential process. Not only must there be the

knowledge of the universal concomitance between the mark and the predicated character, but also the observation of the mark as being present in the subject (*pakṣa*). The former is called *vyāpti-jñāna* and the latter is called *pakṣa-dharmatā-jñāna.*

4. It is also known as a period of time, i.e., fourteen days (a fort-night).

5. Vide *pūrva-pakṣa.*

पक्षाभास - *Pakṣābhāsa* - fallacy of the minor term or subject

पक्षधर्मताज्ञान - *Pakṣa-dharmatā-jñāna* - knowledge of the subject as having the mark

1. It is one of the two factors necessary for an inferential process. It is the observation of the mark as being present in the subject. It is the minor premise or that about which the assertion has been made. It must be invariable and universal for the inference to be valid.

2. Vide *liṅga-parāmarśa.*

पञ्चभेद - *Pañca-bheda* - five differences

According to Dvaita, difference is fivefold: the difference between God and the individual soul; between different individual souls; between Gud and matter; between individual souls and matter; and between matter and matter itself (in its various forms). "*prapañco bhedapañcakaḥ*".

पञ्चभूतविवेक - *Pañca-bhūta-viveka* - enquiry into the five elements

1. The title of the second chapter of the *Pañcadaśī* and a method which enquires into the nature of

the five elements in order to demonstrate that the Real is not the objective world which is made of the five elements.

1. According to Advaita, when all of the elements are denied, only existence (*sat*) remains.

2. The principle employed is: What is grosser and more external is less real then the subtler, more internal, more pervasive. As the Self is the subtlest and innermost being, it is the most supremely real, according to Advaita.

पञ्चाचार - *Pañcācāra* - five codes of conduct

1. According to Vīra Śaivism, there are five ethical codes of conduct: one should daily worship the *liṅga*, remain strickly monotheistic, and admit all rules only on the basis of knowledge (*liṅgācārā*); one must work for one's livelihood, be righteous, and help others (*sadācāra*); one should see everyone as Lord *Śiva śivācāra*); one should be humble to Lord (*Śiva* and his devotees (*bhṛtyācāra*); and one should strive for the upliftment of all (*gaṇācāra*).

2. These are the disciplines necessary as aids which precede *ṣaṭsthala*.

पञ्चाग्निविद्या - *Pañcāgnividyā* - the eshatological doctrine of the five fires taught as a form of meditation in the *Chāndogya Upaniṣad*.

पञ्चकञ्चुक - *Pañca-kañcuka* - five sheaths

According to Kashmir Śaivism, there are five categories; '*kāla*, *niyati*, *rāga*, *vidyā*, and *kalā*', which are called the five sheaths and which envelop the individual soul making for its finitude. The soul which is thus enveloped in the sheaths is called the *puruṣa*.

पञ्चकारणी - *Pañcakāraṇī* - five causes

There are five conditions involved in determining a causal condition; they are: neither the cause nor the effect is perceived; the cause is perceived; in immediate succession the effect is perceived; the cause disappears; in immediate succession the effect disappears.

पञ्चकोशविवेक - *Pañca-kośa-viveka* - enquiry into the five sheaths

The title of the third chapter of the *Pañcadaśī*; it is a method employed to demonstrate that the Self is not the psycho-physical organism. The principle employed is: what is grosser and more external is less real than the subtler, more internal, more pervasive. As the Self is the subtlest and the innermost being, it is the most supremely real, accordng to Advaita.

पञ्चकृत्य - *Pañca-kṛtya* - fivefold activity

According to Kashmir Śaivism, *Śiva* is said to perform five actions: creation (*sṛṣṭi*), maintenance (*sthiti*), dissolution (*saṁhāra*), obscuration (*tirodhāna*), and grace (*anugraha*).

पञ्चमहाव्रत - *Pañca-mahā-vrata* - the five great vows

Vide *mahā-vrata*.

पाञ्चरात्र - *Pāñcarātra* - *Vaiṣṇava Āgama*; a system belonging to the *āgama* class

1. It consists of authoratative source-books according to both Viśiṣṭādvaita and Dvaita which are attributed to Lord Viṣṇu. Some of the more important works include: *Bṛhad-brahma-saṁhitā*, *Īśvara-saṁhitā*, *Pauṣkara-saṁhitā*, *Jñānāmṛtasāra-saṁhitā*, *Ahirbudhnyasaṁhitā*, and *Pādmasaṁhitā*.

2. It is a Vaiṣṇavite sect also known by the names: Nārāyaṇīya, Sāttvata, Ekāntika, and Bhāgavata. They worship *Vāsudeva-Kṛṣṇa*, with his four *vyūhas*.

पञ्चशील - *Pañca-śīla* - five moral precepts

These are the five moral precepts which every Buddhist lay disciple (*upāsaka*) and every monk (*bhikṣu*) must promise to observe. These five precepts are abstinence from: injuring others (*prāṇātipāta*), stealing (*adattanādāna*), incontinence (*abrahmacarya*), lying (*mṛṣāvāda*), and temperance (*surā-maireya-pramāda-sthāna*).

पञ्चस्कन्ध - *Pañca-skandha* - the five aggregates

Vide *skandha*.

पञ्चावयववाक्य - *Pañcāvayava-vākya* - a syllogism with five members

1. These five members are: thesis (*pratijñā*), reason (*hetu*), universal proposition with example (*udāharaṇa*), the application (*upanaya*), and the conclusion (*nigamana*).

2. Vide *anumāna*.

पञ्चीकरण - *Pañcīkaraṇa* - quintuplication

The theory that every physical object contains all the five elements in various proportions. In the

Upaniṣads there was reference only to three elements, but the Vedānta extended it to five elements (vide *Brahma-sūtra,* II. iv. 22). Viśiṣṭādvaita employs this theory to explain *satkhyāti.*

पाणि - *Pāṇi* - hand

1. One of the five organs of action.

2. Vide *karmendriya.*

पाप - *Pāpa* - sin; demerit

1. Actions which produce sorrow.

2. According to Jainism, one of the aspects of *ajīva.*

पापोपदेश - *Pāpopadeśa*? - desisting from advising people to engage in agriculture which leads to the killing of insects

This is a limb of *anarthadaṇḍa,* which is one of the minor duties placed upon householders within Jaina ethics.

पर - *Para* - higher; universal; beyond; supreme

1. According to Sāṅkhya, it is one of the nine kinds of *tuṣṭi.* Here it refers to the idea that no exertion towards liberation is necessary because of the troubles which come of earning one's living.

2. According to Vaiśeṣika, it is a type of *guṇa* representing universality.

परभक्ति - *Parabhakti* - supreme devotion

Supreme devotion is of five types: *śānta, dāsya, sakhya, vātsalya,* and *mādhurya.*

परब्रह्मन् - *Parabrahman* - the Supreme Being; the divine as transcendent; that which is beyond all dualities

According to Advaita, it is the supra-cosmic divine who supports with its timeless and spaceless existence, the entire cosmic manifestation of its own being in time and space. It is infinite, attributeless, and without name and form. Vide *Brahman.*

पराधीनत्व - *Parādhīnatva* - the other-dependent; to be dependent upon God; another-dependent

According to Viśiṣṭādvaita and Dvaita, everything is dependent upon God - "*daivādhīnaṁ jagatsarvam.*"

परजाति - *Parajāti* - highest universal

E.g., *sattā* (being) is the 'highest universal' in the Nyāya-Vaiśeṣika system.

परज्ञान - *Para-jñāna* - supreme knowledge

1. It is devotion awakened by śāstraic knowledge according to Viśiṣṭādvaita.

2. Vide *bhakti.*

पराक् - *Parāk* - external

पराक्दृष्टि - *Parāk-dṛṣṭi* - outward vision

पारलौकिक - *Pāra-laukika* - trans-empirical

परम - *Parama* - highest; supreme

परमभक्ति - *Parama-bhakti* - the quintessence of devotion

1. According to Viśiṣṭādvaita, it is an unquenchable thirst for God.

2. Vide *bhakti.*

परमगुरु - *Parama-guru* – one's teacher's teacher

Within Advaita, Gauḍapāda is known as Śaṅkarācārya's *parama-guru*.

परमाणु - *Paramāṇu* - atom

1. The minutest conceivable particle of matter which cannot be further divided.

2. According to Buddhism, it consists of the fourfold substratum of colour, smell, taste and contact. It is the minutest form of *rūpa*. It cannot be divided, seen, analysed, tasted or felt. Yet it is not permanent, but a mere momentary flash into being. Single atoms are called *dravya-paramāṇu* and compound atoms are called *saṅghāta-paramāṇu*. Seven *paramāṇus* combine together to form an *aṇu* and in this form it becomes visible.

3. According to Vaiśeṣika, the four elements (earth, water, fire and air) comprise the four kinds of atoms. They differ qualitatively with their respective qualities being: smell, taste, colour and touch. Yet the atoms have no parts and are non-spatial. The smallest visible substance is constituted of three dyads called a *tryaṇuka*. Two atoms constitute a dyad (*dvyaṇuka*).

4. According to Sāṅkhya, atoms are fivefold: *ākāśa, vāyu, tejas, ap* and *bhūtādi*. They are generated from the *tanmātras*.

परमपद् - *Paramapada* - the highest abode; the supreme abode (*Vaikuṇṭha*) of Lord Viṣṇu.

It is the immaterial, self-luminous, infinite, realm of *Vaikuṇṭha*.

परामर्श - *Parāmarśa* - subsumptive reflection

1. Understanding the minor premise in relation to the major premise is called subsumptive reflection. It is the ratiocinative process which makes known the fact that the reason which is universally concomitant with the inferred character, is present in the subject. The principle involved in this process is subsumption or the correlation of a particular case with the universal pervading it. E.g., when a particular case of smoke on a hill has been perceived, the presence of fire can be inferred because the smoke is subsumed under the generalization involving the universal pervasion of smoke by fire.

2. Vide *liṅga-parāmarśa*.

परमार्थ - *Paramārtha* - the highest purpose or goal; absolute truth; real

परमार्थसत्य - *Paramārtha-satya* - the transcendental truth according to Mādhyamika Buddhism

पारमार्थिक - *Pāramārthika* - the Absolute; the absolutely real

According to Advaita, it is the highest of the three levels of reality. It represents the absolute truth (Vide *vyāvahārika* and *prātibhāsika*). This term is contextual for it is used with regard to the Absolute for the purpose of distinguishing it from all else.

परमात्मन् - *Paramātman* - the supreme Self; *Brahman*; God

According to Sāṅkhya, the *puruṣa* is called *paramātman*.

परम-अवधि - *Parama-avadhi* - a type of clairvoyance

1. According to Jainism, in this type of clairvoyance, the range is not so limited by spatial and temporal conditions.

2. Vide *avadhi.*

परमेश्वर - *Parameśvara* - the supreme Lord; Śiva

पारमिता - *Pāramitā* - highest ideals of spiritual perfection; virtues

According to Buddhism, these virtues guide and assist the aspirant on the path to perfection. They have three stages: ideals for the worldly life, ideals for the mental life, and ideals for the spiritual life. They are six in number: *dāna* or charity and love; *śīla* or good behaviour; *kṣānti* or patience; *vīrya* or zeal; *dhyāna* or meditation; and *prajñā* or wisdom.

परंज्योति - *Paraṁjyoti* - supreme light

परम्परासम्बन्ध - *Paramparā-sambandha* - indirect relation

परमुक्त - *Paramukta* - highest liberation

1. Individual souls completely liberated according to Śaiva Siddhānta.

2. Vide *jīva* per Śaiva Siddhānta.

परापर - *Parāpara* - one of the nine types of defects

1. According to Sāṅkhya, it is the natural waste of things earned by enjoyment.

2. Vide *tuṣṭi.*

परार्ध - *Parārdha* - one thousand crores of crores

परार्थानुमान - *Parārtha-anumāna* - inference through the help of articulated propositions for convincing others in a debate

1. According to Nyāya, it is one of two classes of inference. It is inference for the sake of another. This type of inference requires the formulation of the five-membered syllogism in order to arrive at a conclusion.

2. Buddhism also makes this twofold division of inference into *svārtha-anumāna* and *parārtha-anumāna.*

3. According to Mīmāṁsā, this type of inference only needs three members of a syllogism (*pratijñā, hetu,* and *dṛṣṭānta*).

4. Vide *anumāna.*

परा संवित् - *Parā saṃvit* - absolute experience; self-luminous knowledge

परस्पराश्रय - *Parasparāśraya* - reciprocal dependence

A type of logical fallacy. Vide *anyonyāśraya.*

परतःप्रामाण्यवाद - *Parataḥ-prāmāṇya-vāda* - the theory of extrinsic validity

1. The theory of the Nyāya school which says that knowledge is not self-evidently valid as it arises, but becomes valid only on fulfilling certain extrinsic conditions. The conditions of validity and invalidity of knowledge are other than the conditions of knowledge itself.

2. Vide *svataḥ-prāmāṇya-vāda.*

परतन्त्र - *Paratantra* - externally valid; dependent

1. One of three types of knowledge according to Āryasaṅgha. It is relative knowledge which exists of the mind and for philosophers. At this level, empirical phenomena are recognized to be relative and interdependent.

2. Vide *parikalpita.*

पारतन्त्र्य - *Pāratantrya* - dependence (on God)

परतस्त्व - *Paratastva* - extrinsicality

परतोग्राह्य - *Paratogrāhya* - made out extrinsically

परत्व - *Paratva* – a type of *guṇa* which gives rise to perception of a long duration of time and remoteness of space

According to Nyāya-Vais'eṣika, it is indicative of spatial and temporal remoteness.

परा विद्या - *Parā vidyā* - the higher knowledge; wisdom

The *Upaniṣads* sometimes make a distinction between the higher and lower truth. In the *Muṇḍaka Upaniṣad,* the former is the knowledge of *Brahman* and the latter is the knowledge of empirical things. Generally it is the supreme knowledge of the Ultimate or imperishable Reality. It is knowledge of the Self.

परिच्छिन्न - *Paricchinna* - finite determination

परिग्रह - *Parigraha* - acceptance

परिहार - *Parihāra* - a logical category

It is a logical category found in the *Caraka-saṁhitā.*

परिकल्प – *Parikalpa* - conceive; to imagine

परिकल्पित - *Parikalpita* - illusory; imaginary

1. One of the three types of knowledge according to Yogâcāra Buddhism. Āryasaṅgha says that this knowledge is as simple, everyday, ignorant individuals hold. At this level, what is imagined, appears as real.

2. Vide *paratantra* and *parinispanna.*

परीक्षा - *Parīkṣa* - enquiry; examination

परिमाण - *Parimāṇa* - size; quantity; measure

Nyāya-Vais'eṣika divides size into: *aṇu-parimāṇa, hrasva-parimāṇa, mahat-parimāṇa.* They also say that the size of the atoms of space, time, ether, mind and *ātman* are eternal and all-pervasive.

पारिमाण्डल्य - *Pārimāṇḍalya* - globular; round; atomic size

According to Nyāya-Vais'eṣika, atomic size is eternal and unchanging in itself. It is the measure of an atom. It is the smallest conceivable size.

परिमिति - *Parimiti* - measure; size

According to Nyāya-Vais'eṣika, it is that entity of quality in things by virtue of which individuals perceive them as great or small and speak of them as such. It is one of the six classes of categories (*padārtha*).

परिणाम - *Pariṇāma* - change; changing; modification

परिणामवाद - *Pariṇāma-vāda* - transformation theory

1 The theory that the cause is continually transforming itself into its effects.

2. According to *Brahma-pariṇāma-vāda*, the world is a transformation of *Brahman*, and according to *prakṛti-pariṇāma-vāda*, the world is a transformation of nature.

3. According to Sāṅkhya, causation is the manifestation of what is in a latent condition in the cause. That is, the effect exists already in the cause in a potential state; and the causal operation only makes patent what is latent in the cause. This theory is also called *satkārya-vāda*. Viśiṣṭādvaita also accepts this theory.

4. Śaiva Siddhānta holds the *prakṛti-pariṇāma-vāda*.

परिनिष्पन्न - *Parinispanna* - Absolute

One of the three types of knowledge in Buddhism, according to Āryasaṅgha. This is the perfect knowledge which the Buddha is said to possess.

परीषहजय - *Parīṣahajaya* - the ability to remain steadfast on the religious path and bear suffering while remaining such

According to Jainism, this is one of the *bhāva-samvaras*. It is employed to control the inrush of *karma*-particles into the individual.

परिसङ्ख्याविधि - *Parisaṅkhyā-vidhi* - exclusive injunction

1. One of the three classes of injunctions. When two or more things of unknown value are enjoined, one must choose according to the Scriptures. What is enjoined is already known, but not necessarily as possible alternatives. For instance, a

mantra may be used in a number of places, but there are cases where it should not be used.

2. Vide *vidhi*.

परिशेष - *Pariśeṣa* - elimination; exclusion; residue

Knowing something by means of elimination.

परिशेषमान - *Pariśeṣamāna* - *reductio ad absurdum*

A type of inference. This type consists in asserting 'anything' because it is already known to be so.

परिस्पन्द् - *Parispanda* - molecular movement

परिव्राजक - *Parivrājaka* - one who has renounced the world; a *sannyāsin*

परोक्ष - *Parokṣa* - non-perceptional; indirect; mediate

परोक्षज्ञान - *Parokṣa-jñāna* - mediate knowledge

पर्याय - *Paryāya* - mode; change

1. A Jaina term applied to the changes which occur in the attributes of substances.

2. The individual (*jīva*) has four modes: *divya*, *manuṣya*, *nārakīya*, and *tiryak*.

3. Modes are of two kinds: *dravya-paryāya*, which gives a vision of unity in the diversity of modes; e.g., a green fruit or a ripe fruit is always fruit. This mode is of two kinds: *samāna-jātīya-dravya-paryāya* and *asamāna-jātīya-dravya-paryāya*. The second type of mode is *jīva-paryāya*.

पर्यायनय - *Paryāya-naya* - Vide *paryāyārthika-naya*

पर्यायार्थिकनय - *Paryāyārthika-naya* - the viewpoint of modes

1. According to Jainism, this is the viewpoint which considers the modifications and conditions of an object. It indicates the infinite standpoints possible when Reality is analysed from the point of view of the modes it possesses.

2. It is of four types: standpoint of momentariness (*ṛjusūtra-naya*), synonyms (*śabda-naya*), etymological standpoint (*samābhirūḍha-naya*), and such-like standpoint (*evambhūta-naya*).

3. Vide *naya*.

पाश - *Pāśa* - bond; fetter

1. Literally it means 'a rope'. It is comprised of three strands or *āṇava*, *karma*, and *māyā*. These three tie the individual soul into bondage. *Āṇava* is ignorance. It is a beginningless, positive, inert entity which causes delusion. It is the original cause of the individual's bondage. It has two powers: *āvāraka-śakti* and *adhonyāmika-śakti*. *Karma* is the bond forged by actions of thought, word, and deed. These produce merit and demerit which tie the individual to the wheel of birth and death. *Māyā* provides the individual with its bodies, instruments, and objects of experience. It creates the universe for one's advancement, though under the influence of ignorance, it is misused and becomes a fetter.

2. Vide *mala*.

पशु - *Paśu* - individual soul; animal

1. The individual soul by nature is infinite, pervasive, and omniscient according to Śaiva Siddhānta. However, due to impurities, individuals experience themselves as finite, limited, and ignorant. These impurities which bind the individual are three: *āṇava*, *karma*, and *māyā* (vide *pāśa*).

2. According to Śaiva Siddhānta, individuals are divided into three classes: *sakala*, *pralayākala*, and *vijñānākala* — as they exist with either all three impurities, only the first two impurities, or only *āṇava*. Individuals are infinite in number and are related to the Lord as a body is related to the soul.

3. Vide *jīva*.

पाशुपत - *Pāśupata* - a philosophical theory of one of the *Śaiva* schools

It is one of the *Śaiva* cults and sometimes *Śaiva* systems are called thus because *Śiva* is the lord of the individual.

पशुपति - *Paśupati* - Lord of individuals; Lord *Śiva*

पाताल - *Pātāla* - hell; nether world

1. The nether pole of *Bhū-loka*. According to Hindu tradition, it is one of the fourteen worlds.

2. Vide *tala* and *loka*.

पति - *Pati* - God; Lord; *Śiva*

Śiva is the Lord of all beings and the highest Reality according to the *Śaiva* schools. He is the only independent substance according to Śaivism. Origination, maintenance, and destruction have their origin in him, but he himself does not undergo any change. He is the unchanging ground of all that changes. He is the efficient cause of the world. He has eight qualities: independence, purity, self-knowledge, omniscience, freedom from impurities, omnipotence, bliss, and grace. He is both immanent and transcendent. He has five functions: creation (*sṛṣṭi*), preservation (*sthiti*), destruction (*saṁhāra*), obscuration (*tirodhāna*), and grace (*anugraha*). He has eight names: *Rudra, Śarva, Ugra, Aśani, Bhava, Paśupati, Mahādeva* and *Īśāna*. See also *rudra* and *Śiva*.

पटुप्रत्यय - *Paṭupratyaya* - vivid cognition

पौद्गल - *Paudgala* - made of material; matter

पौरुषेय - *Pauruṣeya* - personal; what originates from a person

पायु - *Pāyu* - anus; organ of excretion

1. One of the five organs of action.
2. Vide *karmendriya*.

फल - *Phala* - fruit; result

फलभक्ति - *Phala-bhakti* - devotion which is the result of God's grace given spontaneously

Vide *bhakti*.

फलव्याप्यत्व - *Phala-vyāpyatva* - pervasion by knowledge

1. According to Advaita, it is one of the two conditions necessary for something to be an object of knowledge.
2. Vide *vṛtti-vyāpyatva*.

फलीभूतज्ञान - *Phalībhūtajñāna* - resultant cognition

पीलुपाक - *Pīlupāka* – heating of atoms

According to Vais'eṣika, it is the impact of heat upon simple atoms which decomposes *dvyaṇukas* into simpler arrangements so that new characteristics or qualities may arise. There is first a disintegration into simple atoms, then change of atomic qualities, and then a final re-combination. Compare *piṭharapāka.*

पिण्ड - *Piṇḍa* - part of the whole; individual

पिठरपाक - *Piṭharapāka* - heating of molecules

According to Nyāya, heat directly affects the character of molecules and changes their qualities without effecting a change in the atoms. (Compare with *pilūpaka*, as this is one of the few points of difference between the later Nyāya and Vais'eṣika schools.)

पितृयान - *Pitṛyāna* – path of the ancestors or manes

The way of the Fathers in which the individual soul after death jo urneys until it once more enters a womb to be born again.

प्रभा - *Prabhā* - effulgence; shine

प्रभाकरी - *Prabhākarī* - illumination

Vide *bodhisattva.*

प्राचुर्य - *Prācurya* – abundance

प्रदेश - *Prades'a* - extension; body; mode

प्रधान - *Pradhāna* - the originator; primordial matter; the original source of the material universe

Vide *prakṛti*. *cf*., "*Prdhānakṣetrajñapatirguṇes'aḥ.*"

प्रध्वंसाभाव - *Pradhvaṁsābhāva* - annihilative or posterior non-existence

1. The non-existence of a thing after it is destroyed. It has a beginning, but no end according to Nyāya. The Advaitin holds that this type of non-existence has an end also.

2. Vide *abhāva*.

प्रद्युम्न - *Pradyumna* - one of the manifestations of God

1. He creates the universe and introduces all *dharmas*, according to Viśiṣṭādvaita. He emanates from *Saṅkarṣaṇa* and from him emanates *Aniruddha.* He possesses, in the highest degree, lordship and virility. He hypostatizes into *Trivikrama*, *Vāmana*, and *Śrīdhara*.

2. Vide *vyūha*.

प्रागभाव - *Prāg-abhāva* - antecedent or prior non-existence

1. The non-existence of an object before it comes into being. It is said to be beginningless, but this non-existence obviously comes to an end when the object in question is brought into being.

2. Vide *abhāva*.

प्रैरणिकीप्रवृत्ति - *Prairaṇikī-pravṛtti* - imposed volition

प्रज्ञा - *Prajñā* - wisdom; intuitive wisdom

1. The intuitive wisdom or the highest knowledge, according to Mahāyāna Buddhism.

2. It is one of the six virtues of Buddhism. (Vide *pāramitā*).

3. The individual form of the self as the witness of the bare nescience in the state of sleep. It is

also known as *ānandamaya*. The experiencer in deep sleep is called the *prajñā* when there is no determinate knowledge, but only pure bliss and pure consciousness.

प्रज्ञानं ब्रह्म - *Prajñānam-brahma* - 'consciousness is *Brahman*'

A *mahā-vākya* (great saying) which occurs in the *Aitareya Upaniṣad* of the *Ṛg-veda*.

प्रज्ञापारमिता - *Prajñā-pāramitā* - the highest wisdom; the perfection of wisdom

It is the name of the Buddhist Scriptures of the Mahāyāna school which deal with the emptiness of all things.

प्रज्ञप्ति - *Prajñapti* - experience

प्राकाम्य - *Prākāmya* - the power by which impediments to the will power are removed

Vide *aṣṭa-aiśvarya*

प्रकार - *Prakāra* - mode; adjunct

प्रकरण - *Prakaraṇa* - chapter; section; topic

1. It is the context. It is one of the principles by which to decide whether there obtains a subsidiary relation or not.

2. Vide *aṅgatva-bodhaka-pramāṇa*.

प्रकरणग्रन्थ - *Prakaraṇa-grantha* - introductory book or manual

प्रकरणसम - *Prakaraṇa-sama* - similar topic or reason

1. A logical fallacy in an inferential process in which the reason (*hetu*) is contradicted by a

counter-inference; e.g., 'sound is eternal because it is audible' is contradicted by the inference, 'sound is non-eternal because it is produced.'

2. Vide *hetvābhāsa.*

प्रकार-प्रकारिभाव - *Prakāra-prakāribhāva* - the relation between the modes and that which has modes

प्रकाश - *Prakāśa* - shining; luminous; effulgence

प्रख्या - *Prakhyā* - a stage of consciousness *(citta)* which is predominated by the *sattva-guṇa* and in which the *tamo-guṇa* remains in subordination

प्रकृष्टमहत्त्व - *Prakṛṣṭa-mahattva* - higher magnitude

प्रकृति - *Prakṛti* - primal nature

1. According to Sāṅkhya, it is also called *pradhāna* and *avyakta*; matter is one of the two categories basic to its system. It is fundamentally active, but non-conscious. It is fundamentally one and imperceptible. It is the source of the universe and can be inferred from its effects. It is a composite of three constituents called *guṇas (sattva, rajas,* and *tamas*). (Vide chart No. 12).

2. According to Viśiṣṭādvaita, it is one of the six substances. Unlike in Sāṅkhya, the *guṇas* are the qualities of *prakṛti* and not its constituents. These qualities are inseparable from it, but not identical with it. It is inseparably related to *Īśvara* and dependent upon Him, unlike the independent *prakṛti* of Sāṅkhya. It is the dwelling-place of the individual, and through it, of God himself.

Sāṅkhya's *prakṛti* is infinite, but here it is limited above by *nityavibhūti*.

3. According to Advaita, it is a principle of illusion (*māyā*), and therefore not fundamentally real. It is a phenomenon but not a phantasm, however.

4. According to Dvaita, it is the material cause of the world and one of the twenty substances (*dravya*).

प्रलय - *Pralaya* - periodic cosmic dissolution

1. It is a period of repose or reabsorption. It is of three types: *nitya*, which is the sleep in which every effect dissolves for the time-being; *naimittika*, which occurs at the end of a day of *Brahmā*; and *prākṛta*, which occurs at the end of an epoch of *Brahmā*.

2. All the Indian schools except the Mīmāṁsā school accept this theory.

प्रलयकाल - *Pralaya-kāla* - time of dissolution

प्रलयाकल - *Pralayākala* - a kind of *jīva*

One of the seven kinds of knowers, according to Kashmir Śaivism. (Vide *saptapramātṛ*). It is a type of individual soul which is subject to the two bonds of *āṇava* and *karma*. It is the individual as it exists at the time of dissolution.

प्रलयकेवलिन् - *Pralaya-kevalin* - a type of individual soul according to Kashmir Śaivism

प्रमा - *Pramā* - valid knowledge; true knowledge

1. According to Nyāya, it is true presentational knowledge (*yathārthānubhava*). It is a definite and assured cognition of an object which is true and presentational in character.

2. According to the Sautrāntika and Vaibhāṣika schools, it is the identity of content between a cognition and the cognitum This is a realist view which posits that the object determines the cognition's validity.

3. According to Advaita, it is knowledge which possesses non-contradictedness (*abādhita*) and novelty (or sometimes just the former).

4. According to Bhāṭṭa Mīmāṁsā, it is primary and original knowledge (*anadhigata*).

5. According to Prābhākara Mīmāṁsā, it is immediate experience (*anubhūti*).

6. According to Vaiśeṣika, it is the unique operative cause of both true presentational knowledge and memory.

7. According to Jainism, it is immediate presentational knowledge and mediate knowledge in so far as they are true.

8. According to Viśiṣṭādvaita, all knowledge is of the real. Its mark is that it is practically useful.

9. According to Sāṅkhya, it is knowledge not previously known (*anadhigata*), free from error, and above doubt.

प्रमाद् - *Pramāda* - negligence; slip

प्रमादाचारण - *Pramādācaraṇa* - to desist from attending the theatre, music performances, gambling, etc.

This is one limb of the Jaina ethical code *anarthadaṇḍa*.

प्रमाण - *Pramāṇa* - means of valid knowledge

1. It is the instrument (*karaṇa*) of valid knowledge. As the cause, so the effect (*mānādhīnā meya-siddhiḥ*). According to each system, the number of *pramāṇas* accepted as valid will depend upon the types of knowledge that are recognized.

2. The Cārvāka school accepts perception (*pratyakṣa*) as the only means of valid knowledge. The Buddhists and the Vaiśeṣika accept perception and inference (*anumāna*). The Jainas, Sāṅkhya, Yoga, Viśiṣṭādvaita, and Dvaita accept perception, inference, and verbal testimony (*śabda*). Nyāya accepts perception, inference, verbal testimony, and comparison (*upamāna*). The Prabhākara Mīmāṁsā school accepts perception, inference, verbal testimony, comparison, and presumption (*arthāpatti*). The Bhāṭṭa Mīmāṁsā and Advaita accept perception, inference, verbal testimony, comparison, presumption, and non-cognition (*anupalabdhi*). Śaiva Siddhānta accepts *Śiva-cit-śakti* as the only valid means of knowledge, though, as secondary means, it accepts the traditional first three *pramāṇas*. Dvaita calls the sources of valid knowledge as *anu-pramāṇa*; *kevala-pramāṇa* is defined as the knowledge of an object as it is. Dvaita recognizes preception, inference, and verbal testimony as *anupramāṇa*.

3. According to Jainism, the means of vaild knowledge is knowledge of a thing as it is. It is direct (*aparokṣa*), and indirect (*parokṣa*). Direct is either practical (*vyāvahārika*) or other-worldly

(*pāramārthika*). Practical is either *mati* or *sṛta*. Other-worldly is either *kevala* or *vikala*. Indirect is of five types: *smṛti*, *pratyabhijñā*, *tarka*, *anumāna*, and *āgama*. (vide chart no. 11).

4. According to some traditions, inclusion (*sambhava*), tradition (*aitihya*), *pariśeṣa* (supplement or remainder), and *ceṣṭā* (gesticulation) are *pramāṇas*.

प्रमाणमूलक - *Pramāṇa-mūlaka* - right knowledge

प्रामाण्य - *Prāmāṇya* – truth; validity

प्रमाता - *Pramātā* - the cognizer; the subject or the knower who cognizes; vide *tripuṭī*

प्रमत्तनास्तिक - *Pramatta-nāstika* - erring heretic; infatuated atheist

प्रमेय - *Prameya* - object of cognition; object of knowledge

Vide *tripuṭī*.

प्रमिति - *Pramiti* - the act of cognition

Vide *tripuṭī*.

प्रमोद - *Pramoda* – seeing good in all things

According to Sāṅkhya, a type of *siddhi* which leads directly to the separation of *prakṛti* from *puruṣa*.

प्रमूढ - *Pramūḍha* – ignorant

According to Sāṅkhya, a state of the mind (*citta*) revealing ignorant attatchment or instinct.

प्रमुदित - *Pramudita* - joy in one's activities
Vide *bodhisattva.*

प्राण - *Prāṇa* - vital air; life breath; vitality

1. It is that air which is perceptible in the mouth and nostrils. Or, it is the principle of vitality in the individual organism. It is said to be all-pervading, invisible, and the life duration of all — according to the latter idea.

2. The five *prāṇas* are known as: *prāṇa, apāna, vyāna, udāna,* and *samāna, viz.* the air which rises upwards (*prāṇa*); that which moves downwards (*apāna*); that by which these two are held (*vyāna*); that which carries the grosser material of food to *apāna* and brings the subtler material to each limb (*samāna*); and that which brings up or carries down what has been drunk or eaten (*udāna*).

3. Vide *prāṇāyama.*

प्राणलिङ्ग - *Prāṇa-liṅga* - a form of the formless *Śiva*
Vide *liṅga-sthala.*

प्राणलिङ्गिन् - *Prāṇa-liṅgin* - a stage of consciousness
Vide *sthala.*

प्राणमयकोश - *Prāṇamaya-kośa* - the sheath of vital air

1. The second sheath encasing the body, with its instrumentality of vital airs and the nervous system. It is located within the physieal sheath. It is permeated by mental, consciousness, and bliss sheaths.

2. Vide *kośa.*

प्रणव - *Praṇava* - the primeval word; *om*; *oṅkāra*
Vide *om.*

प्राणवादिन् - *Prāṇa-vādin* - a type of Cārvāka who con siders the vital airs as the soul

प्राणायाम - *Prāṇāyama* - control of the breath

1. One of the eight limbs of *rāja-yoga.* (Vide *aṣṭāṅga-yoga*). The control of the breath helps to bring the mind under control. It is the technique of regulating and restrianing the function of breathing.

2. It has three aspects: inhalation (*recaka*), retention (*kumbhaka*), and exhalation (*pūraka*). The practice of *prāṇāyāma* aims at making the span of *pūraka, recaka*, and *kumbhaka* longer. There are also *prāṇāyāmas* for purifying the blood, vitalizing the inner organs, etc.

प्रणिधान – *Praṇidhāna* - the resolution to help beings to universal liberation; a vow taken by a *bodhisattva*

प्रापक - *Prāpaka* - that which makes one attain an end

प्रपञ्च - *Prapañca* – the world; world-appearance

प्रपञ्चनाशन - *Prapañcanāśana* - annihilation of the world

प्रपन्न - *Prapanna* - the capacity of realization; one who has surrendered his self to God; a seeker of God

प्रपत्ति - *Prapatti* - complete and absolute surrender

1. According to Viśiṣṭādvaita, it is one of the means to liberation. It has six constituents: to conceive what is in conformity with the will of *Īśvara* (*ānukūlyasya saṅkalpa*); to reject what is disagreeable to *Īśvara* (*prātikūlyasya varjanam*); to have firm faith that *Īśvara* will save the self

(*rakṣiṣyatīti viśvāsa*); the feeling that one is incapable to follow the prescribed path of *karma, jñāna*, and *bhakti* (*kārpaṇya*); to seek *Īśvara* alone as the protector (*goptṛtva-varaṇam*); and to surrender oneself to *Īśvara* in all meekness (*ātma-nikṣepa*).

2. This concept points to the idea that liberation may be obtained through God's free grace. It is also called *śaraṇāgati* or absolute confidence in the saving grace of the Lord.

3. In this path there are no restrictions of place, time, mode, eligibility, and fruit.

प्राप्तस्य प्राप्तिः - *Prāptasyaprāptiḥ* - attainment of the already attained

E.g., finding the necklace around one's neck which one thought had been lost or discovering that one is the Self when one had thought oneself to be merely the body-mind complex.

प्राप्ति - *Prāpti* - the power to secure whatever is desired

Vide *aṣṭa-aiśvarya.*

प्राप्य - *Prāpya* - that which is to be obtained

प्राप्यकारि - *Prāpyakāri* - the visual sense, being constituted by light, travels to the spot where visible objects happen to be, and perceives them

Except for the visual sense, most of the Indian systems save Nyāya, do not believe that the other senses go out to meet their objects.

प्रारब्ध - *Prārabdha* - *karma*-in-action

1. That part of the accumulated effect of past deeds which has begun to take effect with the

creation of the present physical body, and which is responsible for the continuance of the body even after release is attained. It is destroyed only when its force is spent. It cannot be averted, avoided, or changed, though either by knowledge or by grace, its impact can be minimized or rendered nil to the perceiver as the case may be.

2. Vide *āgāmi* - and *sañcita karma*.

प्रार्थना - *Prārthanā* - prayer; invocation; benediction

प्रसाद् - *Prasāda* - grace

1. According to Dvaita, it is the ultimate cause of liberation.

2. According to many systems, it is the offerings which are first given to the Lord and then partaken of. They are said to purify the taints inherent in all objects. Vide *aṣṭa-āvaraṇa*.

प्रसादलिङ्ग - *Prasāda-liṅga* - one of the forms of the formless *Śiva*

Vide *liṅga-sthala*.

प्रसादि - *Prasādi* - state of consciousness

Vide *sthala*.

प्रसङ्ग - *Prasaṅga* - a method of argument employed only with the view in mind of destroying; *reductio ad absurdum*

This is a method employed by the Mādhyamika system to expose the inner contradictions inherent in any one particular philosophical position.

प्रसङ्ख्यान - *Prasaṅkhyāna* - continued meditation

As a meditation theory (*prasaṅkhyāna-vāda*), it was espoused by Maṇḍana positing that the *Vedas* enjoin both the performance of prescribed acts and meditation on *Brahman* as the means to liberation. He believed that meditation is necessary to get a direct and immediate knowledge of *Brahman.*

प्रसारण - *Prasāraṇa* - expansion

Vide *karma.*

प्रसिद्ध - *Prasiddha* - well-known; well-established

According to Advaita, *avidyā* is well-known but not established by means of valid knowledge (*pramāṇāsiddha*).

प्रसिद्धवृत्ति - *Prasiddha-vṛtti* - primary meaning

Vide *mukhya-vṛtti.*

प्रस्थानत्रय - *Prasthāna-traya* - the triple canon (of Vedānta)

It consists of: the *Upaniṣads*, the *Bhagavad-gītā*, and the *Brahma-sūtra*. These works form the *śruti*, the *smṛti*, and the *nyāya-prasthānas* of Vedānta, and teach the same doctrine.

प्रथमव्यवसाय - *Prathama-vyavasāya* - primary cognition

प्रतिबन्धक - *Pratibandhaka* - counter-agent

प्रतिभा - *Pratibhā* - special mental power; imaginative insight

1. According to Nyāya-Vaiśeṣika, it is the power to know the happening of a future event. Vide *pratibhāna-jñāna*.

2. According to Indian Aesthetics, it is a penetrative imagination which creates or apprehends what is given in a work of art. It is said to be the mental faculty which flashes forth ever new ideas. Thus it belongs both to an artist as well as to a perceptive spectator. This type of imagination is more penetrative than the ordinary kind.

प्रतिभानज्ञान – *Pratibhāna-jñāna* - extra-sensory perception

1. It is a type of perception directly perceived by the mind.

2. It is concerned with objects beyond one's senses, e.g., the intuition that one's father will come tomorrow, and such an event comes to pass. Nyāya-Vaiśeṣika recognises this as a type of perception, while Advaita calls it a case of inference.

प्रातिभासिक - *Prātibhāsika* - apparent; illusory

1. The truth that exists only in appearance, e.g., a mirage or a rope-snake.

2. According to Advaita, it is one of the three levels of reality from the relative point of view. Vide *vyāvahārika* and *pāramārthika*.

प्रतिबिम्बवाद - *Pratibimba-vāda* - reflection theory

The theory that the individual *(jīva)* is an appearance of *Brahman* as reflected in nescience. This theory is propounded by the *Vivaraṇa* school of Advaita. Padmapāda gives an analogy of a reflection in a mirror in contrast to the analogy of the red crystal that is given in *ābhāsa-vāda*.

प्रतिज्ञा - *Pratijñā* - the first member of a five-membered syllogism; the thesis to be proved

1. The premise, what is to be proved, in an inferential argument. Its purpose is to inform the other party of what is sought to be established and where; e.g., the hill has fire.

2. Vide *anumāna.*

प्रतीक - *Pratīka* - symbolic

प्रातिकूल्यस्य वर्जन - *Prātikūlyasya varjana* - rejecting what is disagreeable to *Īśvara*

Vide *prapatti.*

प्रतिपाद्यप्रतिपादकभाव - *Pratipādya-pratipādaka-bhāva* - the relation of a treatise with its subject material

This forms the relation (*sambandha*) in almost all *śāstra* works.

प्रतिपक्षभावना - *Pratipakṣa-bhāvanā* - reflecting on what is contrary to the observances and abstentions (*yama* and *niyama*) and cultivating those traits which are opposed to these obstructions

It is a technique employed by Patañjali in the *rāja-yoga.*

प्रतिसङ्ख्यानिरोध - *Pratisaṅkhyā-nirodha* - a term for *nirvāṇa*

1. It is an unconditional *dharma* in the Vaibhāsika school.

2. It refers to all *dharmas* negated by knowledge (vide *asamskṛta-dharma*).

3. It is the final deliverance from bondage. Its essential characteristic is everlastingness. This

state is brought about through the observance of the eightfold path.

प्रतिसर्ग - *Pratisarga* - dissolution

One of the five topics with which a *Purāṇa* should deal. Vide *purāṇa.*

प्रतिषेध - *Pratiṣedha* - denial; negation

Vide *Pratiṣiddha-karma.*

प्रतिषेध्य - *Pratiṣedhya* – that which is negated; counter-correlate

1. It is also known as the *partiyogin*.

2. Vide *pratiyogin* and *anuyogin.*

प्रतिषेधविषय - *Pratiṣedha-viṣaya* - correlate; the locus of a negated object

1. It is also called *anuyogin.*

2. Vide *anuyogin* and *pratiyogin.*

प्रतिषिद्धकर्म - *Pratiṣiddha-karma* - prohibited actions

Those actions which give sorrow as their results.

Vide *karma.*

प्रतिष्ठा – *Pratiṣṭhā* - gross matter; earth

प्रतिष्ठापना - *Pratiṣṭhāpanā* - a logical category found in Nyāya-Vaiśeṣika

प्रतितन्त्रसिद्धान्त - *Pratitantra-siddhānta* - an established conclusion held by one school, or similar schools, but opposed by others

Vide *siddhānta.*

प्रतीति - *Pratīti* - perception; apprehension

प्रतीत्यसमुत्पाद - *Pratītyasamutpāda* - dependent origination

1. Literally it means: 'this being given, that follows'.

2. It is the central doctrine of the Buddha upon which his other teachings are based. It explains the causes of suffering, both relatively and absolutely. It is comprised of twelve links (*nidānas* which perpetuate the wheel of causation. Those links which are due to one's past life are: ignorance (*avidyā*) and predispositions (*saṁskāra*). Those links which are due to one's present life are: consciousness (*vijñāna*), name and form (*nāmarūpa*), the six fields or the five sense organs and the mind along with their objects (*ṣaḍāyatana*), sense-object contact (*sparśa*), feeling (*vedana*), craving (*taṇha*), and attatchment (*upādāna*). Those links which are due to one's future life are: coming-to-be (*bhāva*), rebirth (*jāti*), and old age and death (*jarāmaraṇa*). From each antecedent factor comes the succeeding one and thus together they form the individual's chain of bondage to the wheel of birth and death. They have four characteristics: objectivity, necessity, invariability, and conditionality.

प्रतियोगिन् - *Pratiyogin* - counter-correlate

1. When two things are related, the correlate exists in the locus, e.g., between a pot and the floor, the pot is the correlate.

2. The object of non-existence is predicated is called the counter-correlate. The non-existence in the locus is known as the counter-correlate.

3. It is also called ***pratiṣedhya.***

4. Vide ***anu-yogin.***

प्रत्यभिज्ञा - *Pratyabhijñā* - recognition.

1. A name for Kashmir Śaivism.

2. The re-cognition or awareness that the individual is identical with the Universal.

3. The means of liberation in Kashmir Śaivism. It is the way that the individual realizes its identity with Lord *Śiva.*

प्रत्यगात्मन् - *Pratyagātman* - the Self whose existence is understood only by turning one's vision inward; the indwelling self

प्रत्यग्दृष्टि - *Pratyag-dṛṣṭi* - inward vision

प्रत्याहार - *Pratyāhāra* - withdrawal of the senses from their objects

1. Control of the mind. It is one of the eight limbs of *rāja-yoga.* By the disciplining of the senses, the mind will be tamed.

2. Literally it means: 'gathering towards oneself'.

3. Vide *aṣṭāṅga-yoga.*

प्रत्यक् - *Pratyak* - internal; subjective

प्रत्यक्ष - *Pratyakṣa* - perception

1. It is a valid means of knowledge (***pramāṇa***) for every school of Indian philosophy.

2. According to Nyāya, it is knowledge generated by sense-object contact. Later Naiyāyikas

defined it as direct apprehension so as to include God's perception and the super-normal perception of *yogins*.

3. What distinguishes it from all other types of cognition is its immediacy. Two stages are distinguished: indeterminate (*nirvikalpa*) and determinate (*savikalpa*). Generally the former is bare awareness of an object while the latter is a cognition of an object that is qualified. The former gives isolated sense-data while the latter compounds these elements and subject-predicate knowledge arises. (For further distinctions, vide *nirvikalpa-pratyakṣa* and infra).

4. The Nyāya school gives six normal (*laukika*) types of perception: *saṁyoga*, *samyukta-samavāya*, *samyukta-samaveta-samavāya*, *samavāya*, *samaveta-samavāya*, and *viśeṣaṇa-viśeṣya-bhāva* or *viśeṣaṇatā*. It also lists three super-normal (*alaukika*) types: *sāmānya-lakṣaṇa*, *jñāna-lakṣaṇa*, and *yogaja*.

6. According to Sāṅkhya, there are two stages in perception, the *nirvikalpa* and the *savikalpa*, but its explanation is different from that of the Nyāya school. Sāṅkhya says that the former is a vague awareness which later becomes clear and distinct through analysis, synthesis, and interpretation. Thus Sāṅkhya does not adhere to a mosaic theory of knowledge but more of an organic growth from the simple to the complex.

7. The Mīmāṁsā agrees with Nyāya's definition, but interprets the two stages in perception differently. Indeterminate perception is simple observation or mere awareness. This knowledge is vague and indefinite. Class characteristics and specific

features are not recognized here whereas they are noted only in determinate perception. Indirect perception is not what has to be inferred on the basis of the subsequent determinate perception as in Nyāya, but is an experienced stage of perception itself. Also Nyāya accepts super-normal modes of perception while Mīmāṁsā does not. To be perceived, an object must be present and fit to be perceived. Thus the sense organs have their limitations and what is beyond them is open only for the *Veda* to reveal.

8. According to Viśiṣṭādvaita, *nirvikalpa* perception is not perception of a mere, unqualified 'that'. All knowledge, in this school, is of a qualified object. Thus indeterminate perception is perception for the first time, while *savikalpa* perception signifies perception of the same object on the second and subsequent occasions.

9. Dvaita accepts only *savikalpa* perception. Knowledge being both unqualified and objectless is held to be impossible. Perception is defined as knowledge generated by sense-object contact with both the sense organ and the object, free from defects.

10. The Buddhists accept only *nirvikalpa* perception.

11. The Nyāya school recognizes both external (*bāhya*) and internal (*manasa*) perceptions.

12. According to Jainism, there are two types of perception: with sense organs (*vyāvahārika*) and without sense organs (*nīja*). *Nīja* is of two types: imperfect (*vikala*) or *avadhi* and *manaḥparyāya-jñāna*; and perfect (*sakala*) or *kevala-jñāna*.

13. According to Advaita, *nirvikalpa* perception presents the Absolute *Brahman* alone as its cognition. It is knowledge which does not apprehend any relatedness of the substantive and its qualifying attribute. Thus it is not necessarily the first or initial perception, but any perception which is indeterminate. Examples of this include: 'Thou art that' (*tat tvam asi*) or 'This is that Devadatta' (*so'yaṁ devadattaḥ*).

प्रात्यक्षिक - *Prātyakṣika* - perceptual

प्रत्यक्त्व - *Pratyaktva* - self-awarencss

प्रत्यवमर्श - *Pratyavamarśa* - retrospection, *viz.* the main diefference between the indeterminate and determinate perceptions in Viśiṣṭādvaita

प्रत्यवाय - *Pratyavāya* - sin

प्रत्यय - *Pratyaya* - suffix; condition

प्रवाहविच्छेद - *Pravāha-viccheda* - uninterrupted tradition

प्रवर्तन - *Pravartana* - imposition

प्रवृत्ति - *Pravṛtti* - action; endeavour; effort

1. The path of active involvement in the world. It is attatched action.

2. According to the Vaiśeṣika school, it is an effort to possess some object.

प्रवृत्तिविज्ञान - *Pravṛtti-vijñāna* - evolving consciousness; sense experience

This is the mind of the common people according to the Yogācāra. It is a product of the storehouse consciousness (*ālaya-vijñāna*).

प्रयत्न - *Prayatna* - effort; conscious activity

According to the Vaiśeṣika school, it has three distinctions: *pravṛtti, nivṛtti* and *jīvanyoni* — effort for possessing some object; effort to get rid of something; and activity for procreation.

प्रयोगनिर्देश - *Prayoga-nirdeśa* - actual discrimination as present, past, and future

Vide *nirdeśa.*

प्रयोजन - *Prayojana* - purpose: the aim of a work

1. It is one of the sixteen categories of the Nyāya school.

2. Vide *padārtha* and chart no 6.

प्रेम - *Prema* - love

प्रेत्यभाव - *Pretyabhāva* - cycle of birth and death

प्रेयस् - *Preyas* - pleasing; worldly gain

Vide *śreyas.*

प्रियम् - *Priyam* - dear; pleasing

प्रोसधोपवास - *Prosadhopavāsa* - a Jaina ethical code of conduct dealing with fasting procedures

पृथक्त्व - *Pṛthakatva* - mutual difference; separateness

पृथ्वी - *Pṛthvī* - the earth

Vide *mahā-bhūta.*

पुच्छब्रह्मवादिन् - *Puccha-brahma-vādin* - one who holds that *Brahman* is the indeterminate bliss and not the blissful (in the *ānandamayādhikaraṇa*)

पुद्गल - *Pudgala* - matter

1. It is a real, non-conscious, independent substance according to Jainism. It is uncreated and eternal. It is that which undergoes modifications by combinations and dissociations.

2. It is of four types: aggregate (*skandha*), aggregate occupying space (*skandha-deśa*), aggregate occupying limited space (*skandha-pradeśa*), and atoms (*paramāṇu*).

पुण्य - *Puṇya* - merit; actions which produce happiness

Vide *ajīva*.

पूरक - *Pūraka* - in-breathing; inhalation

Vide *prāṇāyāma*.

पुराण - *Purāṇa* - ancient

The legendary histories of India and the repositories of popular religious creeds. They are traditionally supposed to deal with five topics: creation (*sarga*), dissolution (*pratisarga*), lineage (*vaṁśa*), epochs (*manvantarāṇi*), and the legends of future lineage (*vaṁśānucaritam*). Eighteen major *Purāṇas* are divided into three categories. Those which are *sāttvic* and honor *Viṣṇu* are: *Viṣṇu*, *Bhāgavata*, *Padma*, *Nāradīya*, *Garuḍa*, and *Varāha*. Those which are *rājasic* and honour *Brahmā* are: *Brāhma*, *Brahmavaivarta*, *Brahmāṇḍa*, *Vāmana*, *Mārkaṇḍeya*, and *Bhaviṣya*. Those which are *tāmasic* and honour *Śiva* are: *Śiva* (*Vāyu*), *Matsya*, *Liṅga*, *Skanda*, *Agni*, and *Kūrma*.

पुरीषह - *Purīṣaha* - bearing all pains arising from hunger, thirst, cold, etc. with fortitude

पूर्ण - *Pūrṇa* - full; complete

पुरुष - *Puruṣa* - spirit; individual soul

1. One of the two basic categories of the Sāṅkhya system. It is pure consciousness, unattached and unrelated to anything. It is non-active, unchanging, eternal, and pure. There are an infinite number of individual souls.

2. According to Kashmir Śaivism, it is enveloped in the five sheaths of: *kāla*, *niyati*, *rāga*, *vidyā*, and *kalā*. It is the universal Self appearing under limitation as the many individual souls.

3. According to Advaita, it is fundamentally one. It is the eternal witness, the modificationless, the one who knows the body. Really speaking, the *paramātman* is the one and only *puruṣa*.

4. The *Puruṣa-sūkta* describes the primal *puruṣa* as thousand-headed, thousand-eyed, thousand-footed, immanent and transcendent, covering the earth on all sides and extending beyond the length of ten fingers, all that is, has been, and will be. One-fourth of him is all beings, three-fourths of him are what is immortal in heaven.

पुरुषकार - *Puruṣakāra* - divine mediator; personal effort

According to Viśiṣṭādvaita, Lakṣmī has the role of *puruṣakāra*.

पुरुषतन्त्र - *Puruṣa-tantra* - person-dependent

1. There are three options open to a doer of an action: a person may do the action, may not do the action, or may do the action otherwise.

2. Action (*karma*) is person-dependent while knowledge, according to Advaita, is object-dependent. Vide *vastu-tantra*.

पुरुषार्थ - *Puruṣārtha* - the four goals of human life

1. The Hindu theory of values. They are: wealth (*artha*), desire (*kāma*), righteousness (*dharma*), and liberation (*mokṣa*). The first is the economic value; the second is the psychological value; the third is the moral value; and the fourth is the spiritual value.

2. Wealth (*artha*), the economic value, and desire (*kāma*), the hedonistic or acquisitive value are the secular values of life. *Dharma* tells how the secular life should be lived. It is the ethical or moral value. And along with *mokṣa*, it is a spiritual value. *Dharma* is the instrumental value leading to *mokṣa*. All the four values are truly vital and must be integrated. *Artha* and *kāma* are means-values or instrumental values for life's goal. *Dharma* is the regulative and integrating value. *Mokṣa* is an intrinsic and end value.

3. *Puruṣārtha* may be viewed from two aspects: primarily it signifies something to be attained for its own sake. This is the intrinsic aspect. It also involves whatever serves as a means to it. This is the instrumental aspect. Thus it may be defind as an end which is consciously sought to be accomblished either for its own sake or for the sake of utilizing it as a means to the accomplishment of a further end.

पुरुषोत्तम - *Puruṣottama* - the supreme self; the Lord

Cf. "*uttamaḥ puruṣastvanyaḥ paramātmetyudāhṛtaḥ*" (*Gītā*)

पूर्व - *Pūrva* - the fourteen canonical books of the Jainas

1. All of these works are lost now.
2. Vide *Aṅgas.*

पूर्वपक्ष - *Pūrva-pakṣa* - *prima facie* view; the opponent's view

Generally, in an Indian philosophical work, first, the opponent's view is given; and then, after this view is rejected, one gives the final view (*siddhānta*).

पूर्ववत् - *Pūrvavat* - like the previous

A classification of *vīta* inference. It proceeds from a perceived cause to an unperceived effect, e.g., the inference of rain from the perception of dark, heavy clouds (vide *anumāna*). It is based on the observed concomitance of the specific major and middle terms.

R

राग - *Rāga* - attachment; greed; passion

1. Vide *pañca-kañcuka.*

2. Vide *kleśa.*

रजस् - *Rajas* - active; energy; passion

One of the three *guṇas.* Vide *guṇa.*

रजतत्वप्रकारकज्ञान - *Rajatatva-prakāraka-jñāna* - silverness-adjunct-cognition

रजतत्वप्रकारकव्यवहार - *Rajatatva-prakāraka-vyavāhara* - silverness-adjunct-edition

रक्षक - *Rakṣaka* - redeemer

रक्षिष्यतीति विश्वासः - *Rakṣiṣyatīti-viśvāsaḥ* - to have firm faith that *Īśvara* will save

Vide *prapatti.*

रस - *Rasa* - taste; savour; juice; nectar of delight

1. One of the five elements. (Vide *tanmātra*). It is of six kinds: sweet, acid, salt, pungent, astringent, bitter.

2. The essence of things. The delight of existence.

3. The supreme delight produced in the mind of an appreciator of a work of art whose content is

an emotion (*bhāva*). It results from the interaction of the objective factors (*vibhāva, anubhāva* and *vyabhicāribhāva*) and the subjective factor, a qualified appreciator (*sahṛdaya*) with their *sthāyibhāva*. The *sthāyibhāva* is the material cause of *rasa*. The *vibhāva, anubhāva*, and *vyabhicāribhāva* are together regarded as the efficient cause of *rasa*. These latter three excite, articulate, and develop the *sthāyibhāva* of the spectator. *Vibhāvas* are of two kinds: *ālambana* and *uddīpana*. The former is made up of the human element and the latter of the natural element in the situation. The former is the main excitant and the latter a contributory one. *Anubhāvas* are of two types: *sāttivikabhāvas* which cannot be produced at will, and all of the other emotions which can be produced at will. *Vyabhicāribhāva* (also called *sañcāribhāva*) is an emotion which accompanies the *sthāyibhāva*.

4. According to Indian aesthetics, there are eight main types of experince: *śṛṅgāra* (the *rasa* based on conjugal love), *hāsya* (the *rasa* based on mirth), *karuṇa* (the *rasa* based on sorrow), *raudra* (the *rasa* based on anger), *vīra* (the *rasa* based on fortitude), *bhayānaka* (the *rasa* based on fear), *bībhatsa* (the *rasa* based on disgust), and *adbhuta* (the *rasa* based on wonder). Sometimes it is said that there are two more *rasas*: *śānta* and *bhakti*.

5. According to Nyāya-Vaiśeṣika, taste is of various types: sweet, sour, pungent (*kaṭu*), astringent (*kaṣāya*), and bitter (*tikta*).

रसना - *Rasanā* - sense of taste

Vide *jñānendriya*.

रसातल - *Rasātala* - hell

1. The nether pole of *mahar-loka.* It is a place of sense enjoyment.

2. Vide *loka* and *tala.*

रसत्याग - *Rasatyāga* - renunciation of delights

An eternal penance in Jainism.

राशि - *Rāśi* - mode (in Bhartṛprapañca's philosophy)

रथिन् - *Rathin* - the master in the chariot

रेचक - *Recaka* - out-breath; exhalation

Vide *prāṇāyāma.*

ऋग्वेद - *Ṛg Veda* - (Vide *veda*)

ऋजुमति - *Ṛju-mati* - telepathy; straightforward

1. According to Jainism, it is a type of telepathy. It is the ability to know the thoughts of other beings that are located within the range of four to eight *krośas* - to four to eight *yojanas.* Temporally, it is within the range of one life-time to eight past and eight future lives.

2. Vide *manaḥparyāya.*

ऋजुसूत्रनय - *Ṛju-sūtra-naya* - the standpoint of momentariness

1. This standpoint considers only the present form of an object to be significant. It is not concerned with an object's past or future. It refers to the fleeting, mathematical, momentary present. The past is past and the future h as not yet come

so it would be non-sensical to entertain these viewpoints from this perspective.

2. Vide *naya.*

ऋणत्रय – *Ṛṇa-traya* - three congenital debts

ऋषि - *Ṛṣi* – seer; a Vedic sage

Individuals who perceived or recorded the Vedic hymns.

ऋत - *Ṛta* - Truth; Law, Right; Order; 'the course of things'

It is the working out of Truth in action. It is the eternal Order, cosmic as well as moral. It is said to be the basis for the later idea of *karma.*

ऋतु - *Ṛtu* – season

In Indian tradition there are six seasons: spring (*vasanta*), summer (*grīṣma*), rainy (*varṣa*), autumn (*śarad*), cloudy (*hemanta*), and winter (*śiśira*).

रूढि - *Rūḍhi* - conventional sense of a word; cf. *samabhirūḍha*

रुद्र - *Rudra* - *Śiva*; God

This term refers to Lord *Śiva.* It is traceable to the *Vedas* and said to be derived from *rud* (*drāvayitā,* he who drives away sin or suffering).

रुद्राक्ष – *Rudrākṣa* - bead of *Śiva* or *Rudra*

1. According to Śaivism, it is the seed which emanates from the eye of *Śiva,* and depicts his grace.

2. Vide *aṣṭa-āvaraṇa.*

रूप - *Rūpa* - form; aggregate; body; matter; sight; colour

1. One of the five aggregates. (Vide ***skandha***).

2. One of the five subtle essence of the elements. (Vide *tanmātra*).

3. According to Nyāya-Vaiśeṣika, the colours are: white, blue, yellow, red, green, brown, and variegated (*citra*). Colour belongs only to earth, water, and fire.

4. Vide *saṁskṛta-dharma*.

रूपारूप - *Rūpārūpa* - form and formless

S

शब्द - *Śabda* - verbal testimony; sound; word

1. It is one of the valid means of knowledge. (Vide *pramāṇa*).

2. It is one of the five subtle essence of the elements. (Vide *tanmātra*).

3. According to Nyāya, it is the testimony of a trustworthy person; one who knows the truth and communicates it correctly.

4. According to Advaita, the truth revealed by *śabda* is the fundamental unity of Being.

5. According to Mīmāṁsā, its purport lies in the injunctive texts of the ritual sections.

6. According to Nyāya-Vaiśeṣika, sound is a quality perceived by the ear. It belongs only to ether and is of two kinds: noise and alphabet, viz. inarticulate noise (*dhvani*) and articulate alphabetic sounds (*varṇa*). Mīmāṁsā holds that *varṇa* is eternal while Nyāya maintains that every *varṇa* is produced by God.

शाब्दबोध - *Śābda-bodha* - verbal cognition

शाब्दज्ञान - *Śābda-jñāna* - verbal knowledge

शाब्दमिति - *Śābdamiti* - verbal knowledge

शब्दनय - *Śabda-naya* - the standpoint of synonyms

According to Jainism, this standpoint refers to the significance of the synonymous words one encounters in any language. Despite differences of tense, case, etc., there exists a similarity of meaning; e.g., *kumbha* and *ghaṭa* both refer to the same object; viz., a jar.

2. Vide *naya.*

शब्दतन्मात्र - *Śabda-tanmātra* - subtle sound (the subtle element of ether)

शब्दवृत्ति - *Śabda-vṛtti* - significative force

शब्दाध्याहारवाद - *Śabdādhyāhāra-vāda* - theory of supplying the eliptical word

सबीज - *Sabīja* - with attributes

सच्चिदानन्द - *Saccidānanda* - existence-knowledge-bliss

1. According to Viśiṣṭādvaita, they are the attributes of *Brahman.*

2. According to Advaita, it is the very essence of *Brahman.*

सदाचार - *Sadācāra* - one should work for one's livelihood, be righteous, and help others

Vide *pañcācāra.*

सादाख्य - *Sādākhya* - the experience of Being

According to Vīra Śaivism, it is a name for the formless form. It is also called *Sadāśiva.* It comes into being when the *Śiva-tattva* comes into contact with the five *śakits*: *Śiva-sādākhya*, *Amūrta-sādākhya*, *Mūrta-sādākhya*, *Kartṛ-sādākhya*, and *Karma-sādākhya.*

षडङ्गयोग - *Ṣaḍaṅga-yoga* - six-fold *yoga*

It is a type of *yoga* referred to in the *Maitrī Upaniṣad.* The six limbs are: *prāṇāyāma, pratyāhāra, dhyāna, dhāraṇā,* and *samādhi.*

सदसद्विलक्षण - *Sad-asad-vilakṣaṇa* - what is other than the real (*sat*) and the unreal (*asat*)

Vide *anirvacanīya.*

सदसत् - *Sad-asat* - real-cum-unreal

षडायतन - *Ṣaḍāyatana* - the six sense organs

1. According to Buddhism, it is one of the links in the causal chain of existence.

2. Vide *pratītya-samutpāda.*

षड्भावविकार - *Ṣaḍbhāva-vikāra* - the six changes applicable to a positive entity

These are: origination, existence, growth, maturity, decline, and death.

षड्दर्शन - *Ṣaḍ-darśana* - the six orthodox schools (*āstika*) of Indian philosophy

They are: Nyāya, Vaiśeṣika, Sāṅkhya, Yoga, Mīmāṁsā, and Vedānta.

साधन - *Sādhana* - self-effort; spiritual discipline; means; the way

1. Generally the means to release.

2. Jainism: it is the *tri-ratna* comprised of right faith, right knowledge, and right conduct.

3. Buddhism: it is the eightfold path.

4. Sāṅkhya: it is discrimination between *puruṣa* and *prakṛti*.

5. Yoga: it is the eight-limbed *yoga* (*aṣṭāṅga-yoga*).

6. Mīmāṁsā: it is action (*karma*).

7. Advaita: it is ultimately knowledge (*jñāna*), with the preliminary aids of the fourfold prerequisites (*sādhana-catuṣṭaya*) and *śravaṇa*, *manana*, and *nididhyāsana*.

8. Viśiṣṭādvaita: it is *karma*- and *jñāna-yogas*, ultimately culminating in devotion (*bhakti-yoga*). The other accepted path is total surrender (*prapatti*).

9. Dvaita: it is discrimination followed by knowledge, followed with by grace (*vairāgya*, *jñāna*, *māhātmya-jñāna*, *niṣkāma-karma*, *bhakti*, and *prasāda*).

10. Śaiva Siddhānta: it is *caryā*, then *kriyā*, then *yoga*, and finally *jñāna*.

11. Vīra Śaivism: it is *aṣṭa-āvaraṇa* and *pañca-ācāra*.

12. Kashmir Śaivism: it is *pratyabhijñā* with the prerequisites of *anupāya*, *śāmbhavopāya*, *śāktopāya*, and *āṇavopāya*.

13. Śivādvaita: it is contemplation.

साधनभक्ति - *Sādhana-bhakti* - devotion with effort

1. One of the two types of devotion according to Viśiṣṭādvaita. It is devotion engendered by spiritual exercises. It consists of the eight-limbed *yoga* (*aṣṭāṅga-yoga*), the sevenfold moral and spiritual requisites (*sādhana-saptaka*), etc. (vide *bhakti*).

2. According to Viśiṣṭādvaita, this path presupposes certain elaborate disciplines in contrast to *phala-bhakti*.

साधनचतुष्टय - *Sādhana-catuṣṭaya* - the fourfold aid to the study of Vedānta; according to Advaita, these four comprise the proximate aid to liberation

They are: the ability to discriminate between the transient and the eternal (*nitya-anitya-vastu-viveka*); the absence of desire for securing pleasure or avoiding pain either here or elsewhere (*iha-amutra-artha-phala-virāga*); the attainment of calmness, temperance, spirit of renunciation, fortitude, power of concentration of mind, and faith (*śama-damādi-sādhana-sampatti*); and the desire for liberation (*mumukṣutva*).

साधनसप्तक - *Sādhana-saptaka* - sevenfold moral and spiritual discipline leading to devotion

According to Viśiṣṭādvaita, these are: discrimination (*viveka*) which is the purification of the body by food that has not become impure either on account of species, abode, or adventitious causes; mental detachment (*vimoka*) which consists of non-attachment to desires; practice (*abhyāsa*) which is the continuous meditation on *Brahman*; action (*kriyā*) which is the performance of the five great sacrifices (*pañca-mahā-yajña*) according to one's capacity; virtues (*kalyāṇa*) which are truthfulness, straightforwardness, compassion, liberality, non-violence, and non-covetousness; cheerfulness (*anavasāda*) which is freedom from dejection; and non-exultation (*anuddharṣa*) which is the absence of exultation.

साधारण - *Sādhāraṇa* - common

A class of fallacious reasoning in which the reason is present in a place where the major term *(sādhya)* is not present, e.g., the mountain has fire because it is knowable.

Vide *savyabhicāra.*

साधारणीकरण - *Sādhāraṇī-karaṇa* - idealization

According to Indian aesthetics, the secret of an artist's achievement consists in idealization. It is the generalizing of the particular. It enables an artist to conform his creation to the highest conception of beauty. It frees the object from ugliness, faults, and mutability.

साधु - *Sādhu* - holy man; saint; virtuous; good

According to Jainism, it is the fourth stage of the ascetic order. They are saints who scrupulously observe the codes of conduct. They are introverts who do not mix freely with others nor give spiritual discourses. Their entire being is fixed on spiritual practice.

साधुमति - *Sādhumati* - good wisdom

Vide *bodhisattva.*

साध्य - *Sādhya* - the subject; the probandum; that which is to be proved; the major term

1. It is the character which is inferred. It is the major term in a syllogism.

2. Vide *anumāna.*

साध्यसम - *Sādhya-sama* - both the reason and the subject are unproved and yet-to-be-proved

A type of fallacious reasoning in which the reason (*hetu*) is unproved and yet-to-be-proved, e.g., "shadow is a substance, because it is characterized by movement." This is unproved because the reason, being characterized by movement, is as unproved as the subject, being a substance.

2. Vide *hetvābhāsa*.

साध्योपाय - *Sādhyopāya* - the means to liberation which has to be effected by the aspirant

षड्लिङ्ग - *Ṣaḍ-linga* - the six marks

There are six marks to be noticed in understanding the scriptures (*Vedas*). They are: beginning and conclusion (*upakrama* and *upasaṁhāra*); novelty (*apūrvatā*); repetition (*abhyāsa*); result or fruit (*phala*); praise or censure (*arthavāda*); and intelligibility in the light of reason (*upapatti*).

सादृश्य - *Sādṛśya* - similarity

1. One of the ten categories of Dvaita. Dvaita claims that inference is made possible because of it.

2. Vide *padārtha* and chart no. 6.

सद्रूप - *Sadrūpa* - existing in a place in a positive relation; perceptible by the senses

षड्विधा शरणागतिः - *Ṣaḍvidhā śaraṇāgatiḥ* - the six limbs of absolute self-surrender

Vide *prapatti*.

सद्विद्या - *Sadvidya* - meditation on *Brahman* as the real (*sat*) without a second, as described in the *Chāndogya Upaniṣad*

सद्विद्यातत्त्व - *Sadvidyā-tattva* - the stage in which the subjective and objective sides of experience are equal according to Kashmir Śaivism.

Vide *tattva.*

षड्विकार - *Ṣaḍvikāra* - the six changes

There are six changes which occur to an object, *viz.*, birth, growth, maturity, decline, death, and dissolution.

सद्योमुक्ति - *Sadyomukti* - immediately on attaining knowledge of the Self (*ātma-jñāna*), one gives up one's physical body

According to Advaita, it is complete liberation from the embodied state which occurs upon realization. The embodied existence is dropped the moment liberation occurs. (*Cf. jīvanmukti*)

सगुण - *Saguṇa* - with attributes; with qualities

सहज - *Sahaja* - natural; innate: inborn

A type of power which exists in things and by virtue of which changes occur, according to Dvaita

सहकारिकारण - *Sahakāri-kāraṇa* - accessory or concomitant cause

The components that help the material cause to produce the effect.

सहोपलम्भ - *Sahopalambha* - simultaneous apprehension

सहृदय - *Sahṛdaya* - a qualified appreciator of a work of art; one of similar heart; connoisseur

According to Indian aesthetics, an appreciator of a work of art has to recreate or reconstruct in his mind the idea implicit in the work. In order to do this, the appreciator himself must be an artist at heart. Thus the appreciator must be a qualified appreciator in order to grasp the true import of a work of art.

शैव - *Śaiva* - a follower of *Śiva*; pertaining to *Śiva*

सजातीय - *Sajātīya* - the difference which exists between two objects belonging to the same class

1. E.g., between one tree and another.

2. Vide *bheda.*

सकल - *Sakala* - determinate

1. A stage of the individual soul, according to Śaiva Siddhānta. (Vide *jīva*). The individual as it exists with the three bonds of *āṇava, karma,* and *māyā* is called *sakala.* Kashmir Śaivism uses the term in the same way.

2. A stage of consciousness — it is the waking state wherein an individual desires to get knowledge.

सकामभावनिर्जरा - *Sakāma-bhāva-nirjarā* - an aspect of *bhāva nirjarā* in which the *karma* particles are destroyed even before their enjoyment is finished

1. It is also called *vipāka.*

2. Vide *nirjarā.*

सकम्पप्रवृत्ति - *Sakampapravṛtti* - halting effort

साकार - *Sākāra* - with form

साकार-उपयोग - *Sākāra-upayoga* - comprehension

1. According to Jainism, it is one of the types of comprehension or understanding.

2. Vide *upayoga*.

शाखा - *Śākhā* - schools; branches

Different branches of the *Brāhmaṇas* which later led to the establishment of the different schools, e.g., *Aitareya*, *Kauṣītakī*, etc.

सख्यम् - *Sakhyam* - friendship

1. One of the emotions (*bhāva*). It is the relationship of friendship.

2. One of the nine forms of devotion. Vide *bhakti*.

सकृद्दर्शन - *Sakṛddarśana* - single observation

सकृदागमिन् - *Sakṛdāgamin* - comes back only once; once returner

A stage in the ethical path of Buddhism wherein an aspirant is only born one more time before attaining perfection.

साक्षात्कार - *Sākṣātkāra* - self-realization; direct experience

साक्षात्प्रतीतिः - *Sākṣāt-pratītiḥ* - direct apprehension

साक्षादुपकारक - *Sākṣād-upakāraka* - direct means (cf. ārādupakāraka)

साक्षिन् - *Sākṣin* - the witness-self; the intuitive faculty

1. According to Dvaita, it is the witness consciousness which is the faculty of direct apprehension or perception. It is the purest sense, without

defects, and always produces absolutely valid knowledge. It indirectly perceives the objects presented to all the other senses, through the senses, as well as directly perceiving the Self (*ātman*), internal organ (*manas*), and the attributes of *manas* (pleasure, pain), ignorance, time, and unmanifested ether. It has two functions: it helps produce knowledge and validity of knowledge. It is the essential attribute of the Self; the Self's own sense-organ.

2. According to Advaita, it is the witness-self and neutral. It is consciousness marked by the internal organ (*antaḥkaraṇa-upahita-caitanya*). It is always in relation to consciousness and the witness thereof. It is self-luminous and ever-present. It corresponds to the *puruṣa* of the Sāṅkhya-Yoga, i.e., as the passive observer of the states of the internal organ. It never appears by itself, but always in association with the internal organ.

साक्षिभास्य - *Sākṣi-bhāsya* - revealed by the witness self
According to Advaita, all things are revealed by the witness-self (*sākṣin*) as assisted by the internal organ (*antaḥkaraṇa*). Three things are revealed by the witness-self alone: *prātibhāsika* objects (e.g., a mirage or a rope/snake), subjective states of the mind (e.g., pleasure or pain), and ignorance (*avidyā*).

साक्षीचैतन्य - *Sākṣī-caitanya* - the witness consciousness

According to Advaita, it is the awareness which underlies and supports all the states of consciousness. It pervades the waking, dreaming, and deep sleep states. It is not a state like one of these three, but being omnipresent, it is the common denominatory which runs throughout them.

शाक्त - *Śākta* - a tradition which, regards *Śakti* as the supreme Deity

It is a philosophy closely allied with Śaivism. It regards *Śakti*, Power, personified as the consort of *Śiva* as the supreme Deity. The basic texts of this school are the *Śākta-āgamas*, also called *Tantras*.

शक्ति - *Śakti* - power; capacity; energy; potency

1. According to Dvaita, it is one of the ten categories (vide *padārtha* and chart no. 6). It is of four kinds: mysterious power (*acintya*), causal or natural (*kāraṇa* or *sahaja*), occasioned (*ādheya*), and word (*pada*).

2. According to Vīra Śaivism, it is of six forms: *cit-śakti*, *parā-śakti*, *ādi-śakti*, *icchā-śakti*, *jñāna-śakti*, and *kriyā-śakti*.

3. According to Śākta philosophy, it is consciousness as dynamic. *Śakti* is one with *Śiva*, being the dynamic aspect as his feminine part.

4. It is the Divine Mother, the latent power of *Śiva*.

5. The potential power latent in human beings is called *kuṇḍalinī-śakti*.

शाक्तोपाय - *Śāktopāya* - one of the steps to liberation per Kashmir Saivism

Vide *upāya*.

सल्लेखन - *Sallekhana* - fasting unto death

According to Jainism, a means to rid oneself of all *karma* particles and to achieve liberation.

सालोक्य - *Sālokya* - to live in the region of God

1. According to Dvaita, it is the first level of release. It is entering the abode of *Viṣṇu* (*Vaikuṇṭha*). Vide *ānanda-tāratamya.*

2. According to Śaiva Siddhānta, the path to release consists of four stages. The first stage is called *dāsa-mārga* and its goal is *sālokya.* In this case, it means residence in the realm of *Śiva* (*Kailāsa*). Vide *mokṣa* per Śaiva Siddhānta and *caryā.*

शम - *Śama* - calmness; tranquillity

1. The method of training the mind by quiet persuasion.

2. Vide *sādhana-catuṣṭaya.*

समभिरूढ - *Samabhirūḍha* - the etymological standpoint

1. This standpoint concentrates on the dissimilarities between words. Even between synonyms, dissimilarity exists when their etymologies are examined. Thus each word has only one exact meaning from this standpoint.

2. It is also said to imply the splitting of words according to their roots. E.g., the literal meaning of the word '*paṅkaja*' is 'one born out of mud' (*paṅka*).

3. Vide *naya.*

शमदमादिसाधनसम्पत्ति - *Śama-damādi-sādhana-sampattiḥ* - the attainment of calmness, temperance, a spirit of renunciation, fortitude, power of concentration of the mind, and faith

1. It comprises: *śama*, *dama*, *uparati*, *titikṣā*, *samādhāna*, and *śraddhā*.

2. Vide *sādhana-catuṣṭaya*.

समाधि - *Samādhi* - concentration; absorption; a calm, desireless fixity; a unifying concentration

1. It is a deep spiritual meditation.

2. A superconscious state where there is complete absorption of the intellect into the object of meditation.

3. A state beyond expression and above all thought. Here speech, and mind cannot reach. It is a state of utter calmness in which consciousness is unwavering.

4. It is a limb of Patañjali's *rāja-yoga*. Vide *aṣṭāṅga-yoga*.

5. According to Yoga, it has four aspects: *vitarka*, *vicāra*. *ānanda*, and *asmitā*. These are called *samādhi* with knowledge of objects (*samprajñāta*). There is also a *samādhi* without any knowledge of objects (*asamprajñāta*).

6. According to Buddhism, it is of three types: *upacāra* or preliminary; *jhāna* or fixed and steady; and *appanā* or achieved meditation.

7. It has also been divided into *samādhi* with the mind (*savikalpa*), and *samādhi* without any mental modifications (*nirvikalpa*).

सामग्री - *Sāmagrī* - collocation; the whole causal apparatus

समाख्या - *Samākhyā* - designation

Vide *aṅgatva-bodhaka-pramāṇa.*

समान - *Samāna* - to breathe equally

1. One of the five vital airs. Vide *prāṇa.*

2. It is the life-breath which controls digestion and assimilation. It keeps an equilibrium in the body. It is located in the region of the navel.

सामानाधिकरण्य - *Sāmānādhikaraṇya* - the principle of grammatical co-ordination

1. The principle which states that one entity may have two aspects. It shows identity as well as difference. It cannot be used wherein there is complete identity or complete difference between the words.

2. Rāmānuja used it to explain his key concept of *apṛthak-siddhi.* According to Rāmānuja, the grammar of language is the grammar of reality. Two terms 'blue' and 'lotus' have distinct meanings but refer to same substance. Distinction is not denied, while at the same time, the organic unity of the whole is affirmed.

3. Advaita uses the same concept to show 'non-difference' or 'identity'.

समानजातीयद्रव्यपर्याय - *Samāna-jātīya-dravya-paryāya* - a type of mode which is the result of the combination of inanimate substances

Vide *paryāya.*

समानतन्त्र - *Samāna-tantra* - allied systems

E.g., Sāṅkhya-Yoga; Nyāya-Vaiśeṣika, Mīmāṁsā-Vedānta.

समन्वय - *Samanvaya* - harmony

सामान्य - *Sāmānya* - generality; class, concept; genus

1. One of the seven categories of the Vaiśeṣika system. (Vide *padārtha* and chart no. 6). It is the generic feature that resides in all the members of a class. It is one, eternal, and resides in the many. It is the common characteristic by virtue of possessing which an individual becomes a member of a class. It is perceptible in perceptible things and imperceptible in imperceptible things. It has a reality of its own, independent of the particulars. It is of different grades: the highest (*para*) is 'being' (*sattā*). The lowest (*apara*) i.e., 'potness' and the intermediate grades (*parāpara*) i.e., 'earthness' are less general than 'being'. It is said to reside in substances, qualities, and activities. The relation between it and an individual is inherence (*samavāya*).

2. According to Jainism, it is neither an abstract entity nor an imposition of the mind, but represents only the accession of similar qualities by a similar development of qualities of atoms forming an aggregate. Vide *ūrdhva-sāmānya.*

3. According to Dvaita, it is one of the ten categories (*padārtha*). It is the nature which characterizes a class. It is eternal in eternal substances and non-eternal in non-eternal substances.

सामान्यलक्षण - *Sāmānya-lakṣaṇa* - relation by generality or class-nature

1. One of the super-normal modes of perception posited by the Nyāya school. It is the relation which is characterized by generality or class-

nature by which, when one perceives a particular of a class, one also perceives, in general, the other particulars; e.g., to see a cow is to see 'cowness' which is present in all cows. Vide *pratyakṣa* per Nyāya.

2. According to the Vaibhāṣika and the Sautrāntika, it is the conceptual elements added by the mind in an act of perception. What is actually perceived is only the bare particular (*svalakṣaṇa*). To the bare particular the mind adds subjective determinations which are of five types: generality (*jāti*), quality (*guṇa*), action (*karma*), name (*nāma*), and substance (*dravya*).

सामान्यतोदृष्ट - *Sāmānyatodṛṣṭa* - inference based on non-causal uniformity

1. A classification of *vīta* inference based on the distinctions of pervasion (*vyāpti*). In this type the inference is based on non-causal uniformity, e.g., when one sees an animal having horns, one infers that it must possess cloven hoofs. It gives knowledge of an imperceptible or unperceived object. It is based, not upon a relation of causality, but upon the fact that the means and the end are always found together.

2. Vide *anumāna*.

सामान्यविशेष - *Sāmānya-viśeṣa* - generic differentia

समाप्ति - *Samāpti* - completion

सामरस्य - *Sāmarasya* - homogeneity (Vide *samāveśa*)

सामर्थ्य - *Sāmarthya* - power; capacity

समष्टि - *Samaṣṭi* - cosmic; collective

समसमुच्चय - *Sama-samuccaya* – simultaneous combination
Vide *jñāna-karma-samuccaya.*

समस्या - *Samasyā* - a type of false knowledge found in *mati* and *sṛta* knowledge which admits of doubt and suspicion

समत्व - *Samatva* - equality; equanimity

समवाय - *Samavāya* – inherence

1. According to Nyāya, it is a normal mode of sense relation in which there is inherence; e.g., contact with sound which inheres in the sense of hearing. Vide *sannikarṣa.*

2. According to Vais'eṣika, it is the intimate relation between inseparables. It is an eternal relationship which is inherent in the objects related. It exists between five kinds of inseparables: substance and quality, substance and activity, particular and generality, eternal substance and particularity, and whole and parts. Of these relations, at least one of the entities cannot remain without its relation to the other. Vide *ayutasiddha.*

3. Vide *padārtha.*

समवायिकारण - *Samavāyi-kāraṇa* - inherent cause

1. The inherent cause is that in which the effect inheres when it is produced; e.g., threads are the inherent cause of cloth.

2. Vide *kāraṇa.*

समवायिन् - *Samavāyin* - constitutive

सामवेद - *Sāma Veda* – (Vide *Veda*)

समावेश - *Samāveśa* - attainment of the original position

The final attainment of the individual according to Kashmir Śaivism. It also signifies the state wherein *Śiva* and *Śakti* are identical (*sāmarasya*).

समवेतसमवाय - *Samaveta-samavāya* - inherence in that which inheres

1. E.g., contact with soundness which inheres in sound, which in turn inheres in the sense of hearing.

2. A normal mode of sense-relation according to the Nyāya school. Vide *sannikarṣa.*

समय - *Samaya* - time (divided into, and perceived as, moments, hours, days, etc.); agreement

1. According to Jainism, this is the appearance of the unchangeable time in so many different forms.

2. Vide *kāla.*

समयाचार्य - *Samayācārya* - the foremost (noteworthy) Śaivite saints (Nāyaṉmārs)

They are: Appar, Sundarar, Sambandhar, and Māṇikkavācakar.

सामयिक - *Sāmayika* - a Jaina ethical code of conduct

It is the practising of being one with the Reality.

सामयिकाभाव - *Sāmayikābhāva* - temporary non-existence

सम्बन्ध - *Sambandha* - relation

Vide *saṁyoga*, *samavāya*, *svarūpa-sambandha* and *tādātmya.*

सम्बन्धोक्ति - *Sambandhokti* - a prose portion of a work which introduces new ideas

सम्भव - *Sambhava* - inclusion

1. The process of knowing something, not directly or immediately, but indirectly on account of its being included in something else which is already known. It is of two types: (i) certain inclusion, e.g., one-thousand includes one-hundred; and (ii) possible inclusion, e.g., a *brahmin* may possess holiness.

2. Vide *pramāṇa*

शाम्भवोपाय - *Śāmbhavopāya* - one of the steps to liberation per Kashmir Śaivism

Vide *upāya*.

सम्भोगकाय - *Sambhogakāya* - the sheath of eonjyment

Vide *tri-kāya*.

संघ - *Saṁgha* - aggregate; compound

1. The substratum of *dharmas* according to the Sarvāstivādins.

2. According to the Vaibhāṣikas, all perceptible things are real and composed of compounds of atoms.

संग्रहनय - *Saṁgraha-naya* - the class point of view

1. According to Jainism, it is the standpoint which is concerned with the general properties or class-characteristics of an object. It is of two kinds: *para-saṁgraha* and *apara-saṁgraha*. While the former is the highest general outlook for which all the objects are part of the extant object the latter dilates upon the general traits of different kinds.

2. Vide *naya.*

संहार - *Saṁhāra* - destruction; dissolution

According to the Śaiva schools, it is one of the five functions of *Śiva.* Vide *Śiva.*

सामीप्य - *Sāmīpya* - nearness to God

1. According to Dvaita, it is the second level of graded release. Vide *ānanda-tāratamya.*

2. According to Śaiva Siddhānta, the path to release consists of four stages. The goal of the path of *satputra-mārga* is to attain the nearness of *Śiva.* Vide *mokṣa* per Śaiva Siddhānta and *kriyā.*

समिति - *Samiti* - moderation

1. According to Jainism, it is of five types: moderation in walking (*trya-samiti*), moderation in speaking (*bhāṣā-samiti*), moderation in bodily wants (*eṣaṇā-samiti*), careful handling of objects (*ādāna-nikṣepaṇa-samiti*), and moderation in answering calls of nature (*utsarga-samiti*).

2. Vide *bhāva-saṁvara.*

संज्ञा - *Saṁjñā* - idea; concept

संज्ञिन् - *Saṁjñin* - rational

सम्प्रदाय - *Sampradāya* - tradition

सम्प्रज्ञात - *Samprajñāta* - a stage in *samādhi* wherein one is conscious of an object

1. The mind functions in this stage, and concentrates on an object of knowledge.

2. Vide *samādhi.*

सम्प्रयुक्त - *Samprayukta* - composite

संसार - *Saṁsāra* - empirical existence; the wheel of birth and death; transmigration

संसर्गाभाव - *Saṁsargābhāva* - relation of non-existence

संसर्ग-अभेद - *Saṁsarga-abheda* - relation of non-duality

One of two types of *abheda-saṁsarga* (*cf. vākyārtha*), according to Advaita. This is oneness by courtesy. There is a oneness with relation, for the oneness exists only on a relational level. The object is one, e.g., a lotus, but it possesses two or more attributes, and/or meanings, viz. lotusness and blueness, etc.

संशय - *Samśaya* - doubt

1. One of the sixteen categories of the Nyāya school. Vide *padārtha* and chart no. 6

2. It is a cognition of conflicting notions with regard to one and the same object. It may be either contradictory [e. g., is it a post or a non-post (*ūha*)], or it may be contrary [e.g., is it a post or is it a man (*anadhyavasāya*)].

3. Doubt is of five types due to whether it arises from: perception of such properties as are common to many things, cognition of a particular and unique property, conflicting testimony, irregularity of perception, and irregularity of non-perception.

4. Doubt is neither true nor false.

संशयज्ञान - *Saṁśaya-jñāna* - doubtful cognition

संशयव्युदास - *Samśaya-vyudāsa* - removal of all doubts about the truth of an inference

सांसिद्धिक - *Sāṁsiddhika* - natural

संस्कार - *Saṁskāra* - predisposition; purificatory rite; consecration

1. It is predisposition from past impressions. It is one of the five aggregates, according to Buddhism. (Vide *skandha*). They are impressions left in the mind after any experience. Vide *vāsanā*.

2. It is one of the twelve links in the causal chain of existence, according to Buddhism. Vide *pratītya-samutpāda*.

3. It is a rite performed with the help of sacred syllables (*mantra*) to restore a thing to its original pure state.

4. It is a purificatory rite in connection with an individual's life in Brahmanical Indian society. It includes the sacred thread ceremony, marriage rites, funeral rites, etc.

5. It is of three kinds: velocity (*vega*), by virtue of which an object possesses motion; feeling (*bhāvanā*) by virtue of which there is memory or recognition; and oscillation (*sthitisthāpakatva*), by means of which a substance returns from a distance to its original position.

संस्कृत - *Saṁskṛta* - coming together; combined cause; compounded thing; perfected; refined; polished

संस्कृतधर्म - *Saṁskṛta-dharma* - ephemeral; impermanent; impure

According to the Vaibhāṣika school, they are of four types: *rūpa*, *citta*, *caitta*, and *cittavip-aryukta*. These are made of subtle elements, physical as well as mental, whose action and reaction cause the creation of the universe. These are born out of the construction of things and are ephemeral, impermanent, and impure. *Rūpa* is of all physical elements and has been divided into eleven kinds: the five external sense organs, their five objects, and *avijñapti*. *Citta* is born out of the interaction of the senses with their objects. All the *saṁskāras* remain in *citta* and it is this which transmigrates from world to world. It changes every moment. *Caitta* are the mental processes releated with *citta*. There are forty-six types of them. *Citta-viparyukta* is the *dharma* which cannot be classified as either *rūpa* or *citta*. It is of fourteen types.

संस्कृति - *Saṁskṛti* – purification

1. The work of action is said to be fourfold and one of those effects is purification.

2. Vide *karma*.

संश्लेष - *Saṁśleṣa* - union

संसृष्टविषय - *Samsṛṣṭa-viṣaya* - relational knowledge

A sentence, by its very nature, conveys relational knowledge, according to Viśiṣṭādvaita. Advaita posits that there are some sentences which convey non-relational knowledge.

समुच्चय - *Samuccaya* - combination

Vide *jñāna-karma-samuccaya*.

समुदायसत्य - *Samudāya-satya* - the apparent reality of the aggregate

The phenomenalistic theory of the Buddhists.

समूहालम्बन - *Samūhālambana* - group cognition

संवाद - *Saṁvāda* - agreement; correspondence

Nyāya holds that validity is ascertained by agreement with the objective facts of experience.

संवादिभ्रम - *Saṁvādi-bhrama* - error which leads to the truth

1. E. g., a man mistakes the light of a gem for the gem itself and thereby actually comes to secure the gem.

2. According to Advaita, God takes the form of *Īśvara* so that a contact may be made which will eventually lead to liberation.

संवर - *Saṁvara* - the Jaina process of reversing the flow of *karma* particles which bind the individual

According to Jainism, it is of two types: *bhāva-samvara* and *dravyasaṁvara*. The former checks one's susceptibility to the inflow of karmic particles while the latter is the actual stoppage of the karmic particles from entering the individual. *Saṁvara* is the means to liberation.

संवेदन - *Saṁvedana* - cognition

संविद् - *Saṁvid* - knowledge

संवृत्ति - *Saṁvṛtti* - a relative point of view

संवृत्ति सत्य - *Samvṛtti-satya* - empirical truth

According to Mādhyamika Buddhism, this is empirical truth. It is of two kinds: worldly truth (*loka-satya*) and illusory truth (*mithyā-satya*). It is the pseudo-truth which relates to the world as phenomena. However, according to Mādhyamika, the distinction between *saṁvṛtti-satya* and *paramārtha-satya* is epistemic and does not import a difference into Reality. The Real is one and non-dual.

सम्यगाजीव - *Samyag-ājīva* - right livelihood

1. One limb of the noble eightfold path of Buddhism.

2. Vide *ārya-aṣṭāṅga-mārga.*

सम्यक्चारित्र - *Samyak-cāritra* - right conduct or character

1. One of the three jewels of Jainism. It is the practice of beneficial activities which lead to liberation and the abstinence of harmful activities which bind the individual. It includes observing the five great vows (*pañca-mahā-vrata*), restraints (*gupti*), *dharma*, etc. It is of two types: partial (*vikala*) for the *śrāvaka* and complete (*sakala*) for the *muni*.

2. Vide *tri-ratna.*

सम्यग्दर्शन - *Samyag-darśana* - right faith

1. One of the three jewels of Jainism. It is considered as the prime cause of liberation as it paves the way for the other two jewels. It is right faith in the seven *tattvas*: *jīva, ajīva, bandha, saṁvara, nirjarā*, and *mokṣa.*

2. Vide *tri-ratna.*

सम्यग्दृष्टि - *Samyag-dṛṣṭi* - right vision

1. One limb of the noble eightfold path of Buddhism.

2. Vide *ārya-aṣṭāṅga-mārga.*

सम्यग्ज्ञान - *Samyag-jñāna* - right knowledge

1. One of the three jewels of Jainism. It is a specialized knowledge of the essence of *jīva* and *ajīva.* It is without any defects and beyond all doubt.

2. Vide *tri-ratna.*

सम्यग्वाक् - *Samyag-vāk* - right speech

1. One limb of the noble eightfold path of Buddhism.

2. Vide *ārya-aṣṭāṅga-mārga.*

सम्यग्व्यायाम - *Samyag-vyāyāma* - right effort

1. One limb of the noble eightfold path of Buddhism.

2. Vide *ārya-aṣṭāṅga-mārga.*

सम्यक्कर्मान्त - *Samyak-karmānta* - right conduct

1. One limb of the noble eightfold path of Buddhism.

2. Vide *ārya-aṣṭāṅga-mārga.*

सम्यक्समाधि - *Samyak-samādhi* - right contemplation

1. One limb of the noble eightfold path of Buddhism.

2. Vide *ārya-aṣṭāṅga-mārga.*

सम्यक्सङ्कल्प - *Samyak-saṅkalpa* - right resolve

1. One limb of the noble eightfold path of Buddhism.

2. Vide *ārya-aṣṭāṅga-mārga.*

सम्यक्स्मृति - *Samyak-smṛti* - right recollection

1. One limb of the noble eightfold path of Buddhism.

2. Vide *ārya-aṣṭāṅga-mārga.*

संयम - *Saṁyama* - self-control; combined practice

The combined practice of the last three steps in *rāja-yoga* (*dhāraṇā, dhyāna,* and *samādhi*).

संयोग - *Saṁyoga* - conjunction

1. A normal mode of sense-relation in Nyāya; *e.g.*, conjunction is represented by the contact of the sense of sight with an object, which is in conjunction therewith.

2. According to Vaiśeṣika, it is of three types: where one substance comes and conjoins with another (*anyatara-karmaja*), where the conjunction takes place as a result of activity on the part of both the substances (*ubhaya-karmaja*), and where the conjunction takes place through the medium of another conjunction (*saṁyogaja*).

3. Vide *sannikarṣa.*

संयोगज - *Saṁyogaja* - a type of conjunction where the conjoining takes place through the medium of another conjunction

Vide *saṁyoga.*

संयुक्तसमवाय - *Saṁyukta-samavāya* - inherence with that which is in conjunction

1. A normal mode of sense-relation according to Nyāya; e. g., contact with the blue colour which is inherent with the sense of sight.

2. Vide *sannikarṣa*.

संयुक्तसमवेतसमवाय - *Saṁyukta-samaveta–samavāya* - inherence in that which inheres in that which is in conjunction

1. A normal mode of sense-relation according to Nyāya; e. g., contact with the blueness which is inherent in the blue colour which inheres in a flower which is in conjunction with the sense of sight.

2. Vide *sannikarṣa*.

सानन्दसमाधि - *Sānanda-samādhi* - a stage in *samādhi* wherein the mind (*citta*) is concentrated on a *sāttvika*, subtle object

This type of meditation renders the mind *sāttvika* and gives bliss.

सनातन - *Sanātana* - eternal; ancient; primeval

सञ्चित - *Sañcita* - *karma*-in-action

1. Actions which have not yet begun to produce their fruits.

2. Vide *karma*, *prārabdha*, and *āgāmin*.

सन्ध्योपासन - *Sandhyopāsana* - the daily worship of God at sunrise, noon, and sunset prescribed for the twice-born

सन्दिग्ध - *Sandigdha* - doubtful middle term

It occurs in an inferential cognition when there is a doubtful connection between the middle term (*hetu*) and the major term (*sādhya*).

सङ्घ - *Saṅgha* - collection

1. The community of monks who followed the Buddha. Its nucleus was formed in the Deer-park when the Buddha gave his first sermon. It is the custodian of the Buddhist *dharma*.

2. The disciples of Mahāvīra formed the Jaina *saṅgha*. They divided themselves into eleven groups called *gaṇa* with each group being led by a *gaṇadhara*.

साङ्ग्रहणी - *Sāṅgrahaṇī* - a type of sacrifice

सञ्ज्ञा - *Saññā* - perception

1. According to Buddhism, one of the five aggregates.

2. Vide *skandha*.

शङ्का - *Śaṅkā* - doubt (vide *saṁśaya*)

सङ्कल्प - *Saṅkalpa* - will; determination

The dynamic energy of *Viṣṇu*.

सङ्कल्पाश्रय - *Saṅkalpāśraya* - dependent on the will of God

साङ्कर्य - *Sāṅkarya* - unwarranted blend

सङ्केत - *Saṅketa* - convention

सङ्क्लेश - *Saṅkleśa* - affliction

सङ्कर्षण - *Saṅkarṣaṇa* - one of the manifestations of *Viṣṇu*

1. His activities are to destroy the universe at the time of dissolution and to propound the Scriptures. He is said to have emanated from *Vāsudeva*, and

Pradyumna emanated from him in turn. He hypostatizes into *Govinda, Viṣṇu* and *Madhusūdana.* He has the qualities of knowledge and strength.

2. Vide *vyūha.*

सङ्खार - *Saṅkhāra* - synthetic mental states and the synthetic functioning of compound sense-affections, compound feeling, and compound concepts

सङ्ख्या - *Saṅkhyā* - number; knowledge

One of the categories of the Prābhākara school. It is one of the qualities of Nyāya-Vaiśeṣika.

साङ्ख्य - *Sāṅkhya* - the philosophical school which enumerates the ultimate object of knowledge

Kapila was the founder of the system, Sāṅkhya and the author of the *Sāṅkhya-sūtra.* The earliest authoritative book on classical Sāṅkhya is the *Sāṅkhya-kārikā* of Īśvarakṛṣṇa. The school professes dualistic realism with its two eternal realilies, being spirit (*puruṣa*) and primordial matter(*prakṛti*). The term 'Sāṅkhya' means both 'discriminative knowledge' and 'enumeration'.

सङ्कोच - *Saṅkoca* - contraction

सङ्क्षेप *Saṅkṣepa* - an external penance in Jainism

सन्मात्रवादिन् - *Sanmātra-vādin* - one who holds the theory of the Aboslute as mere Being

सन्निधान - *Sannidhāna* - proximity

सन्निधि - *Sannidhi* - proximity

1. One of the causes which brings about a valid cognition from a proposition. It consists in the

articulation of words without undue delay. It is also called *āsatti*.

2. Vide *ākāṅkṣā*, *āsatti*, *yogyatā* and *tātparya*.

सान्निध्य - *Sānnidhya* - existing in the proximity of God

1. According to Dvaita, one of the four levels of release (vide *sāmīpya* and *ānanda-tāratamya*).

2. According to Śaiva Siddhānta, it is the goal of the *satputra-mārga* in the stage of *kriyā*. (Vide *mokṣa* per Śaiva Siddhānta)

सन्निकर्ष - *Sannikarṣa* - sense-object contact

1. According to Nyāya, sense-object contact may be of six normal (*laukika*) modes of sense-object relation. This is due to the fact that contact occurs between substances, qualities, class-nature, etc. These six modes are: conjunction (*saṁyoga*), inherence in that which is in conjunction (*samyukta-samavāya*), inherence in that which inheres in that which is in conjunction (*samyukta-samaveta-samavāya*), inherence (*samavāya*), inherence in that which inheres (*samaveta-samavāya*), adjunct-substantive relation (*viśeṣaṇa-viśeṣya-bhāva* or *viśeṣaṇatā*).

2. According to Nyāya, there are also three super-normal (*alaukika*) modes of sense-object relation: relation by generality (*sāmānya-lakṣaṇa*), relation by previous knowledge (*jñāna-lakṣaṇa*), and the perceptive faculty of *yogins* or that is cultivated by *yoga* (*yogaja*).

सन्निपत्य उपकारक - *Sannipatya-upakāraka* - a subsidiary action which is componently helpful to something else; an accessory

सन्न्यास - *Sannyāsa* - monk-hood; renunciantion

The stage of renouncing all worldly possessions and ties. The last stage of human life (vide *āśrama*). It is of two kinds: *vividiṣā-sannyāsa* or renunciation preceded by a sense of detatchment from the world, and *vidvat-sannyāsa* which is renunciation *par excellence* and preceded by the dawn of realization of the Self. In the former, certain rules must be observed, but in the latter, there is absolute freedom.

सान्त - *Sānta* - having an end

शान्त - *Śānta* - peace

Vide *para-bhakti*.

सन्तानाचार्य - *Santanācārya* - the philosophical preceptors of Śaiva Siddhānta

They are: Meykaṇḍār, Aruḷnandi Śivācārya, Umāpati, and Sambandhar.

शान्ति - *Śānti* - peace

सन्तोष - *Santoṣa* - contentment

सपक्ष - *Sapakṣa* - similar instance

1. That which possesses similar attributes of the subject which is desired to be inferred. The subject is known for certain in this case.

2. Vide *pakṣa* and *vipakṣa*.

सप्रपञ्च - *Saprapañca* - the cosmic view of the Absolute

The *Upaniṣads* conceived of *Brahman* as the all-inclusive ground of the universe as well as the reality of which the universe is but an appearance (*niṣprapañca*). The theistic traditions hold the cosmic view.

सप्तभङ्गीनय - *Saptabhaṅgī-naya* - the seven propositions

Vide *syād-vāda.*

सप्तप्रमातृ - *Sapta-pramātṛ* - the seven stages of the individual soul in Kashmir Śaivism

They are: *sakala, pralayākala, vijñānākala, mantra, mantreśvara, mantramāheśvara,* and *śiva.* The individual endowed with three *malas* is called *sakala*; endowed with *karma* and *āṇava-mala* is called *pralayākala*; endowed with only *āṇava* is called *vijñānākala*; as it passes through the *Śivatattva* it is called *śiva* (or *śāmbhava*); as it passes through the *Śakti-tattva* it is called *śaktija*; as it passes through the *Sadāśiva* or *sādākhya-tattva* it is called *mantramāheśvara*; as it passes through the *Īśvara-tattva* it is called *mantreśvara*; and as it passes through the *Sadvidyā-tattva* it is called *mantra.*

सप्तविध-अनुपपत्ति - *Sapta-vidha-anupapatti* - the seven untenabilities

The seven untenabilities are the seven major objections raised by Rāmānuja against the *avidyā* doctrine propounded by Advaita. They are:

the untenability of the locus:	*āśraya-anupapatti*	
,, concealment:	*tirodhāna-*	,,
,, *avidyā's* nature:	*svarūpa-*	,,
,, indefinability:	*anirvacanīya-*	,,
,, *avidyā* per *pramāṇa*:	*pramāṇa-*	,,
,, that which removes:	*nivartaka-*	,,
,, complete cessation:	*nivṛtti-*	,,

(For details refer to the *Śrībhāṣya* and the *Vedārtha-saṅgraha* of Rāmānuja)

शरण - *Śaraṇa* - protection; refuge

It is also a stage of consciousness. Vide *sthala.*

शरणागति - *Śaraṇāgati* - absolute self-surrender

1. Total dependence on God, leaving everything to His will is called total self-surrender, according to Viśiṣṭādvaita. It is an absolute, unconditional, surrender of the self.

2. Vide *prapatti.*

सर्ग - *Sarga* - creation; canto; chapter

1. One of the five topics which a *Purāṇa* deals with.

2. Vide *purāṇa.*

शरीर - *Śarīra* - body; that which perishes

1. According to Viśiṣṭādvaita, the body is that which is supported by the self, controlled by the self, and exists for the sake of the self. It has eight constituents: the five elements, *prakṛti, ahaṅkāra,* and *mahat.*

2. It is divided into the gross body (*sthūla-śarīra*), the subtle body (*liṅga* or *sūkṣma-śarīra*), and the causal body (*kāraṇa-śarīra*).

3. Advaita calls the causal body the sheath of bliss. The subtle body is composed of the mental sheath, the sheath of the intellect and the sheath of breath. The gross body is composed of the food sheath.

4. According to Nyāya-Vaiśeṣika, the body is made up of earth, water, fire, or air and is not constituted of the five elements as postulated by Sāṅkhya and Advaita.

शारीरकसूत्र - *Śārīraka-sūtra* - a name for the *Brahma-sūtra* since it is concerned with the nature and destiny of the embodied individual soul

शरीर-शरीरिभाव - *Śarīra-śarīri-bhāva* - the relation subsisting between the body and the soul (according to Viśiṣṭādvaita)

शरीरशरीरिसम्बन्ध - *Śarīra-śarīri-sambandha* - the vital relation of the body and the indwelling soul, between the finite self and the Absolute, as expounded by Rāmānuja

शरीरव्यापार - *Śarīra-vyāpāra* - physical effort

शरीरेन्द्रिय - *Śarīrendriya* - the psycho-physical complex of the individual

शरीरिन् - *Śarīrin* - the individual soul, Brahman (according to Viśṣṭādvaita)

सारूप्य - *Sārūpya* - to obtain the same form as God

1. According to Dvaita, it is the third level of graded release. (Vide *ānanda-tāratamya* and *mokṣa*).

2. According to Śaiva Siddhānta, it is the goal of *sakhā-mārga* in the stage of *yoga*. (Vide *mokṣa* per Śaiva Siddhānta).

सर्वगत - *Sarvagata* - omnipresent

सर्वज्ञ - *Sarvajña* - omniscient; all knowing

सर्वकर्मत्याग - *Sarva-karma-tyāga* - renunciation of all actions

सर्वास्तिवाद् - *Sarvāsti-vāda* - the theory that all exists

It is an early, realistic school of Buddhism associated with the Theravāda or Hīnayāna tradition. It is also called Vaibhāṣika.

सर्वावधि - *Sarvāvadhi* - clairvoyance

1. An aspect of clairvoyance by which one may perceive the non-sensuous aspects of all the material things of the universe. According to Jainism, it is a type of *vikala* knowledge.

2. Vide *avadhi*.

सर्वज्ञत्व - *Sarvajñatva* - omniscience

सर्वकर्मसन्न्यास - *Sarva-karma-sannyāsa* - renunciation of all actions

It is the renunciation of all actions.

सर्वकर्तृत्व - *Sarva-kartṛtva* - omnipotence

सर्वतन्त्रसिद्धान्त - *Sarvatantra-siddhānta* - an established conclusion accepted by all schools of thought

Vide *siddhānta*.

सर्वोत्तम - *Sarvottama* - the supreme Reality

ससम्बोध - *Sasambodha* - determinate consciousness

सास्मित्समाधि - *Sāsmit-samādhi* - a stage (in *samādhi*) in which the intellect itself becomes the object of concentration

Vide *samādhi*.

शास्त्र - *Śāstra* - Scripture; teaching

The sacred books of Indian thought are divided into four categories: *Śruti*, *Smṛti*, *Purāṇa* and *Ithihāsa*, and *Tantra*.

शास्त्र-अवश्याः - *Śāstra-avaśyāḥ* - those who do nota bide by scriptures

Vide *jīva* per *baddha*.

शास्त्र-वश्याः - *Śāstra-vaśyāḥ* - those individual souls who follow scriptures

1. They are of two kinds: pleasure seekers (*bubhukṣu*) and liberation seekers (*mumukṣu*).

2. Vide *jīva*.

शास्त्रयोनित्वात् - *Śāstra-yonitvā*t - (*brahman* is not known from any other source) since the scriptures (alone) are the means of Brahman knowledge

1. The third *sūtra* of the *Brahmasūtra*.

2. It may also be interpreted as: (*Brahman* is omniscient) because of (Its) being the source of the scriptures.

शाश्वत - *Śāśvata* - eternal

सत् - *Sat* - existence; reality; being

According to Advaita, the Absolute is Being.

सत्-असत् - *Sat-asat* - real-unreal; being-non-being

Vide *sadasat*.

सत्कारणवाद - *Satkāraṇa-vāda* - the theory that cause alone exists

1. Strictly speaking, the Advaita theory of causation should be called this, instead of *satkārya-vāda*.

The cause alone is real and ever-existent, and all effects or phenomena-in-themselves are unreal.

2. Vide *vivarta-vāda.*

सत्कार्यवाद् - *Satkārya-vāda* - the theory of causation that the effect exists prior to its manifestation in a latent state in the cause

1. The causal operation only makes patent the latent effect, according to this theory. It is a theory held by Sāṅkhya school which states that the world is an emanation of *Brahman.* It is also called *pariṇāma-vāda.*

2. Śaiva Siddhānta also holds *satkārya-vāda.*

3. Vide *pariṇāma-vāda* and *asatkārya-vāda.*

सत्कार्यदृष्टि - *Satkārya-dṛṣṭi* - illusory vision

A belief in the permanence of the individual soul. This is an illusory belief according to Buddhism, for there is no soul. The soul is but a name given to an aggregate of elements. It is the first obstacle to an ethical life.

सत्ख्याति - *Sat-khyāti* - cognition of the real

1. A theory of error in which the content of error is, in some sense or other, real. All the systems except the Mādhyamika and Advaita and Dvaita fall into this category, viz., the *ātma-khyāti* of Yogācāra, the *a-khyāti* of Sāṅkhya and Prābhākara Mīmāṁsā, and the *yathārtha khyāti* of Viśiṣṭādvaita.

2. The Viśiṣṭādvaita theory of error is sometimes called *sat-khyāti.* (vide *yathārtha-khyāti*).

3. Vide *khyāti-vāda.*

सत्प्रतिपक्ष - *Satpratipakṣa* - opposable reason

1. A type of fallacious reasoning in which the reason is contradicted by a counter inference. Vide *hetvābhāsa.*

2. Vide *prakaraṇa-sama.*

षट्स्थल - *Ṣaṭ-sthala* - a process in Vīra Śaivism whereby an aspirant grows step by step in various stages until he attains oneness with Lord *Śiva*

1. There are six stages of consciousness: *bhakta-sthala, maheśa-sthala, prasādhi-sthala, prāṇa-liṅgi-sthala, śaraṇa-sthala,* and *aikya-sthala.* To these six correspond six stages of devotion: *sat, niṣṭhā, avadhāna, anubhāva, ānanda,* and *sāmarasa bhaktis.* These six are marked by six stages of *yoga*: *ācāra, guru, jīva, cāra, prasāda,* and *mahāyoga.* Of these 6, the first two are the characteristics of a *tyāga* soul; the next two are of a *bhoga* soul; and the last two are of a *yoga* soul.

2. It is the connecting link between *ātman* and *Brahman*, according to Śrīpati.

3. Vide chart no. 14.

सत्ता - *Sattā* - Being; existence

1. According to the Vaiśeṣika school, being is the highest universal. Vide *jāti.*

2. According to Advaita, Being is the Reality.

सत्त्व - *Sattva* - pure; steady; goodness; illuminating; buoyant; joy; pleasure

One of the three *guṇas.* Its nature is of pleasure and it serves to illumine. Vide *guṇa.*

सत्त्वशून्य - *Sattva-śūnya* - time, in the Viśiṣṭādvaita system, is devoid of all *guṇas*

सत्य - *Satya* - truth

1. The world of the highest truth or being. Vide *loka.*

2. The Golden Age. An age of truth, innocence, and purity. The path to liberation in this age is meditation. Vide *yuga.*

3. One of the abstentions of the *rāja-yoga* discipline. It is absolute truthfulness and abstaining from uttering any falsehood. Vide *yama.*

4. One of the five ethical principles of Jainism. Vide *mahā-vrata.*

सत्यकाम - *Satyakāma* - one who loves the good; the Being with eternal perfections; one whose desires are ever fulfilled

सत्यसङ्कल्प - *Satya-saṅkalpa* - one who wills the true; one whose will is always realised

सत्यस्य सत्यम् - *Satyasya satyam* - the True of the true; real Reality

सत्योपाधि - *Satyopādhi* - true limitation

True limitation is opposed to false limiting adjuncts.

शौच - *Śauca* - purity; cleanliness

1. One of the religious observances of the *rāja-yoga* discipline. Vide *niyama.*

2. One of the ten (*dharmas*), according to Jainism.

सौलभ्य - *Saulabhya* - easy accessibility

According to Viśiṣṭādvaita, God is easily accessible to his devotees.

सावधिक - *Sāvadhika* - limited (opposite to *niravadhika*)

सावकाश - *Sāvakāśa* - that which has had its scope fulfilled

सविचारसमाधि - *Savicāra-samādhi* - a stage in *samādhi* wherein the mind (*citta*) is identified with some subtle object and assumes its form

Vide *samādhi*.

सविकल्प - *Savikalpa* - determinate

Vide *nirvikalpa-pratyakṣa*, and *samādhi*.

सविशेष - *Saviśeṣa* - qualified; with attributes

सविशेष-अभिन्नधर्मिस्वरूपभेदवाद् - *Saviśeṣa-abhinna-dharmi-svarūpa-bheda-vāda* - the Dvaita theory that difference is identical with the essential nature of an object

1. According to Dvaita, difference is the essence of an object, while at the same time providing through attributes, the means of distinguishing the difference from the object as such.
2. Vide *bheda*.

सवितर्कसमाधि - *Savitarka-samādhi* - one of the two types of *vitarka* concentration

1. This is a type of *Samādhi* in which the mind concentrates on objects, remembering their names and qualities.
2. Vide *samādhi* and *vitarka*.

सव्यभिचार - *Savyabhicāra* - a type of fallacious reasoning in which the reason is inconstant

1. For example, when fire is taken as the reason, it turns out inconstant and cannot prove the existence of smoke, for even where there is no smoke there may be fire.

2. It is divided into three types: common (*sādhāraṇa*), uncommon (*asādhāraṇa*), and unsubsuming (*anupasamhārin*).

3. It is otherwise known as *anaikāntika*.

4. Vide *hetvābhāsa*.

सायुज्य - *Sāyujya* - united with God

1. The final level of liberation, according to Dvaita. Vide *ānanda-tāratamya*.

2. The consummate level of liberation, according to Viśiṣṭādvaita.

3. The final stage of liberation, according to Śaiva Siddhānta. It is the goal of *sanmārga* and is the stage of *jñāna* (vide *mokṣa* per Śaiva Siddhānta).

शेष - *Śeṣa* - part, that is left over; accessory; dependent

According to Viśiṣṭādvaita, the relation of God with an individual soul is that of the *śeṣin* (principal) and the *śeṣa* (subordinate).

शेषवत् - *Śeṣavat* - a type of inference which is based on the distinctions of pervasion (*vyāpti*)

1. This type of inference proceeds from a perceived effect to an unperceived cause; e.g., when one infers, on the perception of a river in flood, that it was raining heavily in the mountains which feed

the river. It is essentially negative in character as it is based on the co-absence of the major and middle terms.

2. It is also called *avīta*.

3. Vide *anumāna*.

शेषिन् - *Śeṣin* - principal; God (in Viśiṣṭādvaita)

सिद्ध - *Siddha* - complete; perfect

1. A perfected being. An accomplished one. A seer.

2. According to Jainism, it is one of the sixfold stages in spiritual evolution. It is the final stage which represents the trans-empirical state. *Siddhas* are those who are free from the causal plane and all effects of *karma*. Their state is one of infinite, pure, and unlimited bliss. They have reached the top of the universe and from there, there is no fall.

सिद्धान्त - *Siddhānta* - the final view; the settled conclusion

सिद्धपरवाक्य - *Siddhaparavākya* - an assertive proposition conveying something that is already established

सिद्धार्थवाक्य - *Siddhārtha-vākya* - existential statement; statement which is purely descriptive

Such statements convey knowledge of objects already in existence. Mīmāṁsā says that they are subsidiary to *vidhi-vākyas*. Mīmāṁsā claims that existential statements merely give information about, and clarify, *vidhi-vākyas*, and thereby gain their sole validity. Advaita gives existential statements primary importance as they intimate the existent Brahman. Advaita interprets them qualitatively giving supreme importance to them. Mīmāṁsā gives injunctions the greatest validity due to their being quantitatively greater in the *Vedas*. Mīmāṁsā says that existential statements convey what is already known through other sources of knowledge and hence, they are mere restatements (*anuvāda*).

सिद्धि - *Siddhi* - powers; modes of success; attainment

1. There are eight traditional powers: *aṇimā, laghimā, garimā, mahimā, prāptiḥ, prākāmyam, vaśitvam,* and *yatrakāmāvasāyitvam.* These are: the capacity to grow small and penetrate all things; lightness or the ability to rise up; extreme heaviness; extensive magnitude; extreme reach; obtaining all the objects of one's desire; infallibility of purpose.

2. Other powers include: the ability to fly (*dardura*); the conquest of the death (*mṛtyuñjaya*); the ability to acquire hidden treasure (*pātāla-siddhi*); the ability to fly over the earth (*bhūcari*); the ability to enter into another's body (*kāya-siddhi*); the ability to fly in the sky (*khecari*); knowledge of the past, present, and future (*trikāla-jñāna*); and the power to die at will (*icchā-mṛtyu*).

सिद्धोपाय - *Siddhopāya* - the means to liberation which is self-accomplished

Vide *upāya.*

शिक्षा - *Śikṣā* - teaching; phonetics (one of the six Vedāṅgas)

शिक्षाव्रत - *Śikṣā-vrata* - a Jaina ethical code of conduct

It is comprised of *sāmayika*, *proṣadhopavāsa*, *bhogopabhogaparimāṇa*, and *atithisaṁvibhāga*.

शील - *Śīla* - conduct; right discipline

1. Good behaviour, humility, self-restraint, and self-giving comprise right discipline. It is the desisting from committing all sinful deeds.

2. According to Buddhism, it is one of the six ideals Vide *pāramitā*.

शिल्पशास्त्र - *Śilpa-śāstra* - the scripture which deals with the construction of temples and the fine arts

शिष्ट - *Śiṣṭa* - the disciplined one

शिव - *Śiva* - auspicious; the Ultimate Reality; Lord

1. According to the *Śaiva* schools, *Śiva* is the supreme Godhead. The concept is traced to the *Ṛg Veda*; and He is the same as *Rudra*.

2. Literally *śiva* means 'good' or 'auspicious.'

3. Lord *Śiva* exercises five functions: creation (*sṛṣṭi*), maintenance (*sthiti*), dissolution (*saṁhāra*), obscuration (*tirodhāna*), and grace (*anugraha*).

4. According to Śaiva Siddhānta, *Śiva* has eight qualities: independence, purity, self-knowledge, omniscience, freedom from *mala*, boundless benevolence, omnipotence, and bliss.

5. According to Śaiva Siddhānta, *Śiva* appears in eight forms: earth, water, air, fire, sky, the sun and the moon, and the human beings. Cf. the

benedictory (*nāndī*) verse of the *Abhijñānaśākuntala* of Kālidāsa.

6. According to Vīra Śaivism, *Śiva* manifests in six forms (vide *liṅga-sthala*).

शिवभोग - *Śiva-bhoga* - a stage of liberation in Śaiva Siddhānta

In this stage the individual soul enjoys bliss with Lord *Śiva*.

शिवाचार – *Śivācāra* – seeing everyone as Lord Śiva

1. One of the five codes of conduct in Vīra Śaivism.

2. Vide *pañcācāra*.

शिवलिङ्ग - *Śiva-liṅga* - a form of the formless *Śiva*

1. According to Vīra Śaivism, it is a manifestation of the Divine. Vide *liṅga-sthala.*

2. Vide *liṅga.*

शिवशक्ति - *Śiva-śakti* - the twin truths of Śaktaism affirming the static and dynamic aspects of Reality

शिवयोग - *Śiva-yoga* - a stage of liberation in Śaiva Siddhānta

In this stage the individual soul unites with Lord *Śiva.*

स्कन्ध - *Skandha* - group; an aggregate

1. According to Buddhism, they are aggregates of bodily and psychical states which are immediate to oneself. They are divided into five classes: body (*rūpa*), feelings (*vedanā*), perceptions (*saññā*), predispositions from past impressions (*saṁskāra*),

and consciousness *(vijñāna)*. They constitute what a person is; and being impermanent, they lead only to sorrow. They point to the fact that a person is merely an empirical aggregate and has no essence.

2. *Rūpa* stands for the physical elements, and the other four *skandhas* stand for the psychical elements in the self.

स्मरणम् - *Smaraṇam* - remembering the Lord

Vide *bhakti.*

स्मृति - *Smṛti* - memory; recollection

1. According to Viśiṣṭādvaita, it is included in perception as a valid means of knowledge. It is caused by similarity (*śādṛśya*), unseen effect (*adṛṣṭa*), deep thinking (*cintā*), or association (*sāhacarya*).

2. According to Nyāya, it is non-presentative knowledge which may be either true (*yathārtha*) or false (*ayathārtha*), but not valid (*pramā*).

3. According to the Jainas and the Vaiśeṣikas, it is valid mediate knowledge.

4. According to Nyāya and Mīmāṁsā, it is invalid knowledge (though their reasons for its invalidity differ).

5. According to Advaita, it is either valid or invalid as the case may be.

6. According to Nyāya-Vaiśeṣika, recollection is a cognition caused solely by impressions. Advaita and Bhāṭṭa Mīmāṁsā explain it as a cognitive complex consisting of two parts: perceptual experi-

ence and recollection. Nyāya calls it perceptual experience of a special type.

7. *Smṛti* also refers to traditional scriptures, which include: the *Vedāṅgas*, the *Dharmaśāstras*, the *Itihāsas*, and the *Purāṇas*.

8. The principal law books are: the *Manusmṛti*, *Parāśarasmṛti* and *Vaśiṣṭhasmṛti*. Other *smṛtis* are of: *Śaṅkha*, *Likhita*, *Atri*, *Viṣṇu*, *Hārīta*, *Yama*, *Aṅgirasa*, *Uśanas*, *Saṁvarta*, *Bṛhaspati*, *Kātyāyana*, *Dakṣa*, *Vyāsa*, *Yājñavalkya*, and *Śātātapa*.

स्मृतिप्रस्थान - *Smṛti-prasthāna* - the *Bhagavad-gītā*

1. It is so called according to Vedānta.

2. Vide *prasthāna-traya*.

स्नेह - *Sneha* - smoothness; oiliness; viscidity

According to Nyāya-Vaiśeṣika, viscidity is the quality which causes the lumping up of powder, etc. It causes the particles of powder, etc. to adhere to each other. It belongs only to water.

सोपाधिभ्रम - *Sopādhi-bhrama* - delusion due to an external adjunct

E. g., a crystal appears red in the physical proximity of a red flower.

सोपाधिशेष - *Sopādhi-śeṣa* - a form of *nirvāṇa* in which some impressions remain

Vide *nirupādhi-śeṣa*.

स्पन्द - *Spanda* - vibration; self-movement

1. A name for Kashmir Śaivism.

2. The principle of apparent movement from the state of absolute unity to the plurality of the world.

स्पर्श - *Sparśa* - touch; sense-contact

1. One of the five subtle essences of the elements. Vide *tanmātra.*

2. One of the twelve links in the causal chain of existence. Vide *pratītyasamutpāda.*

स्फटिक - *Sphaṭika* - crystal

One of the substances that *liṅgas* are made out of.

स्फोट - *Sphoṭa* - to burst; manifest

1. The hidden or underlying power behind individual letters of a word which present the meaning of the word to the reader or hearer of it. It is the eternal essence of a word, according to the Grammarians. It is manifested by letters and itself manifests the meaning of a word. It is the single meaningful symbol. The articulated sounds used in linguistic discourse are merely the means by which the symbol is revealed according to the Grammarians who propounded the theory.

2. It is the eternal essence of words both because it is manifested by the letters and because it manifests the meaning. The concept arose due to the need to explain how individual letters form a meaningful word.

श्रद्धा - *Śraddhā* - faith

श्रौत - *Śrauta* - scriptural

1. These are Scriptures based on the *Vedas.*

2. Vide *āgama*.

श्रावक - *Śrāvaka* - listener; disciple

1. A follower of the Hīnayāna monks in Buddhism.

2. A layman in Jainism, who merely expresses his or her (*śrāvikā*) faith in the Jaina doctrines and attempts as best they can to follow the *dharma*.

3. Vide *śrāvaka-dharma*.

श्रावकधर्म - *Śrāvaka-dharma* - the householder's duties

According to Jaina spiritual disciplines, many concessions are allowed to the householder in observing the various virtues.

श्रवण - *Śravaṇa* - hearing; study

1. A proximate aid, according to Advaita, for liberation. An aspirant should hear the Upaniṣadic texts from a qualified teacher. This will remove any doubts one has as to the nature of the *pramāṇa* to know Brahman, i.e., *śruti*. It is the stage of formal study.

2. Vide *mukhya-antaraṅga-sādhana*.

श्रवणम् - *Śravaṇam* - listening to the glory of the Lord

Vide *bhakti*.

श्रेयस् - *Śreyas* - good

In the *Upaniṣads* there is a distinction made between *preyas*, what is pleasing, and *śreyas*, what is good. One is warned never to be lured away by the merely pleasing, for there is no end to the pursuit of pleasure. Vide *preyas*.

श्रीः - *Śrīḥ* - excellent; venerated; wealth; *Lakṣmī*

1. She is the consort of *Viṣṇu*. She is said to be the *puruṣakāra* (an interceder), according to Viśiṣṭādvaita.

2. It is often used as an honorific prefix to the name of deities and holy personages to indicate 'holiness'.

श्रीसम्प्रदाय - *Śrī Sampradāya* - the Viśiṣṭādvaita

स्रोतापन्न - *Sīrotāpanna* - (Pali term) one in the stream of perfection

It is a stage of a Buddhist aspirant on the path to perfection.

श्रोत्र - *Śrotra* - the ear

One of the five sense organs (*jñānendriyas*).

सृष्टि - *Sṛṣṭi* - creation

One of the five functions of *Śiva*. (vide *Śiva*)

सृष्टिवाक्य - *Sṛṣṭi-vākya* - creation texts

According to Advaita, these texts only allude to Reality and do not teach creation *per se*, and explain how creation works only at the empirical level. By employing the method of *adhyāropa* and *apavāda* (superimposition and subsequent denial), these texts lead an aspirant from the known and the familiar to the unknown and the unfamiliar, i.e., *Brahman*.

श्रुतहानि - *Śrutahāni* - distortion of the text; giving up what is actually stated

श्रुतज्ञान - *Śruta-jñāna* - scriptural knowledge

This is a type of mediate knowledge, according to Jainism. It is of two kinds: *Aṅga-bāhya* (not incorporated in the twelve *Aṅgas*), and *Aṅga-praviṣṭa* (incorporated in the twelve *Aṅgas*). Its object of cognition may belong to the past, present, or future, and being the utterance of great ones (*āpta-vacana*), it is pure and beyond change. It is authoritative knowledge whose validity is unchallengeable. It is knowledge derived through words. It is divided into four classes or processes: integration *(labdhi)*, consideration (*bhāvanā*), understanding (*upayoga*), and interpretation (*naya*). A unique feature of the Jaina theory of scriptural knowledge is that it is always preceded by perceptual knowledge (*mati*). No other school maintains that perceptual knowledge is basic to scriptural knowledge.

श्रुतार्थापत्ति - *Śrutārthāpatti* - a type of postulation which helps to explain something which is heard

1. E.g., the fact that the village from which *Kṛṣṇa* hails is on the *Yamunā* can be understood only when this statement is interpreted as meaning that the village is situated on the banks of the river *Yamunā*.

2. Vide *arthāpatti*.

श्रुति - *Śruti* - what is heard; revealed Scripture; direct assertion

1. The *Vedas* are called the *śruti*. They are the Hindu revelatory scripture. The Divine Word (*Veda*) which is heard by the Seer (*Ṛṣi*) constitutes the immemorial truth. Vide *aṅgatvabodhaka-pramāṇa*.

2. It is divided into *bheda-* and *abheda-śrutis.*

श्रुत्यनेक - *Śruti-aneka* - diversity of scriptural statements

According to Advaita, any seeming contradictions which exist in one's mind regarding *Brahman,* are removed by the study (*śravaṇa*) of the Scriptures.

श्रुतिप्रस्थान - *Śruti-prasthāna* - the *Upaniṣads*

1. The *Upaniṣads* are so called by the Vedānta schools because they are the summits of the *Veda* and part of it.

2. Vide *prasthāna-traya.*

श्रुतिसापेक्ष - *Śruti-sāpekṣa* - dependent upon Scripture for authoritativeness

श्रुतिशिरस् - *Śruti-śiras* - the summits of the Scripture

The *Upaniṣads* are called the summits of the *Veda.*

स्थल - *Sthala* - an abode; place

1. The Supreme Reality in Vīra Śaivism.

2. It is a name for consciousness. According to Vīra Śaivism, there are six stages of consciousness: after knowing the world as unreal, one shares the bliss of *Śiva* (*aikya*); one sees God (*liṅga*) in oneself and everywhere (*śaraṇa*); renunciation of the ego (*prāṇaliṅga*); offering all objects of enjoyment to God (*prasādi*); firm belief in the existence of God (*maheśvara*); and performing rituals and possessing devotion (*bhakta*). The first two belong to *yoga-aṅga*; the next two to *bhoga-aṅga*; and the last two stages belong to *tyāga-aṅga.* Vide chart no. 14.

3. According to Vīra Śaivism, *sthala* or *Śiva* divides into *liṅga* and *aṅga*. *Liṅga* is *Śiva* or *Rudra*, and is the object of worship or adoration. *Aṅga* is the individual soul, the worshipper or adorer. Both *liṅga-sthala* and *aṅga-sthala* manifest in six forms. Vide chart no. 14.

स्थान - *Sthāna* - position; proximity

Vide *aṅgatva-bodhaka-pramāṇa*.

स्थावर - *Sthāvara* - non-moving bodies; immobile; stationary

They are said to be of four kinds: stones (*śilā*), shrubs (*gulma*), trees (*vṛkṣa*), and creepers (*latā*).

स्थविरवाद - *Sthaviravāda* - Vide Theravāda

स्थायिभाव - *Sthāyibhāva* - essence of emotion forming the content of a work of art; an emotion located in an appreciator of a work of art

According to Indian aesthetics, it is the material cause of *Rasa* (Vide *rasa*). Such emotions are fit for representation as the theme of a work because these basic emotions may be assumed to be present in the responding spectator. There are nine basic emotions: love (*rati*), mirth (*hāsa*), sorrow (*śoka*), anger (*krodha*), fortitude (*utsāha*), fear (*bhaya*), disgust (*jugupsā*), wonder (*vismaya*), and *śama* (calmness).

स्थितप्रज्ञ - *Sthitaprajña* - one who is established in the divine Consciousness

One who is unmoved by agitated feelings and emotions, whether good or bad, whether pleasurable or painful, who is neither elated by joy nor depressed by sorrow and is stable in the knowledge and awareness of the Reality. Vide the *Bhagavad Gītā* II, 55-57.

स्थिति - *Sthiti* - a state; condition; preservation

स्थितस्थापक - *Sthitasthāpaka* - elasticity

Vide *saṁskāra*.

स्थूलचित् - *Sthūla-cit* - physical consciousness

स्थूलशरीर - *Sthūla-śarīra* - gross body; physical body

1. According to Sāṅkhya, it is constituted of the twenty-five elemental principles: the five *jñānendriyas* (the organs of hearing, touch, sight, taste, and smell), the five *karmendriyas* (the organs of speech, prehenison, movement, excretion, and generation), the five *tanmātras* (the subtle essence of the elements of sound, touch, sight, taste, and smell), the five *mahābhūtas* (ether, air, fire, water, and earth), and the five vital airs (*prāṇa*, *apāna*, *samāna*, *udāna*, and *vyāna*).

2. Vide *śarīra*.

शुद्धाध्वन् - *Śuddhādhvan* - perfect or pure way

1. According to Kashmir Śaivism, it is a name for the pure creation.

2. Vide *tattva*.

शुद्धाद्वैत - *Śuddhādvaita* - pure non-duality

The name of Vallabha's school of Vedānta.

शुद्धावस्था - *Śuddha-avasthā* - pure state

According to Śaiva Siddhānta, it is the state when the individual enters into a non-dual union with *Śiva*. It is twofold: *jīvanmukti* and *paramukti*.

शुद्धभाव - *Śuddha-bhāva* - purity in motive

According to Dvaita, it is an aspect of devotion.

शुद्धजीव - *Śuddha-jīva* - a perfect individual soul (according to Jainism)

Vide *jīva*.

शुद्धमाया - *Śuddha-māyā* - pure *māyā*

According to Śaiva Siddhānta, *māyā* is twofold: pure and impure. Pure *māyā* is *māyā* in its primal state. It gives rise to the five pure principles.

शुद्धनिश्चय - *Śuddha-niścaya* - knowledge of a thing in a particular context

Vide *naya-niścaya*.

शुद्धसत्त्व - *Śuddha-sattva* - pure matter

1. According to Viśiṣṭādvaita, it is a self-luminous, immaterial, spiritual substance which is unconnected with the three *guṇas*. It is infinite in the higher regions and finite in the lower regions. It is the 'matter' out of which the bodies of *Īśvara*, eternals, and liberated individuals are made.

2. Vide *nitya-vibhūti*.

शुद्धाशुद्धमाया - *Śuddhāśuddha-māyā* - pure and impure creation

According to Śaiva Siddhānta, the space-time universe evolves from here. It is an impure creation and is directed by the lesser divinities. It evolves into particle (*kalā*), knowledge (*vidyā*), desire (*rāga*), individual soul (*puruṣa*), and matter (*māyā*). These *tattvas* cause enjoyment for the individual soul. They are also called *miśra-tattvas*. Vide chart no. 9.

शुद्धविद्या - *Śuddha-vidyā* - pure knowledge

It is a category in Śrīkaṇṭha's philosophy. Vide chart no. 9.

सुदुर्बोध - *Sudurbodha* - inexplicable

सुदुर्जय - *Sudurjaya* - supreme invincibility in meditation

Vide *bodhisattva*.

सूक्ष्मचित् - *Sūkṣma-cit* - subtle sentience

According to Śaiva Siddhānta, God needs no support nor experience to understand.

सूक्ष्मेन्द्रिय - *Sūkṣma-indriya* - subtle sense organ

It is a name for the mind.

सूक्ष्मशरीर - *Sūkṣma-śarīra* - subtle body

1. The sheaths of *prāṇa*, *manas*, and *vijñāna*, constitute the subtle body. They are called the *prāṇamaya-kośa*, *manomaya-kośa*, and *vijñānamayakośa*.

2. The subtle body consists of the internal organs (*buddhi*, *ahaṅkāra*, and *manas*), the organs of

knowledge (*jñānendriya*), the organs of action (*karmendriya*), and the five vital airs (*prāṇa*).

3. It is also called the *liṅga-śarīra* or the astral body.

4. Vide *kośa* and *śarīra*.

शून्य - *Śūnya* - the void; non-being; non-existence

According to Mādhyamika Buddhism, there is no Reality nor non-reality. All is *śūnya*, void, as all dualities are disclaimed. Thus whatever is, is not describable by any concept. Being devoid of any phenomenal characteristics, 'void' or 'the indescribable' is the real nature of things.

शून्यता - *Śūnyatā* - voidness; emptiness

According to Buddhism, it is the suchness of existence. Vide *śūnya*.

शून्यवाद - *Śūnyavāda* - the theory of the void

Vide Mādhyamika.

शुष्कयुक्ति - *Śuṣka-yukti* - dry reasoning

सुषुप्ति - *Suṣupti* - deep sleep

1. The state of deep sleep consciousness. There are no objects present, neither of external things of the world, nor of internal ideas. Thus there is no apprehension of duality, though ignorance (*avidyā*) still persists in a latent state.

2. Vide *avasthā*.

सुतल - *Sutala* - hell

1. The nether pole of *Jano-loka*. It is a state of good matter wherein desire and passion rule.

2. Vide *loka* and *tala*.

सूत्र - *Sūtra* - aphorism; 'thread'

1. An extremely condensed and cryptic statement requiring a commentary or explanation to make it intelligible.

2. The sacred thread worn by the members of the three higher castes.

3. The basic text for a philosophical system. It consists of a set of aphorisms setting forth, in an ordered manner, the leading concepts and doctrines of the system concerned. These aphorisms are cryptic and are not expository statements, but aids to memory. Since they are brief, they lend themselves to divergent interpretations. Vide *bhāṣya*.

सुत्तपिटक - *Sutta-piṭaka* - the basket of sermons

This is the Buddhist scripture (compiled by *Ānanda*) which gives the sermons and parables of the Buddha. It is divided into five sections (*nikāya*): *dīgha, majjhima, saṁyutta, anguttara*, and *khuddaka*.

स्वभाव - *Svabhāva* - essential nature

1. The essential law of one's nature.

2. The theory of self-nature (*svabhāva-vāda*) or 'naturalism' which holds that things are as their nature makes them. It acknowledges the universality of causation, while tracing all changes to the thing itself to which it belongs Everything is unique and is predetermined by that uniqueness. Everything is self-determined. What is to happen, must happen, whether one wills it or not.

स्वभावनिर्देश - *Svabhāva-nirdeśa* - natural perceptual discrimination

Vide *nirdeśa.*

स्वधर्म - *Svadharma* - one's own natural duty

1. It arises from one's obligations towards one's nature, class, social position, latent tendencies, place and time.
2. Vide *dharma.*

स्वाध्याय - *Svādhyāya* - study; study of Scripture

1. One of the religious observances of Patañjali's *rāja-yoga.*
2. Vide *niyama.*

स्वगतभेद - *Svagata-bheda* - internal distinctions

1. For example: the difference between the leaves and flowers of a tree.
2. Vide *bheda.*

स्वलक्षण - *Svalakṣaṇa* - the bare particular in perception

According to both the Vaibhāṣika and Sautrāntika schools, what is perceived or postulated is the bare particular, e.g., blue. All the other elements (blueness, peacockness, etc.) are added by the mind and are termed *sāmānya-lakṣaṇa.*

स्वनिर्वाहक - *Svanirvāhaka* - what is self-accomplished

स्वानुभव - *Svānubhava* - self-realization

स्वप्न - *Svapna* - dream

1. It is to be immersed in one's own self. The state of consciousness called dream is also known as *prajñā.*

2. Vide *avasthā*.

स्वप्रकाश - *Svaprakāśa* - self-revealing; self-luminous

स्वारसिक - *Svārasika* - self-evident

स्वारसिकीप्रवृत्ति - *Svārasikī-pravṛtti* - spontaneous volition

स्वर्लोक (स्वर्ग) - *Svarloka* (*Svarga*) - heaven

1. A world of light and delight.

2. Vide *loka* and *tala*.

स्वार्थानुमान - *Svārtha-anumāna* - inference for one's own sake

1. An inference which is intended for the satisfaction of one's own reasoning. It consists of three propositions. The Buddhists, Jainas, and Naiyāyikas — all made this distinction.

2. Vide *anumāna*.

स्वरूप - *Svarūpa* - natural form; actual or essential nature

स्वरूप-अभेद - *Svarūpa-abheda* - non-relational proposition; identity statement

1. According to Advaita, examples of this type of proposition include: *'so'yam devadattaḥ'* (this is that Devadatta) or the *mahā-vākya 'tat tvam asi'*.

2. It is one of the two types of *vākyārthas*. This type is a non-relational sentence in that the two entities referred to, are actually identical.

3. Vide *vākyārtha*.

स्वरूप-अनुपपत्ति - *Svarūpa-anupapatti* - the untenability of the nature (of *avidyā*)

1. One of the seven untenabilities pointed out by Rāmānuja in his criticism of the Advaita concept of *avidyā*.

2. Vide *saptavidha-anupapatti*.

स्वरूपधर्म - *Svarūpa-dharma* - essential attributes of a substance

स्वरूपैक्य - *Svarūpaikya* - absolute identity

स्वरूपज्ञान - *Svarūpa-jñāna* - knowledge which is of the nature of the Self

1. According to Advaita, it is another name for *Brahman*. Advaita makes a distinction between *svarūpa-jñāna* which is *Brahman* and *vṛtti-jñāna* which is cognition or knowledge through a mental mode. *Svarūpa-jñāna* is not opposed to *avidyā*, while *vṛtti-jñāna* is. The type of modal knowledge through which *Brahman* is apprehended is called *akhaṇḍākāra-vṛtti-jñāna*.

2. Vide *vṛtti-jñāna*.

स्वरूपलक्षण - *Svarūpa-lakṣaṇa* - essential nature; inseparable essence

1. The essential nature of a thing lasts as long as the thing persists. Thus, its essential nature distinguishes it from all other things. It is a definition by essence. It defines a thing without the implication of the differentiation entering into the constitution.

2. According to Advaita, existence, knowledge, and bliss (*sat-cit-ānanda*) are the essential nature of *Brahman*. However, it should be noted that the

essential nature of *Brahman*, as defined by Advaita, is interpreted only negatively.

3. Vide *taṭastha-lakṣaṇa*.

स्वरूपनिरूपकधर्म - *Svarūpa-nirūpaka-dharma* - eternal qualities which describe the Lord

According to Viśiṣṭādvaita, these qualities are said to be the Lord's essential nature. They are: *satyatva*, *jñānatva*, and *ānandatva*.

स्वरूपसम्बन्ध - *Svarūpa-sambandha* - self-relation

According to Nyāya, self-relation is of two types: those which limit occupancy (*vṛtti-niyāmaka*) and those which do not limit occupancy (*vṛtty-aniyāmaka*).

स्वरूपासिद्ध - *Svarūpāsiddha* - unestablished in respect of itself

1. A type of unestablished reason (*hetu*) in an inferential process; e.g., sound is a quality, because it is visible, like a colour. Visibility cannot be predicated of sound which is only audible.

2. Vide *asiddha* and *hetvābhāsa*.

स्वरूपस्थिति - *Svarūpa-sthiti* - remaining in one's own natural condition

स्वरूपत्रैविध्य - *Svarūpa-traividhya* - three forms of the self

According to Dvaita, there are three types of individual souls: *sattva*-predominant individuals fit for release (*mukti-yogya*); *rajas*-predominant individuals who are ever within the cycle of birth and death (*nitya-saṁsārin*); and *tamas*-predominant individuals or evil beings (*tamo-yogya*). The second and third types of individuals cannot ever obtain liberation.

स्वरूपोपाधिप्रतिबिम्ब - *Svarūpa-upādhi-pratibimba* - the soul (*jīva*) is a reflection through its own nature functioning as the reflecting medium

According to Dvaita, this is a concept of the individual soul.

स्वरूपविशेष - *Svarūpa-viśeṣa* - special natural forms

स्वसङ्कल्पसहकृतकर्मकृत - *Svasaṅkalpa-sahakṛta-karma-kṛta* - bodies made by one's own will

1. It is said that *yogins* possess the power to make such bodies.

2. Vide *śarīra*.

स्वसिद्ध - *Svasiddha* - self-established

स्वतः निराकार - *Svataḥ nirākāra* - formless in itself

स्वतः प्रामाण्यवाद - *Svataḥ-prāmāṇya-vāda* - the theory of intrinsic validity

1. The theory that the validity of knowledge is present in the material that creates the object and that the awareness of this validity arises spontaneously with that knowledge itself. Vide *parataḥ-prāmāṇya-vāda*.

2. Sāṅkhya holds that validity and invalidity are intrinsic to knowledge. Mīmāṁsā and Advaita hold that validity is intrinsic, but that invalidity is extrinsic to knowledge.

स्वतःसिद्ध - *Svataḥ-siddha* - self-established; self-luminous

स्वतन्त्र - *Svatantra* - independent

स्वतन्त्रतत्त्व - *Svatantra-tattva* - an independent real

According to Dvaita, *Brahman* is an independent real.

स्वातन्त्र्यवाद - *Svātantrya-vāda* - the theory of self-dependence or sovereignty

The unique and chief doctrine of Kashmir Śaivism. It proclaims that *Śiva's* will is responsible for all manifestations. The supreme Reality manifests all from itself, in itself, and by itself as it is self-dependent.

स्वतस्त्व - *Svatastva* - intrinsicality

स्वतोग्राह्य - *Svatogrāhya* - intrinsically made out

स्वतोग्रहण - *Svatograhaṇa* - intrinsic apprehension

स्वतोजन्य - *Svatojanya* - intrinsically brought out

स्वतोव्यावर्तक - *Svatovyāvartaka* - self-discriminating

स्वतोव्यावृत्त - *Svatovyāvṛtta* - self-differentiated

स्वयं-ज्योति - *Svayaṁ-jyoti* - self-luminous

स्वयम्प्रकाश - *Svayam-prakāśa* - self-luminous

स्वयंसिद्ध - *Svayaṁ-siddha* - self-accomplished

1. A type of perception which is independent of the senses and accomplished by *yogic* practices.

2. Vide *arvācīna-pratyakṣa*.

स्वेच्छा - *Svecchā* - free-will

स्वेदज - *Svedaja* - sweat-born

1. Bodies born of sweat.
2. Vide *karma-kṛta.*

श्वेताम्बर - *Śvetāmbara* - white-clad

One of the two principal Jaina sects. Vide *digambara.* Its adherents wear white clothes. They are the most catholic among the Jainas.

स्वेतरभेद - *Svetara-bheda* - different from the rest

स्याद् - *Syād* - 'may-be'

स्यादस्ति - *Syād-asti* - may-be it is

Vide *syād-vāda.*

स्यादस्ति-अवक्तव्य - *Syād-asti-avaktavyam* - may-be it is and is indescribable

Vide *syād-vāda.*

स्यादस्तिनास्ति - *Syād-asti-nāsti* - may-be it is and it is not

Vide *syād-vāda.*

स्यादस्तिनास्ति-अवक्तव्यम् - *Syād-asti-nāsti-avaktavyam* - may-be it is and is not and is indescribable

Vide *syād-vāda.*

स्यादवक्तव्यम् - *Syād-avaktavyam* - may-be it is indescribable

Vide *syād-vāda.*

स्यान्नास्ति - *Syād-nāsti* - may-be it is not

Vide *syād-vāda.*

स्यान्नास्त्यवक्तव्यम् - *Syād-nāsti-avaktavyam* - may-be it is not and is indescribable

Vide *syād-vāda.*

स्याद्वाद - *Syād-vāda* - the theory of 'may be'; conditioned predication

1. As Reality is a complex phenomena, according to the Jainas, no one simple proposition can express the nature of Reality fully. Thus the term 'may be' (*syād*) is prefixed before seven propositions (*saptabhaṅgī*) giving each one a conditional point of view. Each proposition affirms something only in a relative point of view and thus the definite Jaina point of view is that there is no one definite point of view of Reality. All knowldege is relative and may be examined from the point of view of time, space, substance, and mode; e.g., a pot exists, now, from one point of view and does not exist at another time — in the future. From one point of view, a pot doesn't exist (before it is made) and from another point of view, it exists (after it is made). This pot exists from the point of view of its substance, clay, its place, the present moment, and its mode which is its particular shape. The pot does not exist from the point of view of another substance, say gold, etc. To ignore the complexity of objects is to commit the fallacy of dogmatism according to the Jainas.

2. The seven propositions are: *syād-asti*, *syād-nāsti*, *syād-asti-nāsti*, *syād-asti-avaktavyam*, *syād-nāsti-avaktavyam*, *syād-asti-nāsti-avaktavyam*, and *syād-avaktavyam.*

श्येनयाग - *Śyenayāga* - a type of Vedic ritual for bringing about a calamity to one's enemies

T

तदन्यबाधितार्थप्रसङ्ग - *Tadanyabādhitārtha-prasaṅga* - a type of reasoning

Vide *tarka*.

तादात्म्य - *Tādātmya* - identity; empathy

The relation of identity is also referred to as *samsarga*. According to Sāṅkhya, Bhāṭṭa, and Advaita, this is essentially an internal relation.

तैजस - *Taijasa* - the dream self

1. It is the self having a conceit in an individual subtle body in dream-experience. It is so called because it is of the nature of light, and thus can function in the absence of external objects. It knows subtle internal objects and enjoys them through the mind.

2. Vide *viśva* and *prajñā*.

तल - *Tala* - place or world

1. There are seven *talas* in Indian lore; ***pātāla***, the serpent kingdom of the ***Nāgas***; ***atala***, the kingdom of the ***Yakṣas***; ***rasātala***, the abode of the ***asuras***, ***daityas*** and ***dānavas***; ***talātala***, the kingdom of the ***rākṣasas***; ***vitala***, the kingdom of ***Śiva's*** demons; ***sutala***, ruled by ***Bali***; and ***mahātala***, the kingdom of ***pretas*** and demons.

2. Vide *loka*

तलातल - *Talātala* - hell

1. A state of purely outward passions and sense indulgence. It is a place and yet not a place. It is a plane of existence which is not fully material nor fully non-material.

2. Vide *loka* and *tala*.

तमस् - *Tamas* - darkness; inertia; dullness

1. One of the three *guṇas*. It is of the nature of indifference and serves to restrain. It is heavy and enveloping.

2. Vide *guṇa*.

तमोयोगिन् - *Tamo-yogin* - individual souls who are destined to go to hell

1. According to Dvaita, these individuals are *tamas*-predominant, evil beings. They can never obtain liberation.

2. Vide *svarūpa-traividhya*.

तन्हा - *Tanhā* - craving; desire

A Pali term; vide *tṛṣṇā*.

तन्मात्र - *Tanmātra* - the subtle essence of the five elements

1. They are: sound (*śabda*), touch (*sparśa*), sight (*rūpa*), taste (*rasa*), and smell (*gandha*). The five elements (*mahā-bhūta*) are derived from the *tanmātras* as follows: from sound comes ether; from touch comes air; from sight comes fire; from taste comes water; and from smell comes earth. The

tanmātras are said to evolve from the *tāmasa* aspect of egoity according to Sāṅkhya.

2. Vide chart no. 13.

तन्त्र - *Tantra* - rule; ritual, scripture; religious treatise; loom; warp

1. As religious treatises, they are usually in the form of a dialogue between *Śiva* and *Śakti*. Sometimes they are referred to as the 'Fifth *Veda*'.

2. They treat of five subjects: creation, destruction, worship of gods and goddesses, attainment of the six powers, and the four modes of union with the Divine in meditation.

3. They are practical treatises on religion. By means of worship of images (*arcā*), diagrams (*yantra*), repetition of mystic syllables (*mantra*), and meditation (*upāsana*), they provide courses for developing the hidden, latent power in individuals leading to realization. They may also be used for attaining worldly desires.

तनु - *Tanu* - body; person; thin; small

ताप - *Tāpa* - heating; one of the five *saṁskāras* of Śrīvaiṣṇavas

तपस् - *Tapas* - austerity; concentrated discipline; penance

1. A burning enquiry and aspiration. It is a spiritual force of concentrated energy generated by a spiritual aspirant.

2. Vide *niyama*.

तपोलोक - *Tapo-loka* - heaven

1. The world or plane of spiritual force. It is the world of self-conscious energy.

2. Vide *loka* and *tala.*

तारतम्य - *Tāratamya* - gradation

1. According to Dvaita, among individuals there is an intrinsic gradation. There are three grades of individual souls: the ever-free (*nitya*), those who have attained freedom (*mukta*), and those individuals which are bound (*baddha*). Among the latter there are those eligible for release (*mukti-yogya*), those not eligible for release (*nitya-saṁsārin* and *tamo-yogya*). And among the souls eligible for release, there is an intrinsic gradation. Celestial beings, sages, and advanced individuals comprise this latter category.

2. According to Dvaita, all individuals souls who are released enjoy pure bliss. However, this bliss varies in degree, though not in quality. This is based on the theory that individuals differ in their character.

3. Vide *ānanda-tāratamya* and *svarūpa-traividhya.*

तर्क - *Tarka* - reasoning; argumentation

1. It is one of the sixteen categories of the Nyāya school. Vide *padārtha* and chart no. 6.

2. It means deliberation on an unknown thing to discern its real nature. It consists of seeking reasons in support of some supposition to the exclusion of other suppositions. It is employed whenever a doubt is present about the specific nature of anything.

3. It is a hypothetical argument. It is a type of reasoning by which one may test the validity of the conclusion of any reasoning. It consists in deducing an untenable proposition from a given proposition. It takes the contradiction of a proposition as a hypothesis and sees how it leads to a contradiction.

4. It is of five types: *ātmāśraya* which shows the fallacy of self-dependence; *anyonyāśraya* which shows the fallacy of reciprocal dependence; *cakraka* which shows the fallacy of a presupposition explaining another presupposition; *anavasthā* which shows the fallacy of infinite regress; and, *tadanya-bādhitārtha-prasaṅga* which indirectly shows the validity of a reasoning by proving the contradictory of the conclusion absurd.

तर्कशास्त्र - *Tarka-śāstra* - another name for the Nyāya school; the science of reasoning

तत् - *Tat* – 'that'

A neuter pronoun expressing the indescribable Absolute. (Vide *Tat-tvam-asi*)

तटस्थलक्षण - *Taṭastha-lakṣaṇa* – identifying marks; accidental attributes; the definition *per accidens*

According to Advaita, *Brahman* may be defined in one of the two ways, from the relative standpoint and from the absolute standpoint. *Taṭatha-lakṣaṇa* describes the accidental attributes superimposed upon the essential nature of a thing. These attributes remain in that thing only for a time and differentiate it from other things. This definition, *per-accidens,* is from the relative standpoint. Thus to describe *Brahman* as the source and support of the world is to superimpose relational aspects upon the non-relational non-dual Absolute. This technique has a methodological importance for the Advaitin. It is easy for a beginner to understand the nature of a qualified *Brahman*. Then from this known position, it is easier to convey the final Advaitic position of non-duality.

2. Vide *svarūpa-lakṣaṇa*, *adhyāropa* and *apavāda*.

तथता - *Tathatā* - suchness; is-ness; things as they are

According to the Buddhists, that which is beyond all dualities and descriptions. It is a Mādhyamika term for the ultimate Reality.

तथागत - *Tathāgata* - one who has thus gone

1. A title of the Buddha.

2. One of the four meditations (*dhyāna*) spoken of in the *Laṅkāvatāra Sūtra.* It is that state in which the mind lapses into suchness. In this state the nothingness and incomprehensibity of all phenomena is perfectly realized.

तथागतगर्भ - *Tathāgatagarbha* - the womb of the perfect One

1. It is also known as *dharma-kāya.*

2. It is called *ālaya-vijñāna* in Yogācāra Buddhism.

तत्क्रतु - *Tatkratu* - the principle that one who meditates becomes one with the object of their meditation

तात्पर्य - *Tātparya* - purport; intrinsic significance

1. The purport of the Vedic works is determined through six characteristic marks (*ṣaḍliṅga*): the harmony of the initial and concluding passages (*upakrama* and *upasaṁhāra*); repetition (*abhyāsa*); novelty (*apūrvatā*); fruitfulness (*phala*); glorification by eulogistic passages or condemnations by deprecatory passages (*arthavāda*); and intelligibility in the light of reasoning (*upapatti*).

2. It is one of the four conditions which, when fulfilled, produce the meaning of a sentence. (Vide *ākāṅkṣā, yogyatā, sannidhi/āsatti*). Purport is the capacity for generation of the cognition of a particular thing, according to Advaita. According to Nyāya, purport is the intention of the speaker.

तात्पर्यबोधकषड्लिङ्ग - *Tātparya-bodhaka-ṣaḍliṅga* - the six marks which determine the purport of a text's verse

Vide *tātparya*.

तत्तु समन्वयात् - *Tat-tu-samanvayāt* - but that (*Brahman* is to be known only from the Scriptures and not independently by any other means is established) because it is the main purport (of all Vedānta texts)

It is a *sūtra* (I, i, 4) of the *Brahma-sūtra*.

तत्त्व - *Tattva* - category; truth; the essence of things

1. It is the essence of anything. It is a thing's essential being, its 'thatness'.

2. Each school in Indian philosophy names a certain number of *tattvas* as fundamentals in its system of thought. Advaita lists two (from the

empirical, relative point of view): *tat* and *tvam*. Sāṅkhya lists twenty-five: *avyakta*, *buddhi*, *ahaṅkāra*, the five *tanmātras*, the five *mahā-bhūtas*, the five *karmendriyas*, the five *jñānendriyas*, *manas* and *puruṣa*. Kashmir Śaivism lists thirty-six: *Śiva*, *Śakti*, *Sadāśiva* (*sādākhya*), *Īśvara*, *Śuddha-vidyā*, *māyā*, *kāla*, *niyati*, *rāga*, *vidyā*, *kalā*, *puruṣa*, *prakṛti*, *buddhi*, *ahaṅkāra*, *manas*, five *karmendriyas*, five *jñānendriyas*, five *tanmātras*, and five *mahā-bhūtas*. (The first five constitute the pure creation and the latter thirty-one form the impure creation). All the other schools accept similar number - about seven to 26 - of categories.

3. Vide *padārtha* and charts no. 6-9.

तत्त्वाज्ञान - *Tattva-ajñāna* - nonapprehension of the real

तत्त्वदर्शन - *Tattva-darśana* - the absolute level of truth as designated by Gauḍapāda

तत्त्वाध्यवसाय - *Tattvādhyavasāya* - conclusive determination of the truth

तत्त्वज्ञान - *Tattva-jñāna* - Brahman realization; apprehension of the real

तत्त्वमसि - *Tat-tvam-asi* - that thou art

A great saying (*mahā-vākya*) which occurs in the *Chāndogya Upaniṣad* of the *Sāma Veda*.

तत्त्वत्रय - *Tattva-traya* - three realities

According to Viśiṣṭādvaita, three realities exist: living beings (*cit*), inanimate things (*acit*) and the supreme Ruler and Controller (*Īśvara*).

तत्त्वावबोध - *Tattvāvabodha* - apprehension of reality or truth

तेजस् - *Tejas* - fire

1. It is one of the five elements. Vide *mahā-bhūta.*

2. It is of four kinds: terrestrial (*bhauma*), celestial (*divya*), of the stomach (*audarya*), and mineral (*ākaraja*).

तेङ्कलै - *Teṅkalai* - (Tamil term) the Southern sect or school of Viśiṣṭādvaita

1. It was founded by Piḷḷai Lokācārya. This school regards the Tamil *Prabandham* as canonical and is indifferent to the Sanskrit tradition.

2. Vide *Vaḍakalai* and *Ubhaya-vedānta.*

तिमिर - *Timira* - darkness

It is also a disease of the eye producing double vision.

तिरोभाव - *Tirobhāva* - obscuration

तिरोधान - *Tirodhāna* - obscuration; concealment

A type of power (*śakti*) according to the Śaiva Siddhānta, which is active at the time the individual souls are fettered.

तिरोधान-अनुपपत्ति - *Tirodhāna-anupapatti* - the untenability of concealment

1. One of the 7 untenabilities posed by Rāmānuja against the Advaita concept of *avidyā.*

2. Vide *saptavidha-anupapatti.*

तीर्थङ्कर - *Tīrthaṅkara* - ford-crosser; ford-maker

The twenty-four prophets of Jainism who represent the goal of human life. They are called ford-makers because they serve as the ferry-men across the river of transmigration. They are the perfected ones who lead the way to liberation. Ṛṣabha was the first one and he is mentioned even in Vedic lore, though there is no historical evidence available until one comes to the twenty-third preceptor, Pārśvanātha. The list is: Ṛṣabha, Ajita, Sambhava, Abhinandhana, Sumati, Padmaprabha, Supārśva, Candraprabha, Suvidhi, Śītala, Śreyāṁśa, Vasupūjya, Vimala, Ananta, Dharma, Śānti, Kunthu, Ara, Malli, Munisuvrata, Nami, Ariṣṭenemi, Pārśva, and Vardhamāna Mahāvīra.

तिरुवडि-पेरु - *Tiruvaḍippēṛu* - (Tamil term) grace

तिर्यक् - *Tiryak* - animal being

Vide *jaṅgama.*

तितिक्षा - *Titikṣā* - endurance of opposites; forbearance

1. The ability to withstand opposites like pleasure and pain, heat and cold, etc., with equal fortitude.

2. Vide *sādhana-catuṣṭaya.*

तीव्रमुमुक्षु - *Tīvra-mumukṣu* - one who has an earnest and consuming desire for liberation

Vide *jīva.*

त्रैगुणात्मिका - *Traiguṇātmikā* - made of the three *guṇas*

Vide *guṇa.*

त्रैगुण्य - *Traiguṇya* - the three *guṇas* (*sattva, rajas,* and *tamas*)

त्रास - *Trāsa* - individuals who possess more than one sense organ

1. They include human beings, birds, animals, gods, and devils.

2. They are individuals capable of movement.

3. Vide chart no. 8.

त्रसरेणु - *Trasareṇu* - triad; ternary product

1. It is also called *truṭi.* It is the smallest visible substance, according to Nyāya-Vaiśeṣika. It is made up of three dyads (*dvyaṇuka*).

2. Vide *aṇu.*

त्रेतायुग - *Tretā-yuga* - the silver age

1. The age where *dharma* (truth) stands on only three of its four legs. In this age the way to liberation is through sacrifice (*yajña*).

2. Vide *yuga.*

त्रिगुण - *Triguṇa* - the three qualities viz. *sattva, rajas,* and *tamas*

Vide *guṇa.*

त्रिक - *Trika* - triple

1. A name for Kashmir Śaivism.

2. It refers to the triple principle with which the Kashmir Śaivism deals, viz., *pati-pāśa-paśu* or *śiva-śakti-aṇu,* or God-souls-bonds.

त्रिकाय - *Trikāya* - the three sheaths (of the Buddha)

1. *Dharmakāya*: the sheath of the Law. This is the Reality, the Void, the Absolute. It is the universal and transcendent Buddha.

2. *Sambhogakāya*: the sheath of enjoyment. This is the sheath in which a Buddha or *Bodhisattva* dwells on the earth or beyond.

3. *Nirvāṇakāya*: the sheath of the transformation. This is the sheath of the historical Buddha.

4. The first sheath is unmanifest; the second is manifest to the eye of faith, i.e., *bodhisattvas*; and the third sheath is empirically manifest.

त्रिपिटक - *Tri-piṭaka* - the 'three baskets of tradition'

The early Buddhist canon written in Pāli. These are: *Sutta* or utterances of the Buddha himself; *Vinaya* or rules of discipline; and *Abhidhamma* or philosophic discussions.

त्रिप्रदेश - *Tripradeśa* - combination of three atoms

Vide *aṇu.*

त्रिपुटी - *Tripuṭī* - triple form

1. The process of knowing or knowledge implies the subject who knows, and the object which is known. Every act of cognition involves this triple form of: the cognizer, the object cognized, and the means of cognition.

2. The knower, the known, the act of knowledge.

त्रिरत्न - *Tri-ratna* - the three jewels

1. According to Jainism, they are the quintessence of their theory of liberation. They are: right knowledge (*samyag-jñāna*), right vision (*samyag-darśana*), and right conduct (*samyak-cāritra*). Right vision is faith in the Jaina scriptures. Right knowledge is knowledge of the truths taught by Jainism. Right conduct is making one's life conform to the truths learnt. Thus, these are the three principles that exalt life. (For right conduct vide *mahā-vrata*).

2. According to Buddhism, the three jewels are: the Buddha, His doctrine, and the Order. Thus, there is the profession of faith: I go for refuge to the Buddha; I go for refuge to the *Dharma*; I go for refuge to the *Saṅgha*. (*Buddhaṁ śaraṇaṁ gacchāmi*; *dharmaṁ śaraṇaṁ gacchāmi*; *saṅghaṁ śaraṇaṁ gacchāmi*).

3. According to Viśiṣṭādvaita, the three jewels are: (i) *mantraratna* (*Dvaya*), (ii) *purāṇaratna* (Viṣṇu-purāṇa) and (iii) *Stotraratna* (a work of Yāmuna).

त्रिवृत्करण - *Trivṛtkaraṇa* - triplication; all objects are made of three parts

1. The mixture of the three elements, fire, water, and earth, in different proportions, constitutes all the various objects. The *yathārtha-khyāti* of Viśiṣṭādvaita grounds itself on the *trivṛtkaraṇa* texts of the *Upaniṣads*.

2. Vide *pañcī-karaṇa*.

तृष्णा - *Tṛṣṇā* - thirst; craving; desire

1. One of the twelve links in the causal clain of existence. *Upādāna* is an advanced desire which again is the result of pleasure and pain.

2. Vide *pratītya-samutpāda.*

तृतीयलिङ्गपरामर्श - *Tṛtīyaliṅga-parāmarśa* - the two factors necessary in an inferential process; subsumptive reflection

1. There must be knowledge of the universal concomitance between the reason (*hetu*) and the major term (*sādhya*), and there must also be a necessary relation between the reason and the minor term (*pakṣa*) in a valid inferential reasoning.

2. *Vyāpti-jñāna* and *pakṣa-dharmatā-jñāna* must combine so as to serve as the instrument of inference. *Parāmarśa* is the ratiocinative process which makes known the fact that the mark which is universally concomitant with the inferred character is present in the subject. The principle involved in this process is subsumption, the correlation of a particular case with the universal pervading it. *Liṅga* is the *hetu* or probans and should be such that it is related to the probandum (*sādhya*), is known to exist in that which is connected therewith, and does not exist where the *sādhya* is not present.

3. Vide *anumāna.*

त्रुटि - *Truṭi* - triad; ternary product

Vide *trasareṇu.*

त्र्यणुक - *Tryaṇuka* - triad (of atoms); three atoms grouped together

1. The smallest visible substance, according to Vais'eṣika. From these triads, grouped in different ways, all the various things are produced.

2. Vide *aṇu.*

तुच्छम् - *Tuccham* - utterly unreal (*atyanta-asat*)

1. The absolutely non-existent, e.g., the child of a barren woman.

2. According to Advaita, *māyā* is real to the ordinary individual, neither real nor unreal (*anirvacanīya*) to the philosopher, and unreal (*tuccha*) to the enlightened individual.

तुरीय - *Turīya* - the fourth; the transcendental Self; the supreme Reality

1. It is the fourth state of consciousness, according to Advaita. However, it is not really a state, but the underlying substratum of the other three states — the waking, dreaming, and deep sleep.

2. It is the fourth state beyond waking, dream, and sleep. It is the real Self which is beyond the changing modes of existence. It is indivisible, ungraspable, unthinkable, and unnameable. Each of the other three states have their own names (*vaiśvānara, taijasa,* and *prajñā*), but not the Absolute which is merely referred to as the fourth. It is *a-mātra* or modeless.

3. Vide *avāsthā, om,* and *pāda.*

तुरीयातीत - *Turīyātīta* - the state of individual soul in which it is in a totally blissful condition

This is a term used for the individual in Śaiva Siddhānta.

तुष्टि - *Tuṣṭi* - laziness; satisfaction; contentment

There are nine types of laziness, according to Sāṅkhya. They include: no exertion is necessary for an individual since *prakṛti* will herself bring about one's liberation (*ambhas*); it is not necessary to meditate, for it is enough if one merely renounces the householder's life (*salila*); there is no hurry, for salvation will come in its own time (*megha*); salvation will be worked out by fate (*bhāgya*); contentment leading to renunciation proceeds from five causes, e.g., the troubles of earning, the troubles of protecting the earned money, the natural waste of things earned by enjoyment, increase of desires leading to greater disappointments, and all gain leads to the injury of others.

त्वाच-प्रत्यक्ष - *Tvāca-pratyakṣa* - tactual perception

त्वक् - *Tvak* - sense of touch

1. One of the organs of knowledge. It is of three types: cool, hot, and lukewarm.
2. Vide *jñānendriya.*

त्याग - *Tyāga* - abandonment; renunciation

The *Bhagavad-gītā* considers true renunciation to be the relinquishment of the fruits of one's actions.

त्यागाङ्ग - *Tyāgāṅga* - part of the classification scheme of Vīra Śaivism

Vide *ṣaṭsthala*, *aṅga-sthala*, and chart no. 14.

U

उभयकर्मज - *Ubhaya-karmaja* - a type of disjunction where the separation of two conjoined substances takes place through the activity in both the substances

1. E.g., as when two wrestlers break apart (vide *vibhāga*).

2. A type of conjunction where the conjoining takes place due to the activity of both the substances. Vide *saṁyoga*.

उभयलिङ्गत्व - *Ubhaya-liṅgatva* - Brahman's twofold form

1. Śaiva Siddhānta: God is both transcendent and immanent, or both with form and without form.

2. Viśiṣṭādvaita: God has no blemishes and has all good qualities.

उभयवेदान्त - *Ubhaya-vedānta* - the twofold *Vedānta*

According to Viśiṣṭādvaita, the hymns of the *Āḻvārs* (*Divya-prabandha*) constitute the Tamil *Veda* and along with the Sanskrit texts (*prasthāna-traya*), they together constitute the twofold source of authority for the school.

उदाहरण - *Udāharaṇa* - illustration; example; corroboration

1. A member of a syllogism which is essential for establishing the validity of an argument; e.g.,

wherever there is smoke, there is fire, as in a hearth. It substantiates the reason (*hetu*) by citing the universal and an example.

2. Vide *anumāna.*

3. *Udāharaṇa* means 'example' and originally this member of a syllogism only contained the example. But it was realized that there could be no genuine inference from particulars to particulars. Thus, the universal was added to the example, and after the addition, the name of the member, as *udāharaṇa,* was retained. This shows that the Indian syllogism is deductive-inductive.

उडैयवर् - *Uḍaiyavar* - (Tamil term) he who holds the key to the two worlds; a name of Rāmānuja.

उदान - *Udāna* - one of the five vital airs

1. It is the life-breath which directs the vital currents of the body upwards.

2. Vide *prāṇa.*

उद्भिज्ज - *Udbhijja* - sprout-born

1. That whose birth comes out of the earth.

2. Vide *karma-kṛta.*

उद्भूत - *Udbhūta* - perceptible; manifested

उद्बोधक - *Udbodhaka* - that which causes something to manifest; stimulating element

उद्देश - *Uddeśa* - enumeration; object; end

उद्देश्य - *Uddeśya* - subject

ऊह - *Ūha* conjecture; indeterminate sensing

Vide *apoha* and *saṁśaya.*

उपबृंहण - *Upa-bṛṁhaṇa* – *Itihāsas* and *Purāṇas*

उपादान - *Upādāna* - mental clinging; causal substance; material cause

One of the twelve links in the causal chain of existence. Vide *pratītyasamutpāda.*

उपादानकारण - *Upādāna-kāraṇa* - material cause

E.g., thread is the material cause of cloth.

उपदेश – *Upadeśa* - initiation; spiritual instruction

उपाधि - *Upādhi* – adventitious condition; association; vehicle; attribute; support; limiting adjunct

उपाध्याय - *Upādhyāya* - tutor; one of the six stages of the Jaina ascetic order

He is empowered to give discourses on spiritual matters, but not to correct erring individuals.

उपहित - *Upahita* - the conditioned; with attributes; relational; with a mark

उपक्रम - *Upakrama* – the beginning; introduction

Vide *ṣaḍ-liṅga.*

उपक्रमन्याय - *Upakrama-nyāya* – the principle that there is no conflict between the earlier and subsequent cognitions

उपलब्धि - *Upalabdhi* - apprehension; perception

According to Jainism, one type of *mati-jñāna.*

उपमान - *Upamāna* - comparison; analogy

1. The distinctive cause of the valid cognition of similarity. Nyāya, Mīmāṁsā, and Advaita admit comparison as an independent means of valid knowledge (*pramāṇa*).

2. Nyāya says: it is the knowledge which is gained from a word which signifies a thing, hitherto unknown. and on the strength of its similarity with some other known thing, it becomes known.

3. Mīmāṁsā says: it is the knowledge which is gained by inferring that the unknown object which is presently being perceived, is similar to an object which has been perceived before and is remembered.

4. Advaita agrees with Mīmāṁsā as far as it goes. But the former also includes in its definition the knowledge of the similarity between the perceived object to the remembered one. Mīmāṁsā stops with the knowledge of the similarity between the remembered object to the perceived one.

उपमिति - *Upamiti* - assimilative cognition or experience

उपनय - *Upanaya* - subsumptive correlation; the application

1. One of the members of a five-membered syllogism. It shows that the reason (*hetu*), which is known to be concomitant with the major term (*sādhya*), is present in the subject (*pakṣa*); e.g., the hill has smoke which is invariably concomitant with fire.

2. Vide *anumāna*.

उपनीत - *Upanīta* - that which is brought (to the cognition through supernormal relation)

उपनिषद् - *Upaniṣad* - to sit close by devotedly; the last portion of the *Vedas*

1. They are treatises in poetry and prose on spiritual and philosophical subjects.

2. There are ten principal *Upaniṣads*: *Īśa, Kena, Kaṭha, Praśna, Muṇḍaka, Māṇḍūkya, Taittirīya, Aitareya, Chāndogya,* and *Bṛhadāraṇyaka.*

3. They are the concluding portion of the *Vedas.* They are also called *Vedānta* (which in turn bases its theories on the ideas of the *Upaniṣads*).

4. Some hold the view that '*upaniṣad*' literally means 'secret teaching' (*rahasya*); and as the *Upaniṣads* are so varied and difficult to decide as to what their import is, they account for the emergence in later times of the diverse schools of *Vedānta.*

5. Vide *prasthāna-traya.*

उपन्यास - *Upanyāsa* - statement; discourse

उपपत्ति - *Upapatti* - intelligibility in the light of reasoning; explanation; evidence

Vide *ṣaḍ-liṅga.*

उपरति - *Uparati* - (once the senses have been restrained,) the power to ensure that the senses may not once again be tempted towards worldly objects

1. It is a limb of the virtues necessary for an aspirant to be spiritually qualified.

2. Vide *sādhana-catuṣṭaya.*

उपासक - *Upāsaka* - one who meditates; an aspirant

उपसंहार - *Upasamhāra* - the end; recapitulation

Vide *ṣaḍ-liṅga.*

उपासन - *Upāsana* - meditation; worship

उपष्टम्भक - *Upaṣṭambhaka* - supportive

उपस्थ - *Upastha* – organ of generation

1. One of the five organs of action.
2. Vide *karmendriya.*

उपस्थिति - *Upasthiti* - thought, presence

उपाय - *Upāya* - skilful means; means of liberation

1. According to Buddhism, it is a device or way to entice individuals towards perfection. Thus the Buddha was said to be using skilful means whenever he said something, which though not totally true, was nevertheless instrumental in furthering an aspirant's progress.

2. There are four steps to liberation according to Kashmir Śaivism: *āṇavopāya*, *śāktopāya*, *śāmbhavopāya*, and *anupāya.* Among them each preceding step leads to the next naturally. *Āṇavopāya* (also called *kriyopāya*) is the path which uses external aids like the eight-limbed *yoga*, *japa*, etc. *Śāktopāya* (also called *jñānopāya*) is the path by which one attempts to transcend duality. Recognition of one's essential unity is sought. *Śāmbhavopāya* (also called *icchopāya*) is the stage wherein the knowledge of the ultimate Reality arises through a mere exercise of will power. *Anupāya* (also called

ānandopāya) is the last stage and is for advanced individuals. In this stage there is total liberation.

उपायप्रत्ययसमाधि - *Upāya-pratyaya-samādhi* - a type of attributeless *samādhi* in which ignorance is totally destroyed

As wisdom is aroused, all of one's passions (*kleśa*) are destroyed and the mind (*citta*) is established in true knowledge, according to Yoga.

उपयोग - *Upayoga* - understanding; use

1. One of the classes of *śruta-jñāna*, or a stage therein, according to Jainism. It is the stage where there is a proper understanding of a new object of cognition. This stage is preceded by the processes of integration and consideration. It is divided into apprehension (*nirākāra-upayoga*) and comprehension (*sākāra-upayoga*).

2. Determinate understanding is of eight kinds: *mati-jñāna*, *śruta-jñāna*, *avadhi-jñāna*, *manaḥ-paryāya-jñāna*, *kevala-jñāna*, *mati-ajñāna*, *śruta-ajñāna*, and *avadhi-ajñāna*. Indeterminate understanding is of four kinds: *cakṣu-darśana*, *acakṣu-darśana*, *avadhi-darśana*, and *kevala-darśana*.

3. It is a substratum of the faculty of cognition. which is only a manifestation of consciousness in a limited form. It is the defining characteristic of the individual soul.

उपेक्षा - *Upekṣā* - indifference; equanimity resulting from disinterestedness

Vide *brahma-vihāra*.

उपेय - *Upeya* - end to be attained

ऊर्ध्व - *Ūrdhva* - above

Where the gods reside, according to Jainism.

ऊर्ध्वसामान्य - *Ūrdhva-sāmānya* - sameness of qualities in time

उत्क्रमण - *Utkramaṇa* - ascent from the body

उत्क्रान्ति - *Utkrānti* - when the physical body is cast off, the individual soul, according to Dvaita, rises in its subtle body to the world of the gods where it will wait until the world's destruction

उत्क्षेपण - *Utkṣepaṇa* – lifting up; stretching upward

Vide *karma.*

उत्पाद् - *Utpāda* – origination

1. One of the four functions of action.
2. Vide *karma.*

उत्पत्ति - *Utpatti* - origination; generation

1. One of the four possible effects of action.
2. Vide *karma.*

उत्सर्ग - *Utsarga* - general rule

उत्तम - *Uttama* - high; superior; best

उत्तमाधिकारि - *Uttamādhikāri* - one who has the highest qualification for Vedic knowledge

उत्तमाश्रमिन् - *Uttamāśramin* - a *sannyāsin*; a member of the highest stage of life

Vide *āśrama.*

उत्तरमीमांसासूत्र - *Uttara-mīmāṁsā-sūtra* - another name of the *Brahma-sūtra*

The *Brahma-sūtra* is called as such because it is an enquiry into the final sections of the *Vedas*

V

वाच् - *Vāc* - word; divine Word; logos; speech

Vide *karmendriya.*

वचन - *Vacana* - pithy epigrams composed by Vīra Śaivite mystics which expound Vīra Śaivism in a popular and understandable manner

वाद - *Vāda* - debate; argument; theory

1. One of the sixteen categories of the Nyāya school.

2. Vide *padārtha* and chart no. 6.

वडकलै - *Vaḍakalai* (Tamil term) - the Northern sect of Viśiṣṭādvaita

1. The followers of Vedāntadeśika. They accept both the Tamil Prabandham and the Sanskrit tradition as equally authoritative.

2. Vide *teṅkalai.*

वाग्योग - *Vāg-yoga* - sensation of *karma* particles through speech

1. According to Jainism, it is a type of *āsrava.*

2. Vide *āsrava.*

वह्नि - *Vahni* - fire

वैभाषिक - *Vaibhāṣika* - an early school of Buddhism belonging to the Hīnayāna tradition

Their authority is the *Abhidhamma* texts and especially the commentaries written thereon (*vibhāṣās*). They are of a realistic school which holds that both things and ideas are real and that the mind can directly know objects in perception. However, things and ideas are not real as this term is commonly understood, for, what are real are *dharmas* — the ultimate particulars which are neither substances nor attributes. These ultimate elements of existence are real yet momentary. They are the simplest entities and give rise to all else by combining into aggregates.

वैचित्र्य - *Vaicitrya* - the notion that 'I am the doer'

वैदिक - *Vaidika* - Vedic

Vide *veda.*

वैकारिक - *Vaikārika* - the sāttvic aspect of the ego (*ahaṅkāra*)

It is the first development of the intellect (*buddhi*), according to the evolutionary scheme of Sāṅkhya.

वैखानस - *Vaikhānasa* - the *Āgamas* that originate from Lord *Brahmā*

They are valid source books according to Viśiṣṭādvaita and Dvaita. Vide *āgama.*

वैराग्य - *Vairāgya* - dispassion; detachment

वैषम्य - *Vaiṣamya* - partiality

वैशेषिक - *Vaiśeṣika* - one of the six orthodox schools of Indian philosophy

It was founded by Kaṇāda and is closely allied to Nyāya. The term '*Vaiśeṣika*' means excellence or distinction; the system is so-called because, according to its followers, it excels other systems. The peculiar feature of the system is its doctrine of 'particularity'.

वैश्वानर - *Vaiśvānara* - universal being

1. The self of the waking state. It is the self which leads all creatures in diverse ways to the enjoyment of different objects.

2. The place of meditation on it is the right eye.

3. According to Advaita, it stands for the cosmic self in waking, while *viśva* stands for the waking individual self.

4. Vide *pāda*.

वाक् - *Vāk* - (vide *vāc*); *Vāgdevī* the Goddess of Speech

She is the Divine Mother (sound) who became all the words.

वाकोवाक्य - *Vākovākya* - science of logic

1. It is another name of the Nyāya school.

2. It is called the science of logic in the *Chāndogya Upaniṣad*.

वाक्य - *Vākya* - word; syntactical connection

Vide *aṅgatva-bodhaka-pramāṇa*.

वाक्यैकवाक्यता - *Vākyaika-vākyatā* - syntactical unity of sentences

1. When sentences which are complete in respect of their own meanings again combine on the basis of their relationship, one being principal and the others subordinate, they form a syntactic unity.

2. Vide *padaika-vākyatā* and *eka-vākyatā.*

वाक्यार्थ - *Vākyārtha* - verbal sense; primary meaning

1. It is of two kinds: *bheda-saṁsarga* (relation of duality) and *abheda-saṁsarga* (relation of non-duality). In the former, the meaning of a sentence may be conveyed through a relation obtaining among the words conveying difference, e.g., bring the cow by means of a stick. All the words denote and connote different entities. In the latter, oneness is known, or conveyed, through the principle of grammatical co-ordination (*sāmānādhikaraṇya*)- two words which connote different things, denote the same object, e.g., the blue lotus.

2. *Abheda-saṁsarga* is of two kinds according to Advaita: *saṁarga-abheda* (oneness with relation) which is at the relational level and is called oneness by courtesy only. The object may be one (blue lotus), but it has two attributes — blueness and lotusness. *Svarūpa-abheda* (non relational proposition or an identity statement) is true oneness, for the words employed both connote and denote the same entity; e.g., this is that Devadatta or *tat tvam asi.*

3. The primary meaning is also called *śakyārtha, mukhyārtha* and *abhidheyārtha.*

वाक्यार्थबोध - *Vākyārtha-bodha* - verbal judgement; knowledge gained by sentence-meaning

वंश - *Vamśa* - lineage

1. One of the five topics with which a *Purāṇa* should deal.

2. Vide *purāṇa.*

वंशानुचरित - *Vaṁśānucarita* - the future continuance of lineage

1. One of the five topics with which a *Purāṇa* should deal.

2. Vide *purāṇa.*

वानप्रस्थ - *Vānaprastha* - forest-dweller

Vide *āśrama*

वन्दन - *Vandana* - offering gratitude for blessings received from God

Vide *bhakti.*

वर्ण - *Varṇa* - caste; alphabets

1. There are four castes or social classes which divide individuals-in-society, according to one's nature and aptitude. They are: the *brāhmaṇa,* who studies and teaches the *Vedas*; the *kṣatriya,* who protects others; the *vaiśyas,* who are traders and merchants; and the *śūdras,* who serve others. This division is based on the principle of social economy. Its basis is functional. It refers to the social and institutional side of life and gives a horizontal view of society. Each class is relative, though uncondi–

tionally obligatory in the sphere in which it is respectively applicable. One specializes religion, politics, economics, and labour according to one's station in life and individual aptitude.

2. Regarding *varṇa* as alphabetical letters, vide *śabda.*

वर्णक - *Varṇaka* - chapter

वर्तमान - *Vartamāna* - turning; unfolding; present (tense)

1. A type of action.

2. Vide *karma.*

वार्त्तिक - *Vārttika* - verse-commentary

1. These are commentaries whose purpose is to enquire into: what has been said (*ukta*), what has not been said (*anukta*), and what has not been said clearly (*durukta*).

2. Vide *vārttikakāra.*

वार्त्तिककार - *Vārttikakāra* - commentator

1. Sureśvara is the commentator of the Advaita school. He wrote *Bṛhadāraṇyakopaniṣad-bhāṣya-vārttika* and *Taittirīyopaniṣad-bhāṣya-vārttika.*

2. Kumārila Bhaṭṭa is the commentator of the Mīmāṁsā school. He wrote the *Śloka-vārttika,* the *Tantra-vārttika*, and the *Ṭup-ṭīkā.*

वासना - *Vāsanā* - latent tendency

A latent potency or residual impression which clings to the individual. It is also called *saṁskāra.*

वशित्व - *Vaśitva* - the power by which all living beings may be conquered

Vide *aṣṭa-aiśvarya.*

वास्तवी - *Vāstavī* – real

वस्तु - *Vastu* - object; thing

वस्तुतन्त्र - *Vastu* - object-dependent

1. Knowledge is said to be object-dependent according to Advaita.

2. Vide *puruṣa-tantra.*

वासुदेव - *Vāsudeva* - one of the manifestations of *Īśvara*

1. He is the highest Self and possesses all the six attributes: knowledge (*jñāna*), lordship (*aiśvarya*), potency (*śakti*), strength (*bala*), virility (*vīrya*), and splendour (*tejas*). He hypostatizes into: *Keśava*, *Nārāyaṇa*, and *Mādhava.*

2. Vide *vyūha.*

वात्सल्य - *Vātsalya* – love as between parents and child

This is parental love. Vide *bhakti.*

वायु - *Vāyu* - air; life-breath

1. It is of five types: *prāṇa*, *apāna*, *samāna*, *vyāna*, and *udāna.*

2. It is one of the five elements.

3. Vide *mahā-bhūta* and *prāṇa.*

वेद - *Veda* - knowledge; wisdom

1. The sacred scriptures (*śruti*) of the Hindu tradition. They are impersonal (*apauruṣeya*) and eternal (*nitya*). There are four *Vedas* as arranged

by Vyāsa: *Ṛg-veda*, *Yajur-veda*, *Sāma-veda*, and *Atharva-veda*. These are divided into: *mantra*, *brāhmaṇa*, *āraṇyaka*, and *upaniṣad* sections. Strictly the *Veda* stands for the parts known as *mantra* and *brāhmaṇa*. The appendages to the *brāhmaṇa* are the *āraṇyakas* and the concluding portion of the *āraṇyakas* are the *upaniṣads*.

2. There once existed 1131 recensions (*Śākhās*) of the Vedic *Saṁhitās*. The *Ṛg-veda* had 21, the *Yajur-veda* had 101, the *Sāma-veda* had 1000, and the *Atharva-veda* had 9.

3. The *Ṛg-veda* is the *veda* of hymns of wisdom. The *Sāma-veda* is a liturgical collection of hymns, mostly taken from the *Ṛg-veda*, sung to certain melodies. The *Yajur-veda* is the scripture of sacrificial rites. The *Atharva-veda* is comprised of formulas intended mainly to counteract evil, diseases, and other practical events. The *Yajur-veda* is said to be of two recensions: the white (*śukla*) and the black (*kṛṣṇa*).

4. The *Ṛg-veda* is for the priest whose function is to recite the hymns inviting the gods to the sacrificial altar. The *Sāma-veda* is for the *Udgātṛ* priest who sings the hymns. *Yajur-veda* is for the *Adhvaryu* priest who performs the sacrifice according to the rules. The *Atharva-veda* is for the *Brāhmaṇa* priest who is the general supervisor of the sacrifice.

5. The *Ṛg-veda* contains the *Aitareya Upaniṣad*. The *Sāma-veda* contains the *Chāndogya Upaniṣad* and the *Kena Upaniṣad*. The *Yajur-veda* contains the *Īśā*, the *Taittirīya*, the *Bṛhadāraṇyaka*, and the

Kaṭha Upaniṣads. The *Atharva-veda* contains the *Praśna*, the *Muṇḍaka*, and the *Māṇḍūkya Upaniṣads.*

6. Vide chart no. 1.

वेदना - *Vedanā*- sense-experience; sensation; feeling

1. One of the twelve links in the causal chain of existence. Vide *pratītya-samutpāda.*

2. One of the five aggregates. Vide *skandha.*

3. It is caused by sense contact and consists of pleasure, pain, and indifference, according to Buddhism.

वेदाङ्ग - *Vedāṅga* - limbs of the *Vedas*

The limbs of the *Vedas* are: phonetics (*śikṣā*), prosody (*chandas*), grammar (*vyākaraṇa*), etymology (*nirukta*), astronomy (*jyotiṣa*), and ceremonial (*kalpa*). *Kalpa* is of two kinds: *śrauta-sūtra* which relates to the *Vedas* or *śruti*, and *smārta-sūtra* which is based on the *smṛti.*

वेदनीय - *Vedanīya* - feeling producing *karma*

1. According to Jainism, they are one of the eight main types of *karmas.* These are non-obscuring producing actions which generate feelings of pleasure and feelings of pain (*asadvedya*).

2. Vide *karma.*

वेदान्त – *Vedānta* - end of the *Vedas*; Uttara-mīmāṁsā

1. A name of the *Upaniṣads.* Vide *upaniṣad.*

2. A name of the different schools of philosophy, founded on the teachings of the *Upaniṣads.* The

major schools are: Advaita, Viśiṣṭādvaita, and Dvaita.

3. The basic texts of Vedānta are the *Upaniṣads*, the *Bhagavad-gītā*, and the *Brahma-sūtra*. Vide *prasthāna-traya*.

4. The central question considered in the Vedāntic schools concerns the nature of *Brahman*.

वेदान्तसूत्र - *Vedānta-sūtra* - another name of the *Brahma-sūtra*

It is so called because it is the aphoristic text on Vedānta.

वेग - *Vega* - motion; velocity; inerita

According to Vaiśeṣika, it is of three types: *ubhaya-karmaja*, *anyatara-karmaja*, and *vibhāgaja* (vide each listed separately). It is the quality of a moving substance which is responsible for its continuing in the same direction.

विभाग - *Vibhāga* - disjunction; division; separation

According to Vaiśeṣika, it is a type of quality (*guṇa*). It is that entity (or quality) by virtue of which the connection or contact of things is destroyed.

विभागज - *Vibhāgaja* - motion caused by disjunction

1. A type of motion, according to Nyāya-Vaiśeṣika.

2. Vide *vega*.

विभङ्ग - *Vibhaṅga* - a fallacious form of clairvoyance; one of the *Abhidhamma* texts

1. Vide *avadhi.*

2. Vide *Abhidhamma-piṭaka.*

विभव - *Vibhava* - the Descents of Viṣṇu; *avatāras*

1. The descent of *Īśvara* among mankind. It is of ten main advents: *Matsya, Kūrma, Varāha, Nṛsiṁha, Vāmana, Paraśurāma, Rāmacandra, Balabhadra, Kṛṣṇa,* and *Kalki.* Some people substitute *Buddha* for *Kṛṣṇa.* These incarnations originate from the *vyūha, Aniruddha.* The cause for the descent is *Īśvara's* will only, and is for the protection of the good and the destruction of the evils.

2. Vide *vyūha.*

विभाव - *Vibhāva* - one of the three efficient causes of *rasa* (emotion)

It is of two kinds: *ālambana* (main excitant) and *uddīpana* (contributory excitant). Vide *rasa.*

विभ्रम - *Vibhrama* - delusion (vide *bhrama*)

विभु - *Vibhu* - all-pervasive

According to Advaita and Nyāya, the form of the individual soul is all-pervasive.

विभुद्रव्य - *Vibhu-dravya* - all-pervasive substance

विभूति - *Vibhūti* - sacred ash; manifestations of divine power

1. One of the eight aids, according to Vīra Śaivism. It is the smearing of the sacred ash upon one's body. Vide *aṣṭa-āvaraṇa.*

2. Incarnations such as spiritual teachers, etc., who aid mankind, are called *vibhūtis.*

3. According to Viśiṣṭādvaita, the manifestations of *Vāsudeva,* e.g., *Saṅkarṣaṇa*, *Pradyumna*, and *Aniruddha.*

4. Miraculous powers are also called *vibhūtis.*

विचार - *Vicāra* - reflection; enquiry

1. According to the Yoga school, it is a state of *samādhi*. It is of two kinds; *nirvicāra* (when the mind concentrates and is one with the *tanmātras* without any notion of their qualities), and *savicāra* (when the mind concentrates on the *tanmātras* with a remembrance of their qualities).

2. Vide *samādhi.*

विच्छिन्न - *Vicchinna* - limited

विचिकित्सा - *Vicikitsā* - doubt (suspicion)

विदेहमुक्ति - *Videha-mukti* - liberation attained at the time of leaving one's body

विधेय - *Vidheya* - predicate; obedient

विधेयत्व - *Vidheyatva* - the quality of being controlled

According to Viśiṣṭādvaita, all things are controlled by *Īśvara.*

विधि - *Vidhi* - injunction; positive command in the *Vedas,* according to Mīmāṁsā

1. They are of three types: *apūrva-vidhi* (original injunction), *niyama-vidhi* (restrictive injunction), and *parisaṅkhyā-vidhi* (exclusive injunction) (vide each listed separately).

2. There are five classes of injunctions: *karmot-patti-vākya* which enjoins a certain act; *guṇavākya* which enjoins certain necessary details connected with a prescribed act; *phala-vākya* which mentions the result following from the performance of a certain act; *phalaguṇa-vākya* which lays down certain necessary details as conducive to a particular result; *saguṇa-karmotpatti-vākya* which enjoins an action along with an accessory detail.

3. According to Mīmāṁsā, positive commands include: obligatory duties (*nitya-karma*), occasional rites (*naimittika-karma*), and optional rites (*kāmya-karma*). They refer to supra-mundane affairs and are to be understood literally.

विधिवाक्य - *Vidhi-vākya* - injuctive sentence

Vide chart no. 1

विद्वत्सन्न्यास - *Vidvat-sannyāsa* - becoming a renunciant after knowing the truth

1. It is asceticism resorted by *jñānis* and *siddhas*. It is called renunciation by the wise.

2. Vide *sannyāsa*.

विद्या - *Vidyā* - knowledge; meditation; wisdom

1. There are thirty-two types or varieties of *Brahmavidyā* described in the *Upaniṣads* for securing liberation. These are various types of meditation as for instance, meditation on the *praṇava mantra, om*.

2. The chief branches of knowledge are four, according to Vais'eṣika: *ānvīkṣikī* (logic and philo-

sophy), *trayī* (the Vedic religion), *vārtā* (economic science and philosophy of wealth), and *daṇḍanīti* (the science of polity).

विद्यापाद् - *Vidyā-pāda* - that part of the *Āgamas* which sets forth the philosophical doctrines

Vide *āgama.*

विद्यास्थान - *Vidyā-sthāna* - the fourteen sources of knowledge

These are: the four *Vedas*, the six *vedāṅgas*, *Purāṇas*, *mīmāṁsā*, *nyāya*, and *dharma-śāstra.*

विघ्नध्वंस - *Vighna-dhvaṁsa* - destruction of obstacles

विजातीय - *Vijātīya* - one of the three types of difference which exists between things which belong to two different classes

1. E.g., the difference between a tree and a stone.
2. Vide *bheda.*

विज्ञान - *Vijñāna* - wisdom; cognition; intellect; consciousness

1. One of the twelve links in the causal chain of existence. Vide *pratītya-samutpāda.*
2. One of the five aggregates. Vide *skandha.*
3. The intellect. It is also called *buddhi.*

विज्ञानमयकोश - *Vijñānamaya-kośa* - the sheath of the intellect

1. It is located within the mental sheath (*manomaya-kośa*). These two, together with the *prāṇamaya-kośa,* constitute the subtle body.
2. Vide *kośa.*

विज्ञानाकल - *Vijñānākala* - an individual soul in which the bonds of *karma* and *māyā* have been removed and only *āṇava-mala* remains

1. This type of individual soul no longer has to return to empirical existence when it gives up its body, for it is fit for release.

2. Vide *jīva.*

विज्ञानकेवलिन् - *Vijñāna-kevalin* - a liberated individual soul

According to Kashmir Śaivism, it is a term for an individual who has become liberated.

विज्ञप्ति - *Vijñapti* - perceptions

विकलज्ञान - *Vikala-jñāna* - otherworldly knowledge

According to Jainism, it is divided into two: *avadhi* and *manaḥ-paryāya.*

विकल्प - *Vikalpa* - imagination; mental construct; abstraction

According to Śāṅkhya, the mind (*citta*) has five processes, among which are abstraction, construction, and different kinds of imagination.

विकार - *Vikāra* - change; change of form; gluiness

विकास - *Vikāsa* - expansion

विकृति - *Vikṛti* - modification

1. The work of action (*karma*) is fourfold. This is one of its four effects.

2. Vide *karma.*

विक्षेप - *Vikṣepa* - projection; false projection

1. It is the projecting power of ignorance, accordind to Advaita.

2. Vide *avidyā*.

विक्षेपशक्ति - *Vikṣepa-śakti* - the power of *māyā* by which the manifold experiences are projected

विक्षिप्त - *Vikṣipta* - distracted; unsteady

A state of the mind where it is unstable and shifts its attention from object to object.

विमल - *Vimala* - purity; unblemished; without stain

1. One of the ten stages of a *bodhisattva.*

2. Vide *bodhisattva.*

विमोह - *Vimoha* - error; delusion

विनाश - *Vināśa* - destruction; annihilation

विनयपिटक - *Vinaya-piṭaka* - the basket of rules of conduct

1. The Buddhist Scripture (compiled by Upali) which gives the rules of conduct. It governed the life and behaviour of the *saṅgha* and its members.

2. Vide *tri-piṭaka.*

विपाक - *Vipāka* - a type of transformation

विपक्ष - *Vipakṣa* - counter-instance

1. That which is devoid of the probandum as well as anything similar to it. The absence of the subject is known for certain in this type of reasoning.

2. In a ten-membered syllogism, it was the fifth member, e.g., the negative example.

3. Vide *pakṣa.*

विपरीत - *Viparīta* – contrary; contrary to what it is

Uncertainty as to the exact nature of truth. It is a type of delusion.

विपरीतभावना - *Viparīta-bhāvanā* - error; the opposite stream of thought

It is said to be removed by contemplation, according to Advaita.

विपरीतज्ञान - *Viparīta-jñāna* - false knowledge

विपरीतख्याति - *Viparīta-khyāti* - contrary apprehension

1. The theory of error propounded by the Prābhākara Mīmāṁsā school. Error arises when an object appears otherwise than what it is. The object of error is held to be real and it is the identity of its appearance with its basis which is unreal.

2. Vide *khyāti-vāda.*

विपर्यय - *Viparyaya* - erroneous cognition; illusion; mis-apprehension

The *Sāṅkhya-kārikā* lists its causes as 5: ignorance (*avidyā*), egoism (*asmitā*), attatchment (*rāga*), antipathy (*dveṣa*), and self-love (*abhiniveśa*). These five are also called: *tamas, moha, mahāmoha, tāmiśra,* and *andhatāmiśra.*

विपर्ययग्रहण - *Viparyaya-grahaṇa* - mis-apprehension; knowing the truth otherwise

1. It is an aspect of ignorance. To understand ignorance positively as mis-apprehension or to

understand it negatively as non-apprehension (*agrahaṇa*), is a question asked of the Advaitin's concept of *avidyā*.

2. Vide *avidyā*.

विप्रलम्भ - *Vipralambha* - separation from the beloved one

विपुलमति - *Vipula-mati* - a type of telepathy

1. According to Jainism, it has a spatial range between four *yojanas* and two and a half *dvīpas*. Its temporal range is between eight and an infinite number of incarnations. It lasts until the dawn of omniscience.

2. Vide *mati*.

वीर - *Vīra* - heroic; strength

According to Jainism, it is a stage wherein one becomes master of oneself

विराग - *Virāga* - non-attatchment

विराज् - *Virāj* - the macrocosm; the manifested universe; the world-man

According to Advaita, *viśva* (*sthūla*) and *vaiśvānara* are equated with *virāj*.

विरक्ति - *Virakti* - self-renouncement

The first pre-requisite for those who seek *Brahman*.

विराट् - *Virāṭ* - the cosmic form of the Self as the cause of the gross world

Vide *virāj*.

विरोध - *Virodha* - opposition

विरुद्ध - *Viruddha* - contradictory

A type of fallacious reasoning in which the reason (*hetu*) is contradictory. Here, the reason proves the contradictory of what is intended to be proved; e.g., 'sound is eternal because it is produced' only proves the non-eternality of sound because whatever is produced is necessarily non-eternal.

2. Vide *hetvābhāsa.*

वीर्य - *Vīrya* - strength; zeal

1. One of the six *pāramitās* of Buddhism.
2. One of the six attributes of *Īśvara.*

विषाद् - *Viṣāda* - depression; dullness

विसंवादिव्यवहार - *Visaṁvādi-vyavahāra* - unsuccessful volition

विशय - *Viśaya* - doubt

विषय - *Viṣaya* - object; subject-matter; content

विषयवाक्य - *Viṣaya-vākya* - a Vedic statement which is taken up as the subject for investigation

विषयविषयिभाव - *Viṣaya-viṣayi-bhāva* - the relation between the revealed and the revealer, or the relation between the object and its knowledge

विषयिन् - *Viṣayin* - the subject who knows

विशेष - *Viśeṣa* – the qualified; particularity

1. A category in Vaiśeṣika metaphysics. It is the feature which distinguishes one individual from another. *Viśeṣas* are innumerable, eternal and

partless. The Vaiśeṣika system depends upon this category for its pluralism. It is the differentia of ultimate things which are otherwise alike.

2. It is the basic concept of Dvaita. It justifies their concept of pluralism. They hold that every substance has an infinite number of particulars, with one for each quality. It is the power by which a quality is distinguished from a substance. They distinguish the different aspects which they qualify, and as they are self-distinguishing, they do not need another quality to distinguish themselves.

विशेषगुण - *Viśeṣa-guṇa* - specific quality

विशेषण - *Viśeṣaṇa* - qualification; attributive element

विशेषणता - *Viśeṣaṇatā* - that mode of contact which leads to the perception of non-existence

1. It is also called *viśeṣaṇa-viśeṣya-bhāva.*

2. Vide *sannikarṣa.*

विशेषणविशेष्यभाव - *Viśeṣaṇa-viśeṣya-bhāva* - the relation of the qualification and the qualified; a mode of contact

1. It is also called *viśeṣaṇatā.*

2. According to Nyāya, this is the contact for the perception of non-existence (*abhāva*).

3. Vide *sannikarṣa* and *viśeṣaṇatā.*

विशेषणविशेष्यताज्ञान - *Viśeṣaṇa-viśeṣyatā-jñāna* - knowledge which has a subject-predicate relation

Vide *vākyārtha.*

विशेषाप्ति - *Viśeṣāpti* - the emergence of new features

The Dvaita theory of causation. The world originates from matter with newer and newer forms. At every stage this emergence is dependent upon God's will.

विशेष्य - *Viśeṣya* - the substantive element; the qualified

विशेष्यतावच्छेदक - *Viśeṣyatāvacchedaka* - determinant of substantiveness

विशिष्ट - *Viśiṣṭa* - that which is qualified; determinate

1. According to Dvaita, it is the form a thing aequires when it gets related to its attributes. It is the substance and quality taken together. It is one of the ten categories of Dvaita. Vide *padārtha*.

2. According to Viśiṣṭādvaita, the qualified is one, but the factors qualifying it are quite distinct, though inseparable, from it.

विशिष्टाद्वैत - *Viśiṣṭādvaita* - qualified non-dualism; pan-synthetic monism

A theistic school of Vedānta whose great consolidator and exponent is Rāmānuja. It posits three ultimate realities: *Īśvara, cit,* and *acit,* which exist in an inseparable relationship, though *cit* and *acit* are dependent upon the independent *Īśvara.* The complex whole forms an organic unity and thus its name, Viśiṣṭādvaita.

विशिष्टैक्य - *Viśiṣṭaikya* - unity in the form of an organic whole involving several attributes

विशिष्टज्ञान - *Viśiṣṭa-jñāna* - qualified knowledge

विशिष्टप्रतीति - *Viśiṣṭa-pratīti* - determinant cognition

विशिष्टविषय - *Viśiṣṭa-viṣaya* - qualified object

विश्लेष - *Viśleṣa* - separation

विशिष्टबुद्धि - *Viśiṣṭa-buddhi* - qualified cognition

विष्णु - *Viṣṇu* - the Supreme Lord; the all-pervading

1. According to Viśiṣṭādvaita, he is the sole Reality, one without a second, having the sentient *(cit)* and insentient *(acit)* for his qualifications. He is the means to liberation and the goal to be attained.

2. He abides in a fivefold form as: *para*, *vyūha*, *vibhava*, *antaryāmin*, and *arcā*.

3. He has six divine qualities: knowledge (*jñāna*), strength (*bala*), lordship (*aiśvarya*), power (*śakti*) virility (*vīrya*), and splendour (*tejas*).

4. Among His manifestations are: *Saṅkarṣaṇa*, *Pradyumna*, *Aniruddha*, and *Vāsudeva*.

5. His weapons include: the conch (*śaṅkha*), discus (*cakra*), club (*gadā*), sword (*khaḍga*), and bow (*śārṅga*).

6. One of the names of the Law Books. Vide *smrti*.

विष्फुलिङ्गन्याय - *Viṣphuliṅga-nyāya* - the analogy of fire and its sparks

विशुद्धि - *Viśuddhi* - purity; *cakra*

One of the seven *cakras*. It is located in the throat centre. Vide *cakra*.

विश्व - *Viśva* - the individual form of the Self having egoism in a gross body while awake; universe

1. It is the form of the Self in its waking state according to Advaita.

2. It is pervasive of the entire body but for purposes of meditation, it has its seat in the right eye. Its limiting adjunct is the gross body (*sthūla-śarīra*).

3. Vide *pāda*.

विश्वाधिक - *Viśvādhika* - more than the universe; transcendent

विश्वमाया - *Viśva-māyā* - universal nescience

विश्वरूप - *Viśva-rūpa* - of the form of the universe

विश्वातिग - *Viśvātiga* - transcendent

विश्वोत्तीर्ण - *Viśvottīrṇa* - transcendent

वीत - *Vīta* - a type of inference

1. Inference is classified into two types, according to Sāṅkhya. The *vīta* type is where there is a positive concomitance between the reason (*hetu*) and the major term (*sādhya*). It is divided into two varieties: (i) *pūrvavat*, which is based on the observed concomitance of the specified reason and the major term, i.e., smoke and fire, and which is known through prior perception, as observed in a hearth; (ii) *sāmānyato-dṛṣṭa* is the concomitance which is known through similarity.

2. Vide *anumāna*.

वितल - *Vitala* - hell

1. The nether pole of *Tapo-loka*. It is a state changing towards materiality.

2. Vide *loka* and *tala*.

वितण्डा - *Vitaṇḍā* - destructive criticism; destructive argument

1. One of the sixteen categories of the Nyāya school. Vide *padārtha* and chart no. 6.

2. This is a destructive criticism which seeks to refute an opponent's doctrine without seeking to establish or formulate any new doctrine of one's own.

वितर्क - *Vitarka* - a state of *samādhi*

1. It is of two kinds: *savitarka* and *nirvitarka*.

2. Vide *samādhi*.

वीतसन्देह - *Vīta-sandeha* - free from doubt

विवाद - *Vivāda* - dispute

विवरण - *Vivaraṇa* - explanation

विवरणकार - *Vivaraṇakāra* - a name of Prakāśātman, the author of the *Pañcapādikā-vivaraṇa*, a commentary on Padmapāda's *Pañcapādikā*

विवरणप्रस्थान - *Vivaraṇa-prasthāna* - the *Vivaraṇa* school of Advaita

1. It is one of the two schools of Advaita. Vide *Bhāmatī*.

2. Its most important works are: the *Pañcapādikā* of Padmapāda, the *Pañcapādikā-vivaraṇa* of

Prakāsātman, and the *Vivaraṇa-prameya-saṅgraha* of Vidyāraṇya.

3. Suresvara's works are reputed to have been the inspiration of the school.

विवर्त - *Vivarta* - transfiguration; apparent change; illusory appearance

विवर्तवाद - *Vivarta-vāda* - the theory of apparent change; the theory of phenomenal appearance

1. The Advaita theory of causation which posits that the world is an illusory appearance superimposed by ignorance (*avidyā*) on *Brahman.*

2. Vide *pariṇāma-vāda* and *ābhāsa-vāda.*

विवेक - *Viveka* - discrimination

विविदिषासन्न्यास - *Vividiṣā-sannyāsa* - renunciation for the purpose of desire to know

1. According to Visiṣṭādvaita, it is renunciation for seekers and *sādhakas.* It is a preliminary renunciation and is renunciation with a desire to know.

2. Vide *vidvat-sannyāsa* and *sannyāsa.*

विविक्तशय्यासन - *Vivikta-Śayyāsana* - an external penance in Jainism; to keep thoroughly aloof with regard to abode and seat

व्रत - *Vrata* - vow; rule of conduct

वृत्ति - *Vṛtti* - mental mode; a modification of the mind whose function is to manifest objects

It is what makes knowledge possible, according to Advaita. It serves as the connection link between the knowing subject and the known object. It is a transformation of either the internal organ or of nescience (*avidyā*). It goes out through the senses and pervades the object.

वृत्तिज्ञान - *Vṛtti-jñāna* - empirical knowledge

1. According to Advaita, it is a blend of a modification of the mind and the reflection of consciousness therein.

2. It is of two kinds: immediate (*aparokṣa*) and mediate (*parokṣa*).

3. It is opposed to *avidyā*. Vide *svarūpa-jñāna*.

वृत्तिनियामक - *Vṛtti-niyāmaka* - Vide *svarūpa-sambandha*

वृत्तिव्याप्यत्व - *Vṛtti-vyāpyatva* - pervasion by a mental modification

1. According to Advaita, it is one of the two conditions necessary for an entity to be an object of knowledge.

2. Vide *phala-vyāpyatva*.

वृत्यनियामक - *Vṛttyaniyāmaka* - Vide *svarūpa-sambandha*

व्यभिचार - *Vyabhicāra* - deviation

व्याघात - *Vyāghāta* - given up; dispensed with

व्याज - *Vyāja* - occasion; indirect cause

व्याकरण - *Vyākaraṇa* - grammar

1. One of the limbs of the *Vedas*.

2. Vide *vedāṅga*.

व्यान - *Vyāna* - a vital air

1. The life-breath which governs the circulation of blood in the body.

2. Vide *prāṇa*.

व्यङ्ग्यार्थ - *Vyaṅgyārtha* - suggested meaning

1. According to Indian aesthetics, besides the primary meaning (*mukhyārtha*) and the secondary meaning (*laksyārtha*), words may also have a suggested meaning. In this type of meaning, the primary meaning stands as a stepping stone to it. The primary meaning suggests, or hints, or indicates, to the mind of the listener what the meaning is, but this meaning is not necessarily related or connected to the primary meaning. For example, by saying that the village is on the Ganges, the idea may be to convey that it is cool and holy.

2. In poetry, this type of meaning is indispensable where the content is emotion.

व्यापक - *Vyāpaka* - pervader; probandum (*sādhya*)

व्यापार - *Vyāpāra* - activity; intermediate cause

व्याप्ति - *Vyāpti* - invariable concomitance; universal pervasion between the middle term and the major term

1. This relation must be unconditional or necessary. It is the central essence of an inferential cognition. It is a correlation between two terms, of which one is the pervaded and the other is the pervader. The *hetu* is the pervaded and

the *sādhya* is the pervader in a *vyāpti.* It is the relation of co-existence of the *hetu* and the *sādhya.* This relation must also be free from and adventitious circumstance.

2. Vide *anumāna.*

व्याप्य - *Vyāpya* - pervaded; probans (*sādhaka-sādhana*)

व्याप्यत्वासिद्ध - *Vyāpyatvāsiddha* - unestablished in respect of its concomitance

1. One type of unestablished reason. Here the reason is associated with an adventitious condition.

2. Vide *asiddha* and *hetvābhāsa.*

व्याप्यवृत्ति - *Vyāpya-vṛtti* - pervasive

व्यासज्यवृत्ति - *Vyāsajya-vṛtti* - partially contained

व्यतिरेकदृष्टान्त - *Vyatireka-dṛṣṭānta* - negative example

व्यतिरेकसहचार - *Vyatireka-sahacāra* - concomitance of negation

व्यतिरेकव्याप्ति - *Vyatireka-vyāpti* - negative pervasion

1. A type of inference in which only agreement in absence of the middle and major terms has been observed; e.g., where there is no fire, there is no smoke.

2. Vide *kevala-vyatireka* and *anumāna.*

व्यवहार - *Vyavahāra* - empirical; worldly life; practice

1. That on which is based all of one's practical movements.

2. Empirical discourse.

व्यवहारनय - *Vyavahāra-naya* - a type of viewpoint in Jainism

Vide *naya.*

व्यावहारिक - *Vyāvahārika* - the relative viewpoint; empi rical

1. The standpoint of ignorance, according to Advaita. At this level, the Absolute is with attributes (*saguṇa*), one individual differs from another, and the entire pluralistic universe exists.

2. Vide *prātibhāsika* and *pāramārthika.*

व्यावहारिकसत्य - *Vyāvahārika-satya* - phenomenal (or relative) reality

व्यवहित - *Vyavahita* - mediate

व्यावर्तक - *Vyāvartaka* - differentiating feature

व्यवसाय - *Vyavasāya* - determinate cognition

A determinate cognition gives only the cognition of the object. Vide *anu-vyavasāya.*

व्यवसायज्ञान - *Vyavasāya-jñāna* - original cognition

1. According to Nyāya, a determinate cognition which gives only the cognition of an object and not the awareness that one is aware of such a cognition is called *vyavasāya-jñāna.*

2. Vide *anu-vyavasāya.*

व्यवस्था - *Vyavasthā* - order; restriction

व्यावृत्त - *Vyāvṛtta* - discontinunity

व्यावृत्ति - *Vyāvṛtti* - differentiation

व्यय - *Vyaya* - disappearance; loss; expenditure

व्यूह - *Vyūha* - manifestation; emanation

1. According to Viśiṣṭādvaita, it is one of the fivefold forms which *Īśvara* takes. There are four manifestations (for the purposes of meditation by the devotees and for the creation, etc. of the universe): *Vāsudeva*, *Saṅkarṣaṇa*, *Pradyumna*, and *Aniruddha*. Each emanates from the former, with *Vāsudeva* as the highest self. They are all manifestations of *Vāsudeva*, the one divine person.

2. From *jñāna* and the capacity for unceasing work or never-ending creation (*bala*) evolves *Saṅkarṣaṇa*. From *aiśvarya* and *vīrya* evolves *Pradyumna*. From *śakti* and *tejas* evolves *Aniruddha*. Vide *Īśvara*.

3. *Saṅkarṣaṇa* fulfils the function of creation, maintenance, and dissolution of the world and exists as the deity superintending all the individual souls. *Pradymna* protects the individual souls and superintends their birth and gives them instruction regarding spiritual matters. *Aniruddha* helps individuals towards liberation and protects the world. Vide each listed individually.

व्युत्सर्ग - *Vyutsarga* - indifference to objects

Y

यज्ञ - *Yajña* - sacrifice; sacrificial ceremony

Every twice-born Hindu is enjoined to perform regularly the five great sacrifices (*pañca-mahā-yajña*). *Deva-yajña* is deity worship; *Brahma-yajña* is worship of *Brahma*, a sacrifice to the sages by studying, teaching, or meditating on the *Vedas*; *Pitṛ-yajña* is ancestor worship; *Bhūta-yajña* refers to gratification of living beings *viz* animals and birds and *Nara-yajña* consistsin welcoming the guests and honouring them.

यम - *Yama* - abstentions; self-control

The first limb of Patañjali's *rāja-yoga*. It is comprised of non-injury (*ahiṁsā*), truth (*satya*), non-stealing (*asteya*), celebacy (*brahmacarya*) and non-possession (*aparigraha*). Vide *aṣṭāṅga-yoga*.

यन्त्र - *Yantra* - mystic diagram

Geometrical diagrams designed to channel psychic forces by concentrating them on a pattern such that it (the pattern) becomes reproduced by the devotee's visualizing power.

यथार्थख्याति - *Yathārtha-khyāti* - apprehension of the real

1. This theory of error is propounded by Viśiṣṭādvaita. All that is presented in experience

is real. Thus illusory knowledge or error is not unreal because it has an unreal object, but because it fails in life. The object of error is real and existent, but the error arises and is explained by the theory of quintuplication. What is perceived in error is but a minor portion of an existent entity.

2. Vide *khyāti-vāda.*

यतिराज - *Yatirāja* - king of ascetics

A name of Rāmānuja; cf. the *Yatirāja-saptati* of Vedāntadeśika and the *Yatirāja-viṁśati* of Varavaramuni.

यत्रकामावसायित्व - *Yatra-kāmāvasāyitva* - the power by which all desires are fulfilled

Vide *aṣṭa-aiśvarya.*

यौगिक - *Yaugika* - derivative

योग - *Yoga* - union; a process or path or discipline leading to oneness with the Divine or with oneself

1. The chief systems of *yoga* are: *haṭha-yoga* (the *yoga* of body and life-breath), *karma-yoga* (the path of action), *bhakti-yoga* (the path of devotion), *rāja-yoga* (the kingly *yoga*), *japa-yoga* or *mantra-yoga* (the *yoga* of repeating God's names or of repeating holy words), *kuṇḍalinī-yoga* (the serpent power *yoga*), *jñāna-yoga* (path of knowledge).

2. It is also the name for the school of philosophy founded by Patañjali. Its object is the union of individual soul with the divine Self within. It is one of the six orthodox systems of Indian philosophy. Vide *ṣaḍdarśana.*

3. According to Śaiva Siddhānta, it is a path to liberation which is characterized by contemplation and internal worship. It is called the path of friendship to God (*sakhā-mārga*). Its goal is gaining the form of God (*sārūpya*). Vide *mokṣa.*

योगाचार - *Yogācāra* - practice of *yoga*

A Mahāyāna school of Buddhism which advocates subjective idealism. It asserts that consciousness alone is real and emphasizes *yoga* practices to achieve its ideal. Its two most famous exponents are: Asaṅga and Vasubandhu. It is also called *Vijñānavāda.*

योगाङ्ग - *Yogāṅga* - the stages of *yoga* in Vīra Śaivism

Vide *ṣaṭsthala.*

योगज - *Yogaja* - extra-sensory perception

One of the super-normal modes of sense perception, according to Nyāya. It is cultivated by *yoga* and by means of it, one is able to perceive things beyond the reach of the senses. Vide *pratyakṣa.*

योगजलक्षण - *Yogaja-lakṣaṇa* - (contact) originated from yogic powers

योगपाद - *Yogapāda* - that part of the *Āgamas* which teaches practices of meditation

Vide *Āgama.*

योगरूढ - *Yoga-rūḍha* - derivative-conventional

योग्यानुपलब्धि - *Yogyānupalabdhi* - effectual non-cognition

योग्यता - *Yogyatā* - special fitness; congruity

1. One of the causes which bring about a valid cognition from a proposition. It consists in there being no contradiction among the meanings of the words of a sentence, e.g., 'fire is cold' (vide *āsatti*, *ākāṅkṣā*, *tātparya*).

2. The transcendent touch of the *puruṣa* which sets in motion the original nature (*prakṛti*) in Sāṅkhya.

युग - *Yuga* - age or cycle; aeon

1. Four ages are said to exist: the Golden Age (*satya* or *kṛta*), the Silver Age (*treta*), the Bronze Age (*dvāpara*), and the Iron Age (*kali*).

2. In a day of *Brahmā* (vide *kalpa*) there are four *yugas*, and each *yuga* is preceded by a period called its *Sandhyā* (evening twilight). Four *yugas* make a half *kalpa* (or 4,320,000,000 years) which is the duration of one day or one night of *Brahmā*.

युगधर्म - *Yuga-dharma* - the law of time

During each Age, there is a particular code of law to be followed which is suited to it. In *Kṛta-yuga* one follows the *Manudharmaśāstra*. In *Treta-yuga* one follows the *Gautamadharmaśāstra*. In *Dvāpara-yuga* one follows the *Śaṅkhalikhitadharmaśāstra*. In *Kali-yuga* one follows the *Parāśarasmṛti*.

युगपत् - *Yugapat* - simultaneous

An aspect of designate time. Vide *kāla*.

युक्ति - *Yukti* - reasoning

According to Advaita, the truth is realized through *śruti*, *yukti* and *anubhava*.

युक्तिदर्शन - *Yukti-darśana* - the empirical level of Reality

CHARTS

Chart 1

THE VEDAS

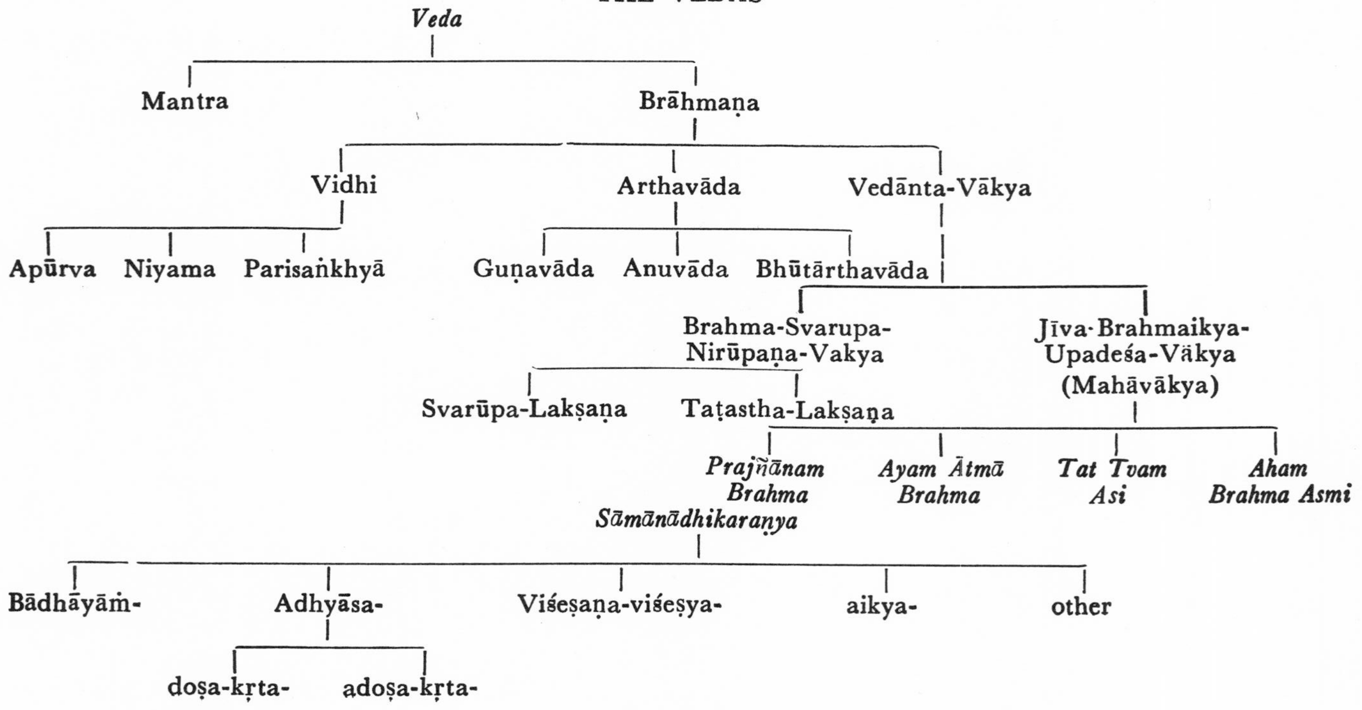

Chart 2

SOURCE - BOOKS OF NĀSTIKA SYSTEMS

Cārvāka

Bārhaspatya-sūtra (not extant)
references in :

(i) *Sarva-darśana-saṅgraha* of Mādhavācārya

(ii) *Ṣaḍ-darśana-samuccaya* of Haribhadrasūri

(iii) *Cārvāka-ṣaṣṭi* of Dakṣiṇarañjan Śāstri

Jainism

Fourteen *Pūrvas* (not extant)

Eleven *Aṅgas*

- Ācāra
- Sūtrakṛta
- Sthāna
- Samavāya
- Bhagavatī
- Jñāta-Dharmakathās
- Upāsakadaśās
- Antakṛtadaśās
- Anuttara-Upapātikadaśās
- Praśnavyākaraṇa
- Vipāka

Twelve *Upāṅgas*

Ten *Prakīrṇas*

Six *Chedasūtras*

Four *Mūlasūtras*

(For Source-Books of *Buddhism*, see next page)

Chart 2 (*contd.*)

- ***Buddhism***
  - ***Hīnayāna***
    - Pali Canon
      - Tripiṭaka
        - ***Vinayapiṭaka***
          - Suttavibhaṅga
          - Khandhakas
          - Mahāvagga
          - Chullavagga
          - Parivāra
        - ***Suttapiṭaka***
          - Dīgha Nikāya
          - Majjhima Nikāya
          - Saṁyutta Nikāya
          - Aṅguttara Nikāya
          - Khuddaka Nikāya
        - ***Abhidhammapiṭaka***
          - Paṭṭhāṇa
          - Dhammasaṅgaṇi
          - Dhātukathā
          - Puggaḷapaññatti
          - Vibhaṅgi
          - Yamaka
          - Kathāvatthu
  - ***Mahāyāna***
    - Prajñāpāramita Sūtras
      - Mahāprajñāpāramitāsūtra
      - Aṣṭasāhasrikā-prajñāpāramitā
      - Vajracchedika
    - Saddharmapuṇḍarīka
    - Mahāparinirvāṇasūtra
    - Avataṁsaka
    - Gaṇḍavyūha
    - Daśabhūmika
    - Laṅkāvatārasūtra
    - Vimalakīrtti Nirdeśa
    - Lalita Vistara
    - Vajraśekharasūtra, etc.

Chart 3

SOURCE - BOOKS OF ĀSTIKA SYSTEMS (i)

Nyāya	*Vaiśeṣika*	*Sāṅkhya*	*Yoga*	*Mīmāṁsā*
Nyāya-sūtra of Gautama	*Vaiśeṣika-sūtra* of Kaṇāda	*Sāṅkhya-sūtra* of Kapila (not extant)	*Yoga-sūtra* of Patañjali	*Pūrva-mīmāṁsā-sūtra* of Jaimini
Nyāya-sūtra-bhāṣya of Vātsyāyana	*Vaiśeṣika-sūtra-bhāṣya* or *Padārtha-dharma-saṅgraha* of Praśastapāda	*Sāṅkhya-kārikā* of Īśvarakṛṣṇa	*Yoga-sūtra-bhāṣya* of Vyāsa	*Pūrva-mīmāṁsā-sūtra-bhāṣya* of Śabara-svāmin
Nyāya-sūtra-vārttika of Uddyotakara	*Rāvaṇa-bhāṣya* (not extant)	*Sāṅkhya-kārikā-bhāṣya* of Gauḍapāda	*Tattva-vaiśāradī* of Vācaspati	*Śloka-vārttika* of Kumārila Bhaṭṭa
Nyāya-vārttika-tātparyaṭīkā of Vācaspati	*Bhāradvāja-bhāṣya* (not extant)	*Tattva-kaumudī* of Vācaspati	*Yogasāra-saṅgraha* of Vijñānabhikṣu	*Tantra-vārttika* of Kumārila Bhaṭṭa
Nyāya-vārttika-tātparya-pariśuddhi of Udayana	*Kiraṇāvalī* of Udayana	*Sāṅkhya-pravacana-bhāṣya* of Vijñānabhikṣu	*Bhoja-vṛtti* of Bhojarāja	*Tupṭīkā* of Kumārila Bhaṭṭa

(Chart continued on next page)

Chart 3 *(contd.)*

Nyāya	*Vaiśeṣika*	*Mīmāṁsā*
Nyāyamañjari of Jayanta	*Nyāya-kandalī* of Śrīdhara	*Bṛhatī* of Prabhākara
Tattvacintāmaṇi of Gaṅgeśa	*Bhāṣāpariccheda* of Viśvanātha	*Ṛjuvimala* of Śālikanātha
		Prakaraṇa-pañcikā of Śālikanātha
		Nyāya-ratnākara of Pārthasarāthi Miśra
		Kāśikā of Sucarita Miśra
		Nyāyasudhā of Someśvara

Chart 4

SOURCE - BOOKS OF ĀSTIKA SYSTEMS (ii)

Advaita	*Viśiṣṭādvaita*	*Dvaita*
Upaniṣads	*Upaniṣads*	*Upaniṣads*
Bhagavad-gītā	*Bhagavad-gītā*	*Bhagavad-gītā*
Brahma-sūtra of Bādarāyaṇa	*Brahma-sūtra* of Bādarāyaṇa	*Brahma-sūtra* of Bādarāyaṇa
Śārīraka-bhāṣya of Śaṅkarācārya	*Nālāyira Divya Prabandham* of Āḻvārs	Vaiṣṇava Purāṇas
		Vaiṣṇava Āgamas
Bṛhadāraṇyaka-bhāṣya-vārttika of Sureśvara	Vaiṣṇava Purāṇas	*Brahma-sūtra-bhāṣya* of Madhva
	Vaiṣṇava Āgamas	*Anuvyākhyāna* of Madhva
Taittirīya-bhāṣya-vārttika of Sureśvara	*Āgama-prāmāṇya* of Yāmunācārya	*Daśa-prakaraṇa* of Madhva
	Gītārtha-saṅgraha of Yāmunācārya	*Bhāratatātparyanirṇaya* of Madhva
Pañcapādikā of Padmapāda	*Siddhi-traya* of Yāmunācārya	*Tattva Prakāśikā* of Jayatīrtha
	Śrī-bhāṣya of Rāmānuja	*Nyāyasudhā* of Jayatīrtha
Bhāmatī Catuḥsūtrī of Vācaspati	*Vedārthasaṅgraha* of Rāmānuja	*Tātparya Candrikā* of Vyāsarāya
	Vedāntasāra of Rāmānuja	*Tattvamuktāvali* of Pūrṇānanda
Pañcapādikā-vivaraṇa of Prakāśātman	*Vedāntadīpa* of Rāmānuja	*Candrikā Prakāśa* of Rāghavendra Yati
	6000-paḍi of Piḷḷāṉ	
Kalpataru of Amalānanda	*36000-paḍi* or *Īḍu* of Vaḍakkut-tiruvīthip-piḷḷai	
Vivaraṇa-prameya-saṅgraha of Vidyāraṇya		

(Chart continued on next page)

Chart 4 (*contd.*)

Advaita	*Viśiṣṭādvaita*
Kalpataru-parimala of Appayya Dīkṣita	*Śrutaprakāśikā* of Sudarśanasūri
Brahmasiddhi of Maṇḍana	*Artha-pañcaka* of Piḷḷai-lokācārya
Naiṣkarmyasiddhi of Sureśvara	*Tattva-traya* of Piḷḷai-lokācārya
Iṣṭasiddhi of Vimuktātman	*Rahasya-trayasāra* of Vedāntadeśika
Advaitasiddhi of Madhusūdana Sarasvatī	*Tattva-ṭīkā* of Vedāntadeśika
Māṇḍūkya-kārikā of Gauḍapāda	
Pañcadaśī of Vidyāraṇya	
Vedānta-sāra of Sadānanda	
Vedānta-paribhāṣā of Dharmarāja	
Siddhānta-leśa-saṅgraha of Appayya Dīkṣita	
Upadeśasāhasrī of Śaṅkarācārya	
Vivekacūḍāmaṇi of Śaṅkarācārya	
Ātmabodha of Śaṅkarācārya	

Chart 5

SOURCE - BOOKS OF SCHOOLS OF ŚAIVISM

Śaiva Siddhānta	*Vīra Śaivism*	*Śivādvaita*
Vedas	*Vedas*	*Brahma-sūtra-bhāṣya* of Śrīkaṇṭha
Śaiva Āgamas	*Śaiva Āgamas*	Commentary on the above by Appayya Dīkṣita
Tolkāppiyam	*Purāṇas*	
(Twelve *Tirumurais*:)	*Vacanas* of Basava and others	
Tēvāram of Sambandhar, Appar and Sundarar		
Tiruvācakam of Māṇikkavācakar		
Tirumantiram of Tirumūlar		
Periya Purāṇam of Śēkkiḻār		
Śiva Jñāna Bodham of Meykaṇḍār		
Śiva Jñāna Siddhiyār of Aruḷnandi Śivācārya		
Siddhānta Aṣṭakam of Umāpati Śivācārya		

(For source-books of Kashmir Śaivism see next page)

Chart 5 (*contd.*)

Kashmir Śaivism

ĀGAMA ŚĀSTRA (Saivāgamas)	SPANDA ŚĀSTRA (Spandakārikās)	PRATYABHIJÑĀ ŚĀSTRA
Svachchanda	*Vivṛti* of Rāmakaṇṭha	*Īśvara Pratyabhijñā* of Utpaladeva
Mṛgendra	*Pradīpikā* of Utpala Vaiṣṇava	*Pratyabhijñā Vimarśinī* of Abhinavagupta
Rudra Yāmala	*Spanda Śandoha* of Kṣemarāja	*Pratyabhijñā Vivṛtti Vimarśinī* of Abhinavagupta
Mālinī Vijaya	*Spanda Nirṇaya* of Kṣemarāja	*Pratyabhijñā Hṛdayam* of Kṣemarāja
Vijñāna Bhairava		*Śiva Sūtra* of Vasugupta
		Spanda Sarvasa of Kallaṭa
		Śiva Dṛṣṭi of Somānanda
		Paramārthasāra of Abhinavagupta
		Īśvara Pratyabhijñā Kārikā of Utpaladeva

Chart 6

PADĀRTHAS (CATEGORIES)

I. *Nyāya*	II. *Prābhākara*	III. *Bhāṭṭa*	IV. *Sāṅkhya*
1. Pramāṇa	1. Dravya	1. Dravya	1. Puruṣa
2. Prameya	2. Guṇa	2. Guṇa	2. Prakṛti
3. Saṁśaya	3. Karma	3. Karma	
4. Prayojana	4. Sāmānya	4. Sāmānya	
5. Dṛṣṭānta	5. Paratantratā	5. Abhāva	
6. Siddhānta	6. Śakti		
7. Avayava	7. Sādṛśya		
8. Tarka	8. Saṅkhyā		
9. Nirṇaya			
10. Vāda			
11. Jalpa			
12. Vitaṇḍā			
13. Hetvābhāsa			
14. Chala			
15. Jāti			
16. Nigraha-sthāna			

(Chart continued on next page)

Chart 6 (*contd.*)

V. *Viśiṣṭādvaita*

(i) *Adravya*

1. Śabda
2. Sparśa
3. Rūpa
4. Rasa
5. Gandha
6. Sattva
7. Rajas
8. Tamas
9. Śakti
10. Saṁyoga

(ii) *Dravya*

1. Prakṛti
2. Kāla
3. Śuddha-sattva
4. Dharma-bhūta-jñāna
5. Jīva
6. Īśvara

VI. *Dvaita*

(i) *Padārthas*

1. Dravya
2. Guṇa
3. Karma
4. Sāmānya
5. Viśeṣa
6. Viśiṣṭa
7. Amśin
8. Śakti
9. Sādṛśya
10. Abhāva

(ii) *Dravyas*

1. Paramātman
2. Lakṣmī
3. Jīva
4. Avyākṛtākāśa
5. Prakṛti
6. Guṇatraya
7. Mahat
8. Ahaṅkāra
9. Buddhi
10. Manas
11. Indriya(s)
12. Tanmātra(s)
13. Mahābhūta(s)
14. Brahmāṇḍa
15. Avidyā
16. Varṇa
17. Timira
18. Vāsanā
19. Kāla
20. Pratibimba

Chart 7

VAIŚEṢIKA CATEGORIES

(i) *Dravya* (*substance*)	(ii) *Guṇa* (*quality*)	(iii) *Karma* (*activity*)
pṛthivī (earth)	*rūpa* (colour)	*utkṣepaṇa* (upward)
ap (water)	*rasa* (taste)	*avakṣepaṇa* (downward)
tejas (fire)	*gandha* (smell)	*ākuñcana* (contraction)
vāyu (air)	*sparśa* (touch)	*prasāraṇa* (expansion)
ākāśa (ether)	*śabda* (sound)	*gamana* (locomotion)
kāla (time)	*saṅkhyā* (number)	
dik (space)	*parimāṇa* (size)	
ātman (self)	*pṛthaktva* (separateness)	
manas (mind)	*saṁyoga* (conjunction)	
	vibhāga (disjunction)	
	paratva (remoteness)	
	aparatva (proximity)	
	buddhi (cognition)	
	sukha (pleasure)	
	duḥkha (pain)	
	icchā (desire)	
	dveṣa (aversion)	
	prayatna (effort)	
	gurutva (heaviness)	
	dravatva (fluidity)	
	sneha (viscidity)	
	saṁskāra (faculty)	
	dharma (merit)	
	adharma (demerit)	

(For *Vaiśeṣika categories* (iv)—(vii), see next page)

Chart 7 (contd.)

(iv) *Sāmānya (generality)*	(v) *Viśeṣa (particularity)* (innumerable)	(vi) *Samavāya (inherence)*	(vii) *Abhāva (non-existence)*
		It obtains between five kinds of inseparables:	*prāg-abhāva* (prior non-existence)
		substance and quality substance and activity particular and generality	*pradhvaṁsābhāva* (annihilative non-existence)
		eternal substance and particularity whole and parts	*anyonyābhāva* (reciprocal non-existence)
			atyantābhāva (absolute non-existence)

Chart 8

JAINISM CATEGORIES

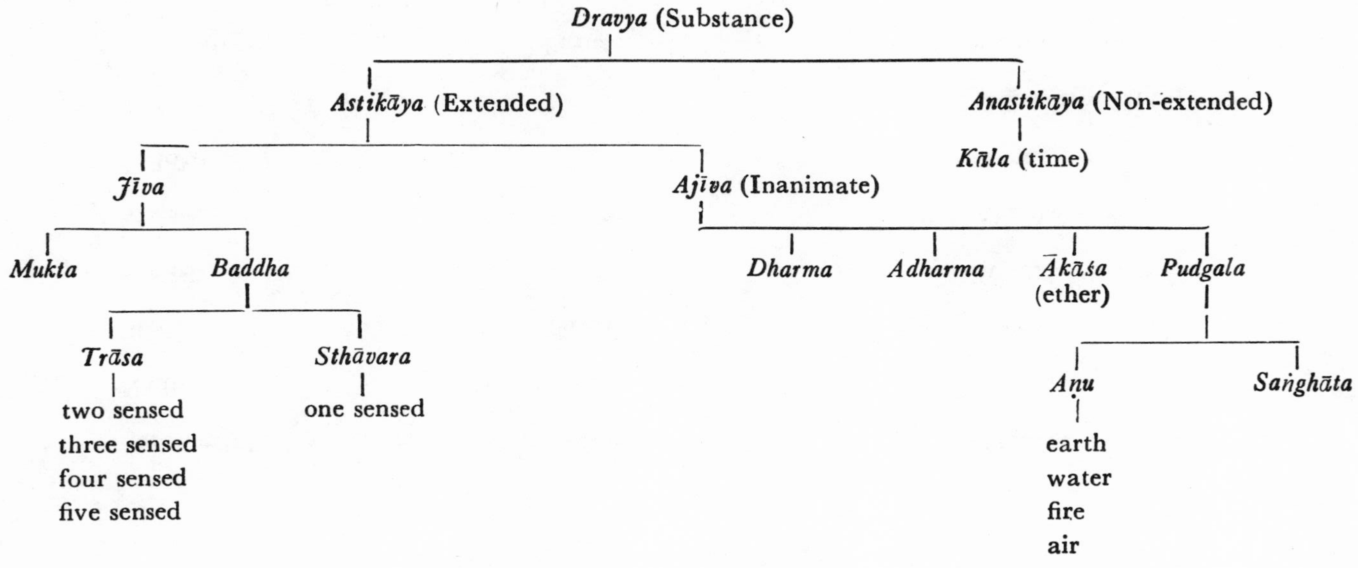

Dravya (Substance)
Astikāya (Extended)
Anastikāya (Non-extended)
Kāla (time)
Jīva
Ajīva (Inanimate)
Mukta
Baddha
Trāsa
Sthāvara
two sensed
three sensed
four sensed
five sensed
one sensed
Dharma
Adharma
Ākāśa
(ether)
Pudgala
Aṇu
Saṅghāta
earth
water
fire
air

Chart 9

ŚAIVA SIDDHĀNTA TATTVA(S)

MĀYĀ

Śuddhamāyā	*Śuddhāśuddhamāyā*	*Aśuddhamāyā*
Nāda	Kāla	(Kāla)
Bindu	Niyati	Prakṛti
Sadāśiva	Kalā	Buddhi
Maheśvara	Vidyā	Ahaṅkāra
Śuddhāvidyā	Rāga	Manas
	Māyā	Jñānendriya(s) (5)
(Śiva-tattvas)	Puruṣa	Karmendriya(s) (5)
		Tanmātra(s) (5)
	(Vidyā-tattvas)	Pañcabhūta(s) (5)
		(Ātma-tattvas)

Chart 9 (*contd.*)

KASHMIR ŚAIVISM TATTVA(S)

Śuddha-tattva(s)

[Anāśrita-tattva(s)]

Śiva
Śakti
Sadāśiva
Īśvara
Sadvidyā

Aśuddha-tattva(s)

[Āśrita-tattva(s)]

Māyā
|
Kāla, Niyati, Rāga, Vidyā, Kalā
|
Puruṣa
Prakṛti
Buddhi
Ahaṅkāra
|
Manas, Jñānendriya(s), Karmendriya(s)
|
Tanmātra(s)
|
Mahābhūta(s)

Chart 10

SCHEME OF VIŚIṢṬĀDVAITA

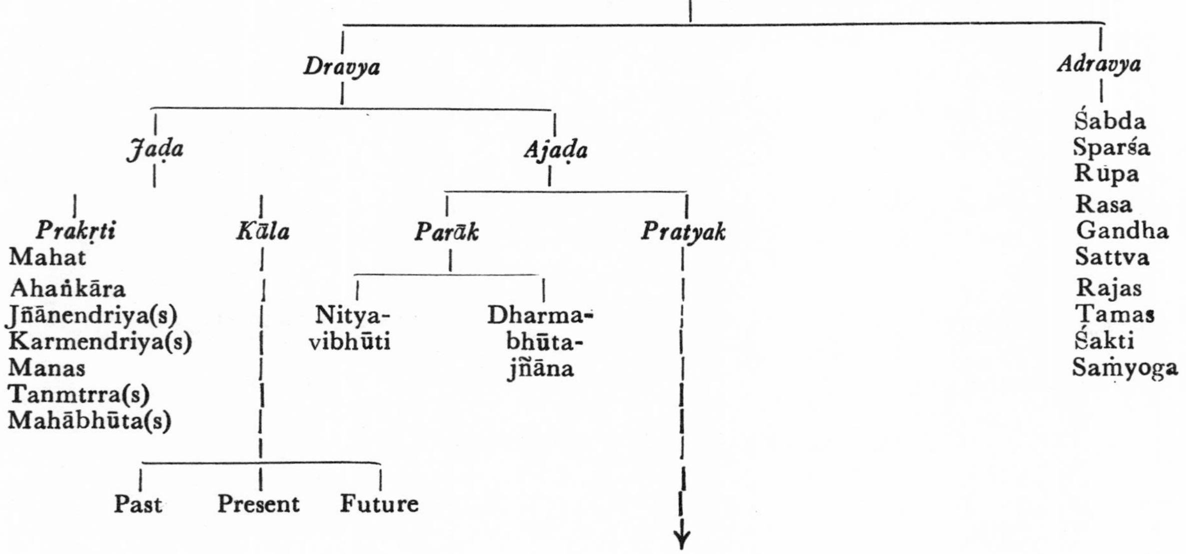

Chart 10 (*contd.*)

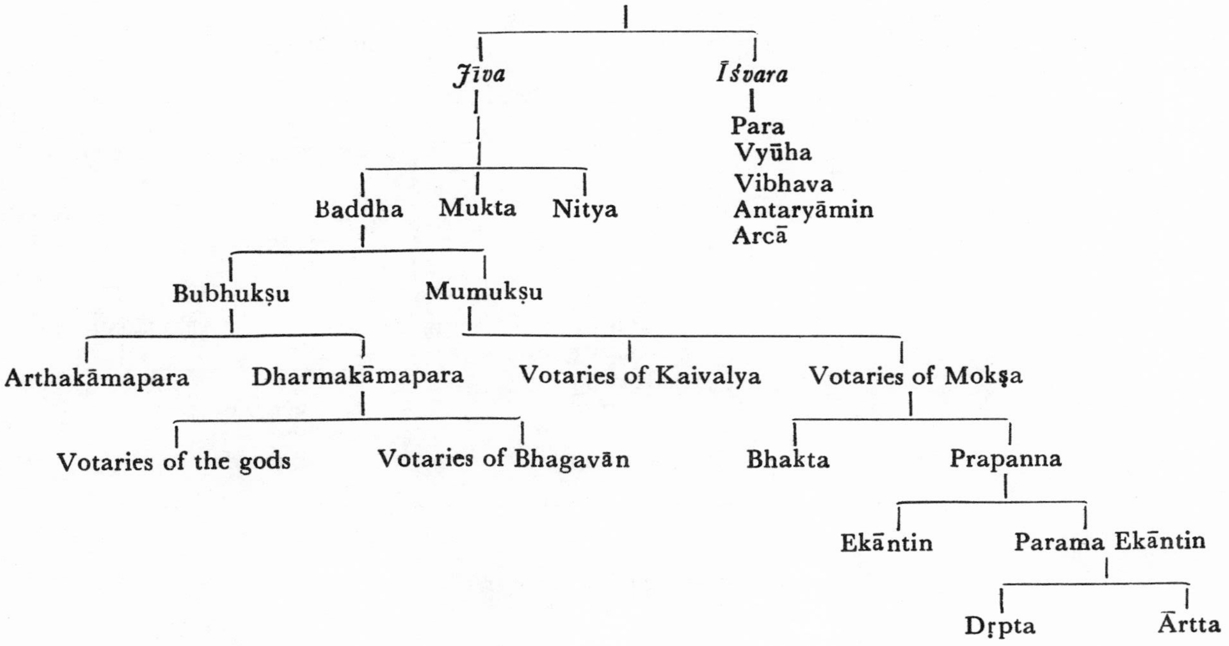

Jīva
Īśvara
Para
Vyūha
Vibhava
Antaryāmin
Arcā
Baddha
Mukta
Nitya
Bubhukṣu
Mumukṣu
Arthakāmapara
Dharmakāmapara
Votaries of Kaivalya
Votaries of Mokṣa
Votaries of the gods
Votaries of Bhagavān
Bhakta
Prapanna
Ekāntin
Parama Ekāntin
Dṛpta
Ārtta

Chart 11

JAINA EPISTEMOLOGY

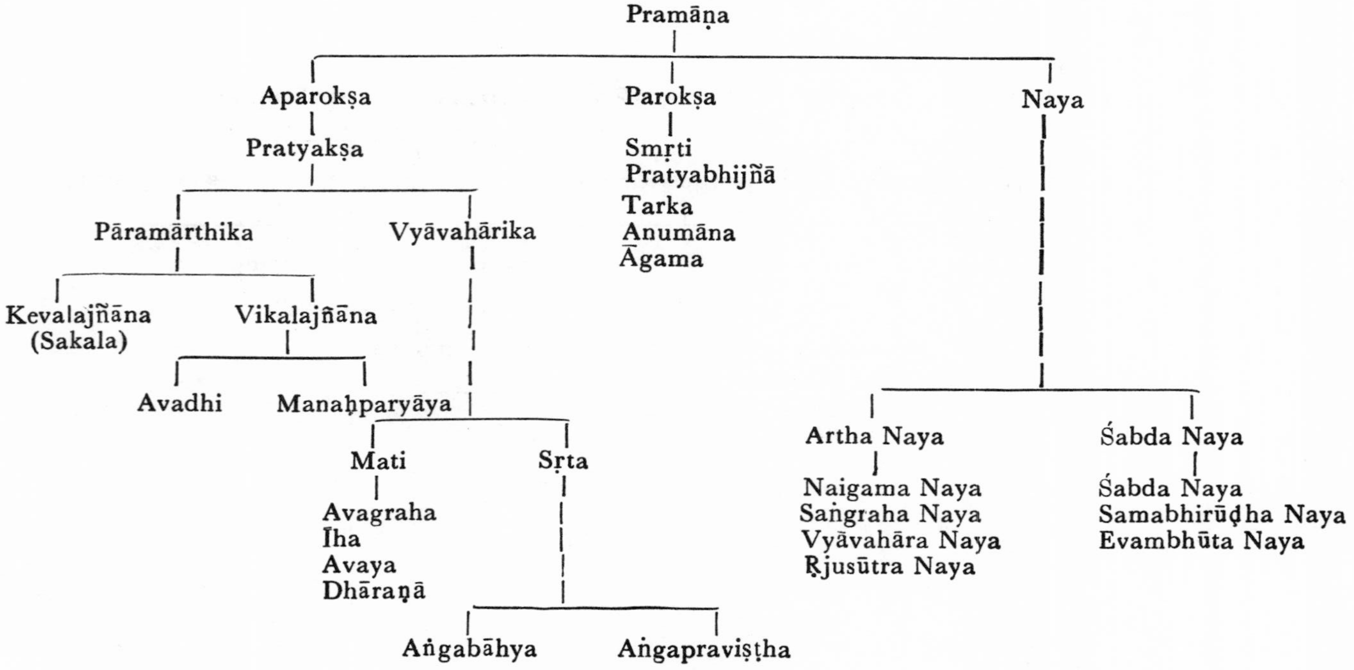
Pramāṇa
Aparokṣa
Pratyakṣa
Pāramārthika
Kevalajñāna
(Sakala)
Vikalajñāna
Avadhi
Manaḥparyāya
Vyāvahārika
Mati
Avagraha
Īha
Avaya
Dhāraṇā
Sṛta
Aṅgabāhya
Aṅgapraviṣṭha
Parokṣa
Smṛti
Pratyabhijñā
Tarka
Anumāna
Āgama
Naya
Artha Naya
Naigama Naya
Saṅgraha Naya
Vyāvahāra Naya
Ṛjusūtra Naya
Śabda Naya
Śabda Naya
Samabhirūḍha Naya
Evambhūta Naya

Chart 12

EVOLUTION OF PRAKṚTI ACCORDING TO SĀṄKHYA

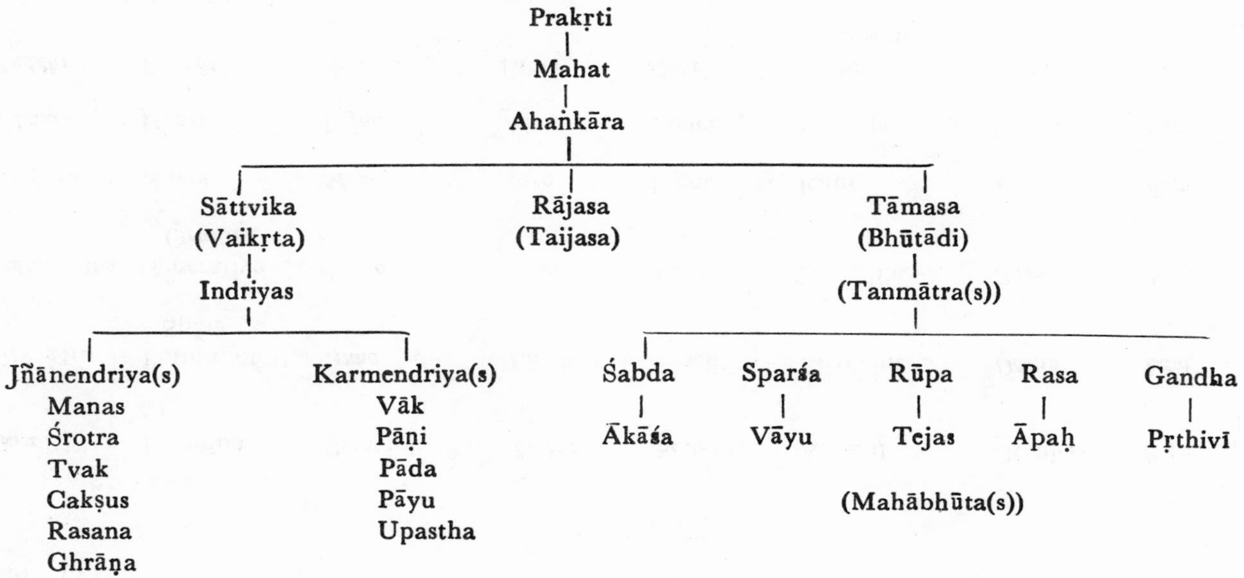

Chart 13

CAKRA(S)

Cakra	Location	Principle	*Tattva*	Sense	Animal	Goddess	*Bīja*	Number of Petals
Mūlādhāra	Bottom of Spine	*Anna*	Earth	Smell	Elephant	*Ḍākinī*	*Lam*	4
Svādhiṣṭhāna	Generative Organ	*Prāṇa*	Water	Taste	Crocodile	*Rākinī*	*Vam*	6
Maṇipūra	Navel	*Manas*	Fire	Sight	Ram	*Lākinī*	*Ram*	10
Anāhata	Heart	*Vijñāna*	Air	Touch	Antelope	*Kākinī*	*Yam*	12
Viśuddhi	Throat	*Ānanda*	Ether	Hearing	White Elephant	*Śākinī*	*Ham*	16
Ājñā	Between Eyebrows	*Cit*	*Mahat*	Mind	Swan	*Hākinī*	*Om*	2
Ṣahasrāra	Top of ḥead	*Ṣat*	...	...	...	...	...	1000

Chart 14

AṄGASTHALA

	Yogāṅga		Bhogāṅga		Tyāgāṅga	
Stage of Consiousness	Aikya	Śaraṇa	Prāṇaliṅgi	Prasādi	Maheśvara	Bhakta
Aspect of Lord Worshipped	Mahā	Prasāda	Cāra	Śiva	Guru	Acāra
Attendant Sakti	Cit	Para	Ādhi	Icchā	Jñāna	Kriyā
Name of Bhakti	Samarāsa	Ānanda	Anubhāva	Avadhāna	Niṣṭhā	Śraddhā

(For *Liṅgasthala*, see next page)

Chart 14 (*contd.*)

LIṄGASTHALA

Bhāvaliṅga		Prāṇaliṅga		Iṣṭaliṅga	
Mahālinga	Prasādaliṅga	Cāraliṅga	Śivaliṅga	Guruliṅga	Acāraliṅga
Vedhā Dīkṣā		Mantra Dīkṣā		Kriyā Dīkṣā	

AN INDEX OF SOME IMPORTANT WORDS

Abhinandhana, 364
Ajita, 364
ājñā, 104
anāgāmi-mārga, 57
anāhata, 104
ananta, 100
Ananta, 364
Āṇḍāḷ, 25
aṅguttara, 346
Aniruddha, 257, 389, 390, 400, 408
antya-vṛtti, 21
anukta, 384
anuṣṭup, 200
aparatva, 50, 136
apipāsaḥ, 137
Ara, 364
Ariṣṭanemi, 364
artha-adhyāsa, 11
artha-avagraha, 79
Aruḷnandi, 319
aśru, 39
asti, 92
aṣṭi, 201
atidhṛti, 201
atijagatī, 201
atiśakvarī, 201
avijjāsava, 66

Balabhadra, 389
Balarāma, 81
Bhadrāśva, 176
Bhārata, 176
Bhartṛprapañca, 95
bhavāsava, 66
Bhīma, 131
bhūcari, 331
Bṛhaspati, 105
bṛhatī, 200
Bhūtattāḻvār, 25
Buddha, 81, 84, 126, 389

Candraprabha, 364
chandas, 387

Dāmodara, 34
daṇḍanīti, 392
dardura, 331
dāsa-mārga, 105, 202, 299
devī, 14
Dharma, 364
dharma-adhyāsa, 11
dharmi-adhyāsa, 11
dhṛti, 201
dīgha, 346
ditthāsava, 66
durukta, 384
dvīpa, 396

gadā, 400

Gauḍapāda, 8, 18, 19, 23, 66, 245, 362
gāyatrī, 200
Govinda, 317
guṇa-vākya, 391

Hari, 176
Hiraṇyaka, 176
Hṛṣīkeśa, 34

icchā-mṛtyu, 331
Ilāvarta, 176

jagatī, 200
Jambū-dvīpa, 176
jñāna-adhyāsa, 11
jñāna-agni, 15
jyotiṣa, 387

Kalki, 81, 389
kāmāsava, 66
karma-sāmya, 145
karmotpatti-vākya, 391
kāya-siddhi, 331
Ketumāla, 176
khaḍga, 400
khecari, 331
khuddaka, 346
Kimpuruṣa, 176
kopa-agni, 15
Kṛṣṇa, 81, 389
Kṣudhā-agni, 15
Kulaśekhara Āḻvār, 25
Kunthu, 364
Kūrma, 81, 389
Kuru, 176

Madhusūdana, 317
Madhurakavi Āḻvār, 25
majjhima, 346
Malli, 364
maṇipūra, 104
Matsya, 81, 389
Meykaṇḍār, 319
mṛtyuñjaya, 331
mūlādhāra, 104
Munisuvrata, 364

Nālāyiradivyaprabandham, 25
Nami, 364
Nammāḻvār, 25
Narasiṁha, 81, 389
nirvitarka, 402

Padmanābha, 34
Padmaprabha, 364
paratantratā, 423 (chart)
Paraśurāma, 81, 389
Pārśva, 364
pātāla-siddhi, 331
Patañjali, 31, 270, 300, 347, 410
Periyāḻvār, 25
Pēyāḻvār, 25
phalaguṇavākya, 391
phalavākya, 391
Piḻḻai Lokācārya, 363
Poygaiyāḻvār, 25
Pradyumna, 33, 317, 389, 400 408
pratyaya, 213
purohita, 102
putra-mārga, 202

rāja-yoga, 31
Rāmacandra, 81, 389
Rāmānuja, 34, 67, 91, 102, 177, 203, 231, 301, 321, 322, 349, 363, 372, 410
Ramyaka, 176
romāñca, 39
Ṛṣabha, 364

Sadāśiva, 288
Sādhāra, 119
sadurjayā, 99
saguṇa-karmotpatti-vākya, 391
sahasrāra, 104
sakhā-mārga, 91, 202, 243, 411
sakṛdāgāmi-mārga, 57
Sambandhar, 319
Sambhava, 364
saṁsarga-adhyāsa, 11
samyutta, 346
Śaṅkarācārya, 72, 91, 102, 203, 245
Saṅkarṣaṇa, 257, 390, 400, 408
Śaṅkha, 400
samārga, 202, 329
saṁsargābhāva, 1
śānti, 364
śārṅga, 400
satputra-mārga, 307
satyakāmaḥ, 137
satyasaṅkalpaḥ, 137
savitarka, 202
śīta-agni, 15
Śītala, 364
Śivācārya, 319
Śreyāṁśa, 364
Śrī Caitanya, 6
Śrīdhara, 257
srotāpatti-mārga, 57
stambha, 39
śūdra, 383
Sumati, 364
Supārśva, 364
Suvidhi, 364
svādhiṣṭhāna, 104
svarūpa-adhyāsa, 11
sveda, 39

Tirumangaiyāḻvār, 25
Tirumaḻiśaiyāḻvār, 25
Tiruppāṇāḻvār, 25
Toṇḍaraḍippoḍiyāḻvār, 25
trayī, 392
triṣṭup, 200
trikāla-jñāna, 331
Trivikrama, 257

ukta, 384
Umāpati, 319
uṣṇik, 200
uttara-pakṣa, 9

Vācaspati, 91, 106
Vaikuṇṭha, 207
vaiśya, 383
vaivarṇya, 39
Vāmana, 81, 257, 389
Varāha, 81, 389
Vardhamāna Mahāvīra, 132, 152, 364
vārtā, 392

Vāsudeva, 316, 400, 408
Vāsupūjya, 364
Vedāntadeśika, 133
vepathu, 39
vijaraḥ, 137
vijighatsaḥ, 137
vijñāna-avagraha, 79
vimalā, 99
Vimala, 364
vimṛtyuḥ, 137
Vipranārāyaṇa, 25
viśokaḥ, 137
viśuddhi, 104
vyākaraṇa, 387

Yādava, 14
yojana, 396